Library of
Davidson College
VOID

# POLISH RENAISSANCE LITERATURE
# AN ANTHOLOGY

# POLISH RENAISSANCE LITERATURE
# AN ANTHOLOGY

## MICHAEL J. MIKOŚ

Slavica Publishers, Inc.

Slavica publishes a wide variety of scholarly books and textbooks on the languages, peoples, literatures, cultures, history, etc. of the former USSR and Eastern Europe. For a complete catalog of books and journals from Slavica, with prices and ordering information, write to:

> Slavica Publishers, Inc.
> PO Box 14388
> Columbus, Ohio 43214

ISBN: 0-89357-257-8.

Copyright © 1995 by Michael J. Mikoś. All rights reserved.

All statements of fact or opinion are those of the authors and do not necessarily agree with those of the publisher, which takes no responsibility for them.

Printed in the United States of America.

# TABLE OF CONTENTS

| | |
|---|---|
| List of Illustrations | 10 |
| Foreword | 12 |
| Introduction | 16 |
| Select Bibliography | 41 |

**Andrzej Krzycki**

| | |
|---|---|
| *Four-line Poem on Queen Barbara* | 57 |
| *On the Armory of King Zygmunt* | 57 |
| *On the Picture of Life at Court* | 58 |
| *On Jan Zambocki* | 58 |
| *How a Girl Answered a Priest* | 58 |
| *On a Girl Lidia* | 59 |

**Mikołaj Hussowski**

| | |
|---|---|
| *A Poem on Bison* | 60 |

**Klemens Janiciusz**

| | |
|---|---|
| *Amo* | 62 |
| *Andrzej Krzycki, a Pole* | 62 |
| *Elegy VII. About Myself to Posterity* | 63 |

**Biernat of Lublin**

| | |
|---|---|
| *A Short Description of Aesop's Life* | 69 |

Fables

| | |
|---|---|
| *He Who Holds the Sword Has Peace* | 71 |
| *He Who Loves Books Is Not Bored* | 71 |
| *He Who Is Diligent Won't Go Wrong* | 72 |

**Marcin Bielski**

| | |
|---|---|
| *A Chronicle of the Whole World Death and Funeral of Zygmunt the Old* | 74 |
| *Parliament of Women* | 77 |

Anonymous
>    Owlgass, Facetious and Amusing    79

Jan of Kijany
>    Wolves    83
>    Hares    83

Nicholas Copernicus
>    On the Revolutions of the Heavenly Spheres
>    >    To His Holiness Pope Paul III    86

Marcin Kromer
>    Polonia    92

Andrzej Frycz Modrzewski
>    On the Reform of the Commonwealth
>    >    How to Care About Good Upbringing of Children and Youth    98
>    >    On Guardians of the Poor    103

Stanisław Orzechowski
>    Chimera or on the Shameful Heresy in the Kingdom of Poland    108

Łukasz Górnicki
>    The Polish Courtier
>    >    On Language    112

Wawrzyniec Goślicki
>    The Accomplished Senator    118

Piotr Skarga Powęski
>    Sermons to the Diet
>    >    Eighth Sermon    123

Mikołaj Rej
>    A Short Conversation    139
>
>    Life of an Honest Man
>    >    What Children's Clothes Should Be Like    143

## Table of Contents

When the Summer Comes — 144
Reading--a Great Pleasure — 145

### The Bestiary
Mikołaj Rej of Nagłowice — 147
Jan Kochanowski — 147
Martin Luther, the Doctor — 147
The Republic or the General Sejm — 148

### Trifles or Pranks
Old Woman Who Cried During the Passion of Christ — 148
On an Uncertain Conciliation — 149
A Parson Buried a Dog at a Graveyard — 149
The Blacksmith Who Lived Beside the Merchant — 149

## Jan Kochanowski
The Mountain of Beautiful Calliope — 151

### Latin Epigrams
On Petrarch's Writings — 153
To Łukasz Górnicki — 153
On Homer — 154

### Latin Elegies
Book II
Elegy VI — 154

### The Muse — 155

### Trifles
Book I
3. On Human Life — 156
21. On a Pious Woman — 157
53. On a Mathematician — 157
57. On Drunkards — 157
79. On a Spanish Doctor — 157
82. On Youth — 158
83. On Old Age — 158
87. On Trifles — 158

| | | |
|---|---|---|
| 97. | *To His Lady* | 158 |
| 98. | *On Love* | 159 |
| 101. | On Human Life | 159 |

Book II
| | | |
|---|---|---|
| 6. | *On the Linden Tree* | 160 |
| 19. | *On a Chaplain* | 160 |
| 37. | *To Sleep* | 160 |
| 66. | *To Hanna* | 161 |
| 87. | *To a Doctor* | 161 |

Book III
| | | |
|---|---|---|
| 1. | *To the Mountains and Forests* | 161 |
| 17. | *On My Poems* | 163 |
| 37. | *On My House at Czarnolas* | 163 |
| 38. | *To the Lord* | 163 |
| 50. | *To a Guest* | 164 |
| 54. | *On Health* | 164 |
| 72. | *Prayer for Rain* | 164 |
| 82. | *To a Maid* | 165 |

Songs
  Book I
| | |
|---|---|
| *Song II* | 165 |
| *Song VII* | 166 |
| *Song IX* | 167 |
| *Song XXIV* | 168 |

  Book II
| | |
|---|---|
| *Song VII* | 170 |
| *Song VIII* | 170 |
| *Song XXIV* | 171 |

| | |
|---|---|
| *Saint John's Eve Song* | 173 |
| *First Maiden* | 173 |
| *Second Maiden* | 174 |
| *Twelfth Maiden* | 175 |

| | |
|---|---|
| *Song* | 177 |

*David's Psalter*
| | |
|---|---|
| *Psalm 91* | 178 |

# Table of Contents

|  |  |
|---|---|
| Laments I-XIX | 180 |
| The Dismissal of the Greek Envoys | 212 |
| A Treatise on Virtue | 239 |

Mikołaj Sęp-Szarzyński
- Sonnets I-V ... 242
- On the Picture of Stefan Batory, Polish King ... 248
- On Katie and Annie ... 249

Sebastian Grabowiecki
- A Hundred Spiritual Rhymes
  - Book I
    - VII ... 250
    - XI ... 251
    - LXXXII ... 251
  - Book II
    - CXII Octonarius ... 252

Sebastian Klonowic
- Lament V ... 253
- Sailing, That Is Navigating Boats on the Vistula ... 255
- Judas's Bag ... 259

Szymon Szymonowic
- The Reapers ... 262

Szymon Zimorowic
- Roxolans
  - Cycerina ... 270

Kasper Miaskowski
- The Elegy of Penitence to the Holiest Virgin and Mother ... 273
- On a Painted Glass Goblet ... 274
- On Harvest ... 275

## LIST OF ILLUSTRATIONS

I. Zygmunt's Chapel in Cracow, 1519-1533 (Photograph by M. Moraczewska, courtesy of Instytut Sztuki PAN in Warsaw), p. 25.

II. Baranów palace courtyard, 1579-1602 (Photograph by M. Moraczewska, courtesy of Instytut Sztuki PAN in Warsaw), p. 26.

III. Title page of Mikołaj Gomółka's *Melodies for the Polish Psalter*, Cracow, 1580 (Photograph by St. Turski, courtesy of Biblioteka Narodowa in Warsaw), p. 29.

IV. Title page of the Wujek *Bible*, Cracow, 1599 (Photograph by Krzysztof Konopka, courtesy of Biblioteka Narodowa in Warsaw), p. 30.

V. Title page of Biernat's *A Short Description of Aesop's Life*, Cracow, 1578 ((Photograph by Andrzej Szypowski, courtesy of Biblioteka Kórnicka PAN), p. 70.

VI. King Zygmunt August, engraved portrait from Kromer's *De origine et rebus gestis Polonorum*, Basilea, 1555 (Photograph by J. Jaworski, courtesy of Instytut Sztuki Polskiej Akademii Nauk in Warsaw), p. 76.

VII. Nicholas Copernicus, portrait from Frombork Museum (Photograph by Ewa Kozłowska-Tomczyk, courtesy of Instytut Sztuki PAN in Warsaw), p. 85.

VIII. Title page of Andrzej Frycz Modrzewski's *Commentariorum de Republica emendanda,* Basilea, 1554 (Photograph by St. Turski, courtesy of Biblioteka Narodowa in Warsaw), p. 97.

IX. Mikołaj Rej, engraved portrait, Cracow, 1568 (Photograph by Krzysztof Konopka, courtesy of Biblioteka Narodowa in Warsaw), p. 137.

*List of Illustrations*

X. Title page of Mikołaj Rej's *A Short Conversation*, Cracow, 1543 (Photograph by Henryk Romanowski, courtesy of Biblioteka Narodowa in Warsaw), p. 138.

XI. Jan Kochanowski, portrait from his tomb in Zwoleń (Photograph by M. Kopydłowski, courtesy of Instytut Sztuki PAN in Warsaw), p. 152.

XII. Title page of Jan Kochanowski's *Laments*, Cracow, 1583 (Photograph by Maria Wesołowska, courtesy of Fundacja Książąt Czartoryskich in Cracow), p. 181.

XIII. Title page of Jan Kochanowski's *The Dismissal of the Greek Envoys*, Cracow, 1578 (Photograph by Zbigniew Kamykowski, courtesy of Biblioteka Narodowa in Warsaw), p. 213.

XIV. Title page of Mikołaj Sęp Szarzyński's *Rhythms or Polish Poems*, 1601 (Photograph by Zbigniew Kamykowski, courtesy of Biblioteka Kórnicka PAN), p. 243.

XV. Granary in Kazimierz (Photograph by J. Szandomirski, courtesy of Instytut Sztuki PAN in Warsaw), p. 256.

XVI. Engraved view of Cracow from Braun and Hogenberg's *Civitates orbis terrarum*, 1572-1617 (Photograph by Alan Magayne-Roshak, author's collection), p. 271.

# FOREWORD

This volume, a sequel to *Medieval Literature of Poland. An Anthology* (New York and London, Garland Publishing, 1992), is addressed to students of Polish literature and culture, scholars, and the general public. It is the first ever collection of English texts devoted solely to Polish Renaissance poetry and prose. It can be argued that the achievements of European Renaissance literature cannot be fully appreciated until the major Polish works, surpassing those of other Slavic nations in quality and range, become accessible to foreign critics and readers.

Sixteen poems and prose works included in this annotated anthology were written originally in Latin, attesting to the essentially bilingual character of Polish Renaissance literature. Some writers who wrote exclusively in Latin, for example, Janiciusz, Copernicus, and Frycz Modrzewski, gained prominence in literary and scientific circles in Europe. Others, most notably Kochanowski, Klonowic, and Szymonowic, wrote with equal facility in Latin and in Polish throughout their lives. And yet with the ascent and eventual supremacy of the vernacular, the literary canon that emerged and retained its hold on generations of readers consists mostly of works written in Polish, less often translated from Latin into Polish. Reflecting the present dominance of the literature created in the national language, this book contains over one hundred texts that were composed in the native idiom.

Texts originally written in Latin were consulted, but the translations have been made from their Polish renditions. Latin texts of Janiciusz, Kochanowski, Frycz Modrzewski, and others are still studied in their original form by scholars of the Renaissance. However, the general public as well as high school and University students read them only in the vernacular. Many excellent and richly annotated translations created by prominent writers, to mention only Władysław Syrokomla, Leopold Staff, and Zygmunt Kubiak, became an integral part of the Polish literary canon.

The anthology encompasses poetry, prose, and drama. The texts include epigrams, fables, songs, sonnets, and elegies as well as letters, sermons, tales, treatises, and chronicles. They are richly diverse and display the virtuosity of many writers. They range from short poems, for example, a rhymed fable by Biernat of Lublin, to longer prose sections, for example, Piotr Skarga's sermon to the Diet deputies. Some poems and stories describe personal experiences, others depict the mores, still others deal with the political issues of the day, for example, with the Reformation disputes. Two larger works by Jan Kochanowski: a cycle of nineteen *Laments* and a play, *The Dismissal of the Greek Envoys*, are translated here in their entirety for the first time since 1928.

I have attempted to make *Polish Renaissance Literature* as comprehensive as possible. Because of space limitation, however, I was able to include in this volume only a limited number of poems and prose excerpts. My main criteria in selecting them were the literary quality and representativeness of content, as reflected in the abundance of styles and genres. Needless to say that in a collection of this scope the artistic quality of poems is not even. Biernat's *Fables*, written in a simple and irregular syllabic verse, cannot be compared with Kochanowski's sublime and elaborate poems, in which he used as many as fifteen different types of rhymed syllabic verse as well as blank verse. Similarly, Krzycki's refined Latin epigrams, which recorded important events at the royal court, seem pale in comparison with Sęp Szarzyński's sonnets expressing his intense personal struggle. The same holds true for prose, as evidenced by the juxtaposition of the plain narrative in Bielski's *Chronicle* with the fiery oratory of Skarga's *Sermons*.

Out of one hundred and twenty two works I have translated, sixty-three have been done for the first time, while the remaining fifty-nine, most of them by Kochanowski, have been rendered into English before. Useful as those texts were, I have retranslated the original works for a number of reasons. Some old renditions were not accurate. Others did not convey the rhymed endings and meter of the original poems. The remaining selections were retranslated so that I could maintain the uniformity of style in the book. The texts have been translated from authoritative editions or if those were lacking from the best available sources. I have compared variant readings in different editions of a poet or writer, selected one, and commented upon the other readings in footnotes.

My main goal was to provide faithful and philologically accurate translations, preserving at the same time metric and stanzaic regularity. The original meters of the poems have been rendered into a variety of metrical patterns, most often into the iambic pentameter, not unlike natural, simple couplets used by Chaucer in most of *The Canterbury Tales*.

In general, modern poets, influenced by T.S. Eliot and Ezra Pound, tend to avoid rhyme, as they consider it an insignificant addition to English verse. Much of English great poetry is indeed not rhymed. It has been pointed out that it is extremely difficult to manage rhyme in English and easy to create artificial and false effects, particularly when dealing with traditional forms, for example, the sonnet.

The use of rhyme in verse with regular stress-pattern was, however, a characteristic feature of English Renaissance poetry, to mention only the poems of Wyatt, Spenser, and Ralegh. For the lyric poets like Kochanowski, Szymonowic, and Szarzyński, regular meters and precise rhymes were not mere conventional devices, but the integral components of rhetorical and aesthetic expression, crucial elements of classical discipline required of a Renaissance artist.

I have chosen to maintain stanzaic regularity and rhyme in most poems, even though it involved the challenge of finding satisfactory patterns for thousands of verses. I strove for exact rhymes, but in many cases used imperfect rhymes and assonances in an effort to gain greater naturalness. Rhymes in Polish are overwhelmingly feminine, with stress falling on the last but one syllable of words. In English, because of the predominance of rising and monosyllabic phrases, masculine rhymes are by far the most common type, especially in short lines of two, three or four feet, creating an acoustically "heavier" effect.

These goals of faithfulness to the original and of metrical and stanzaic regularity limited considerably my freedom of translation. So did the constraint of conveying the eleven and thirteeen syllable lines of some Polish poems in a customary ten and twelve syllable English verse. Yet in order to do justice to the significant literary achievement of the Polish Renaissance, I endeavored to reproduce the character and spirit of the original works in the most natural language.

A word of warning is in order to those who will consult the original texts in Polish, while reading these translations.

# Foreword

Many sixteenth century words, identical in form to present day words, differ substantially in meaning from their contemporary counterparts. Thus, for example, 'prawie' did not mean 'almost, nearly', but 'truly', 'smok' was often not 'a dragon', but 'a snake', and 'barwa' was not only 'color', but also 'a feigned shape'. My authority in these matters was *Słownik polszczyzny XVI wieku*, which provides not only various meanings of the word, but also cites contexts in which it appears.

I would like to thank Zygmunt Kubiak and Stefan Nieznanowski, my colleagues in Poland, who answered many questions and offered advice. James Shey, my colleague at the University of Wisconsin-Milwaukee, was always ready to listen to a new version of the text, read the whole manuscript, and made many valuable suggestions. I am grateful to Samuel Fiszman, Halina Filipowicz, James Liddy, and Ewa Thompson for their comments and help at various stages of this project. I wish to thank the anonymous readers as well as several colleagues, who used my translations of Kochanowski's *Laments* in their classes, for giving me the benefit of their comments. I am thankful to John W. Bowden for his technical expertise in getting the text ready for publication. The preparation of this volume was made possible in part by a grant from the Graduate School of the University of Wisconsin-Milwaukee and by a grant from the National Endowment for the Humanities.

M.J.M.

University of Wisconsin-Milwaukee    February 1995

# INTRODUCTION

## HISTORICAL BACKGROUND

At the end of the fifteenth century and the beginning of the sixteenth century Europe enjoyed a period of rapid growth and prosperity. The population was increasing by 4-5 per mill each year. Thousands of people settled down in the burgeoning cities of Italy, France, England, and the Netherlands, and engaged in crafts, industry, and trade. Explorers and merchants brought to Europe rich supplies of gold and spices and established profitable new markets throughout the world.

Poland participated actively in this new age of expansion and growth. The powerful monarchs of the Jagiellonian dynasty ruled over a large country, stretching from the Baltic Sea to the environs of the Black Sea, and over adjacent Lithuania, Bohemia, and Hungary. A century without a major war allowed the multinational commonwealth to unify and to gain strength. The battles against Muscovy and Turkey were fought upon remote eastern frontiers, the Reformation brought no bloodshed.

Living conditions in Poland, just as in the rest of Europe, improved significantly. The number of city dwellers increased to 23% of the country population, as the major cities, Cracow, Gdańsk, and Wrocław grew to 20,000 people each in the middle of the sixteenth century. Agricultural production flourished. The expanding industrial and mercantile centers in Europe needed food and raw materials for their inhabitants. The prices for agricultural goods rose rapidly, allowing Poland to export lucratively its surplus, mainly grain, lumber, and cattle. Other exports included potash, wool, and products made of furs and hides.

These trade profits gave opportunity to the Polish gentry, who constituted about ten percent of the population but owned more than sixty percent of the land, to raise considerably their standard of living and to accumulate wealth. Gradually they began to assert their political power. The Sejm formed itself into the General Assembly, which consisted of two chambers: the Senate and the Chamber of Deputies composed of delegates chosen at the land diets. With a series of decrees, the deputies curtailed the freedom of peasants by tying them to their land and increasing their work load. They restricted the privileges of the clergy, limiting all the senior Church appointments to candidates of noble birth. They reduced the rights of the burghers by preventing them from purchasing land and by imposing high taxes on trade, while granting for themselves a duty free status. In 1504 the Sejm passed resolutions directed against the magnates, and in 1505 against the king. The decree of *Nihil Novi* ("nothing new") stipulated that the king would not levy taxes or pass new laws without the consent of the Senate and the Chamber of Deputies. Later, when the Sejm began to exercise a rule according to which any new law could be vetoed by a single deputy on behalf of the opposition (the *liberum veto*), the royal authority became further restricted.

The challenge to the Polish monarchs ruling over the largest territory in Europe, which by 1634 extended over 386,719 square miles (ca. 1,000,000 square kilometers) and was inhabited by eleven million people, came not only from within but also from without. In 1497, King Jan Olbracht (1492-1501) sent a military expedition to stop the growing threat posed by Turkey. The Turks conquered Constantinople in 1453, then Genua, and seized the Black Sea ports of Kilia and Akkerman, important for the Polish trade. The defeat of the expeditionary forces in Bukowina exposed Poland's ineffectiveness and encouraged the Turks to launch devastating raids against the south-east territories of the country.

When Aleksander Jagiellon (1501-1506), who ruled Lithuania, was elected King of Poland, the personal union between the two countries was re-established. This alliance, which originated with the 1385 Union of Krewo and became confirmed a year later, when Jogaila, Grand Duke of Lithuania, accepted Christianity, married Jadwiga, and with the name of Władysław Jagiełło was crowned King of Poland, brought both states into a direct conflict with Ivan III, Grand Duke of Muscovy, who wrested Novgorod and Pskov from Lithuanian control. Poland's situation became even more precarious when Maximilian I, the Habsburg Emperor, allied himself with Muscovy and with the Teutonic Knights in order to gain influence in Hungary and Bohemia, ruled by Władysław Jagiellon.

The basic principle of the policy pursued by Zygmunt the Old during his long reign (1506-1548) was to ensure, mostly by diplomatic means, Poland's security and stablility. By signing the Treaty of Vienna (1515), Zygmunt approved his brother Władysław's dynastic concessions to the Habsburgs with regard to Hungary and Bohemia. In return Maximilian withdrew his support for Muscovy and the Teutonic Order. When Albrecht von Hohenzollern, Grand Master of the Teutonic Order, challenged the suzerainty of Poland and allied himself with Muscovy, the Polish army attacked Koenigsberg in 1519. Albrecht, threatened with defeat, sued for peace. The Teutonic Order was transformed into the secular Duchy of Prussia, becoming dependent on Poland. In 1525, in an act of submission, Duke Albrecht paid homage to Zygmunt the Old at the Market Square in Cracow.

Supported by his influential second wife, Bona Sforza of Italy, King Zygmunt attempted to strengthen Poland's defenses of the south-eastern territories. He was hampered in his efforts by the gentry, who were unwilling to provide adequate financial means for permanent armed forces. His son, Zygmunt II August (1548-1572), succeeded in establishing a royal treasury, from which one quarter of the revenues was set aside to maintain the standing army.

The need for a strong army and navy was apparent. In 1558, Ivan the Terrible, seeking the access to the Baltic Sea for Muscovy, attacked Livonia, ruled by the Order of the Livonian Knights. When in 1561 Gotthard von Kettler, the Grand Master of the Livonian Order, ceded his country to King Zygmunt August, Ivan the Terrible, supported by Sweden, waged war for the domination of the Baltic Sea against Poland, Lithuania, and their ally Denmark.

The military threat posed by Muscovy compelled Poland and the Grand Duchy of Lithuania to seek a closer alliance. Even though Lithuanian magnates, fearful to lose their privileges, opposed the political union, they were unable to resist the combined pressure of the King and the gentry of both countries, strongly in favor of uniting as "the free with the free, the equal with the equal." On July 1 1569, at a meeting of the Sejm in Lublin, the delegates of Poland and Lithuania accepted the Act of Union, creating the Commonwealth of the Two Nations. The new state would have one king, a common Sejm and monetary system, but maintain separate treasuries, administrations, judicial systems, and armed forces. Thus the process of unification, begun by the personal union between Władysław Jagiełło and Jadwiga, the founders of the dynasty, bound Poland and Lithuania into one multinational commonwealth during the reign of Zygmunt August, the last Jagiellon monarch.

The power of the kings and the authority of the Church were challenged by the dynamic movement of the Reformation that swept across many countries of Western Europe. The news of Martin Luther's 1517 declaration in Wittenberg quickly reached Prussia and Silesia, then other parts of Poland. The country became a sanctuary for people persecuted elsewhere. The Anabaptists, mostly from Holland, the Bohemian Brethren, expelled from Prague, the Calvinists, and other groups, found shelter and support among the burghers, gentry, and magnates in various regions of Poland.

The most radical champions of the Reformation were the Polish Brethren (also known as the Arians or the Socinians). They rejected the concepts of the Holy Trinity and of original sin. They applied the teachings of Christ to their lives, advocating the dignity and freedom of man, and common ownership of material goods. They condemned serfdom, participation in war, and holding of office. Within a short period of time, the Arians gained close to 20,000 converts who practiced in up to 100 temples all over the country. They established their own Academy and publishing house in Raków. When they were expelled from Poland for political reasons in 1658, they settled throughout Europe, contributing to the ideas embraced later by Unitarianism and the Age of Reason.

But in spite of the intellectual fervor brought by the Reformation and the strong convictions of its adherents, the movement spent itself in a relatively short period of time without achieving its goals of causing a break with Rome and establishing a Polish national church. The royal court, the magnates, the gentry, and even the Church, liberal in their attitudes, did not feel threatened by the Protestant causes to a degree that would justify a militant reaction. The new ideas did not appeal to the broad masses of the population. Multiethnic and multireligious, Poland was well prepared to accept and absorb new religious denominations and sects. At the Warsaw Confederation of 1573, the deputies pledged that "we who differ in matters of religion, will keep peace among ourselves" and "will not shed blood or punish others by depriving them of property and good name, imprisonment and exile, nor assist at all any authority or office in such a deed." When the act was incorporated into the constitution, no religious issue was allowed to take precedence over a legal one. Consequently, the Poles tolerated various religions, refrained from persecution, and produced no martyrs.

In addition, while the Reformation movement was splintered and ever-changing, the Catholic Church responded with a cohesive program of the reaffirmation of faith. The Counter Reformation, led by Cardinal Hosius, Bishop of Warmia, and author of a popular *Confessio fidei Catholicae Christianae* (1553), was spearheaded by the Jesuits, brought to Poland in 1564. Well educated and disciplined, they organized about fifty schools, gaining increasing influence on education. By the end of the reign of Zygmunt August, the Reformation began to recede.

The results of the first election, held after a long interregnum following Zygmunt August's death, were not auspicious. In order to restrain the autocratic tendencies of the contending Habsburg, French, and Russian candidates and to secure their own privileges, the gentry submitted to Henri de Valois, the future king, numerous conditions, known as the Henrician Articles. The elected king agreed, for example, not to call a general levy or proclaim new taxes without the consent of the Sejm. More importantly, he was required to reaffirm all the privileges won so far by the gentry. In 1574, after four months' residence in Poland, Henri de Valois learned of his brother's death and fled secretly from Cracow to become the King of France.

The election of Stefan Batory (1576-1586), a gifted strategist and an accomplished military leader, proved much more beneficial for Poland. The new ruler was knowledgeable about contemporary political affairs, well read in history, and fluent in many languages, especially Latin. Supported by the Grand Chancellor of the Crown Jan Zamoyski, Batory reformed the judicial system and the royal army. After breaking the resistance of Gdańsk, which supported the Habsburg candidacy to the Polish throne and attempted to secure for itself a semi-independent position, Batory fought for years against the forces of Ivan the Terrible. After defeating him at Duneberg and Połock, Batory regained Livonia and the region of Połock. He was unable, however, to reform during his short reign the political institutions in Poland.

The inherent weakness of the electoral process became apparent again during the interregnum following Batory's death. Supporters of Zygmunt III Vasa of Sweden, led by Jan Zamoyski, clashed on the battlefield with the army of the Habsburg Archduke Maximilian and his Polish adherents. Zamoyski's victory in 1588 paved the way for Zygmunt, son of the Swedish King John III and Catherine Jagiellon, to the throne of Poland (1587-1632). But the deep conflict between the King and a large faction of the gentry led by Mikołaj Zebrzydowski erupted into rebellion in 1606, undermining further the royal authority and the political system of the Commonwealth.

The gentry accused the King not only of striving to increase his powers but also of involving Poland in ill-advised military adventures. Zygmunt's desire to ascend the Swedish throne, particularly fervent after his father's death in 1592, caused a protracted war with Sweden, which lasted with intervals from 1600 to 1629. In spite of the Polish victories at Kirchholm in 1605 and near Oliwa in 1627, Zygmunt failed in his dynastic bid. This resulted in Poland's loss of a large part of Livonia and of several strongholds on the Baltic coast.

Equally unsuccessful were the attempts of some magnates and of the King to influence the struggle for succession in Muscovy. Taking advantage of a civil war, the Polish forces managed in 1605 to elevate their candidate to the throne of the Tsar. The reign of 'the false Demetrius' was brief--he and his Polish followers were killed in 1606. Other costly campaigns ended in failure and the truce in 1629 put an end to this Polish confrontation with Russia.

Thus the golden age enjoyed by Poland during the reign of the last Jagiellons was drawing to a close under the first king of the Vasa dynasty. But even the political abuses, military defeats, and territorial losses suffered by the country in the seventeenth and eighteenth centuries did not diminish the luster of the Polish Renaissance, since it had left behind a fertile and diverse heritage, preserved most permanently in its culture and literature.

## CULTURAL BACKGROUND

The Renaissance belief in the dignity of man and power of his reason found a receptive ground in Poland. The revival of interest in antiquity and learning stimulated a new world view. It manifested itself in the expanding studies of classical Latin, Greek, and Hebrew. It led to an increased interest in the disciplines of rhetoric, epistolography, and history. Important works of ancient writers, e.g., by Cicero and Seneca, were translated into Polish and imitated. So were the seminal Italian texts, e.g., *The Book of the Courtier*, Castiglione's treatise on the ideal Renaissance man, who lives in harmony with himself and the world.

Between 1500 and 1535, the Cracow Academy enjoyed a period of growth and international recognition. In the first ten years of the sixteenth century, 3215 students matriculated in the university, a record not surpassed until after the reform of 1777-1786. Many foreign students settled in Cracow, some of them attracted by the reputation enjoyed by the Academy professors. One of the most outstanding teachers was Maciej of Miechów, the erudite author of *Chronica Polonorum* and of the *Tractatus de duabus Sarmatiis*, published in Cracow in 1517. The *Tractatus*, the first accurate geographical and ethnographical description of Eastern Europe, was translated into many languages, and went through eighteen editions in the sixteenth century. It also popularized a theory of the ancient, Sarmatian heritage of Poland.

It is not a coincidence that the fertile intellectual milieu of Cracow produced many outstanding scientists, political writers, and poets. Among Polish students at the Cracow Academy was Nicholas Copernicus, who in his opus *De revolutionibus orbium coelestium* (1543) developed a new scientific theory of the universe. His colleague and friend, Bernard Wapowski, a historian and cartographer, drafted the maps of the Polish and Ruthenian lands which appeared in the the 1507 and 1508 editions of Ptolemy's *Geography*. Marcin Kromer, the author of *De origine et rebus gestis Polonorum libri III* (1555) and *Polonia* (written about 1558) described the historical development of Poland as well as its geography, nationalities, customs, and institutions. Andrzej Frycz Modrzewski, another prominent graduate of the

Academy, advanced novel political and social theories concerning the whole state. Jan Kochanowski perfected Polish poetic language and became recognized as the most eminent Slavic poet until the beginning of the nineteenth century.

In the middle of the sixteenth century, a network of more than 2500 parish schools provided elementary education to Polish children. Some gymnasia, mainly Protestant and later Jesuit, especially in Gdańsk, Toruń, Poznań, and Pińczów, offered advanced programs for students of law, medicine, theology, and mathematics. In 1579, thanks to the efforts of King Stefan Batory, the Jesuit gymnasium of Wilno was transformed into the Wilno Academy, and in 1595 Chancellor Jan Zamoyski founded the Academy of Zamość which promoted a program in the humanities and prepared its students for state offices.

Young Poles, in general sons of the gentry and of the burghers, traveled abroad to complete their education, most often to Padua, Bologna, Rome, Louvain, Paris, Wittenberg, or Basel. The university bonds were cultivated through personal contacts, official activities, and correspondence. Members of the Polish intellectual elite, e.g., Jan Dantyszek, a distinguished diplomat and poet, Jan Łaski, a religious reformer and patron of the arts, or Andrzej Frycz Modrzewski, maintained contacts with leading European luminaries, including Thomas More, Erasmus of Rotterdam, and Philip Melanchthon. Through this exchange of ideas, Poland not only participated in major scientific and political developments but also propagated Western heritage and art among the East Slavic nations, especially in Byelorussia and Ukraine, from where they were transmitted to the Duchy of Muscovy.

The main incentive for the development of Renaissance art and architecture came from the royal court at Wawel. King Zygmunt the Old fell under the spell of Italian art, when as a young prince he visited the court of his brother Władysław in Buda. Crowned in 1507 King of Poland, Zygmunt launched an ambitious project of transforming the royal castle into a Renaissance residence. The new palace, with slim columns and three levels of light galleries, built by Bartolommeo Berrecci from Florence, his compatriots, and local artists, became a model accomplishment of the Polish

Renaissance. Inside, residential chambers and halls were embellished with ornamental wall paintings and large tapestries from Brussels, embroidered with gold. A richly carved wooden ceiling in the Deputies Hall was decorated with one hundred and ninety four sculptures in the shape of human heads, an innovative idea which most likely originated with the King or his wife Bona Sforza of Italy, while the whole project was designed and carried out by Sebastian Tauerbach and his coworkers. The sepulchar chapel (1551), called Zygmunt's Chapel, another masterpiece of Berrecci, became the mausoleum for Zygmunt the Old and his son Zygmunt August. The two great patrons of the arts who made Wawel a truly royal residence rested there in the marble tombs, surrounded by figures of saints beneath the splendidly decorated gilded dome.

Magnates and wealthy burghers were also eager to display their artistic tastes and patronage. Foreign architects, sculptors, and craftsmen brought to Poland by King Zygmunt and Queen Bona were employed side by side with native artists to build and embellish castles, palaces, and manor houses throughout the country. Many designs imitated the arcaded courtyard and arched loggias of the Wawel palace. The Gothic castle in Pieskowa Skała near Cracow, for example, was reconstructed by the Szafraniec family in 1542-1544, its double arched loggias looking down at the courtyard and an exterior loggia overlooking the river valley. The richly decorated castles built by Santi Gucci and Galeazzo Appiani (or Appiano) for the Firlejs in Janowiec, the Krasickis in Krasiczyn, and the Leszczyńskis in Baranów, the last one known for its quadrangular courtyard and a double open stairway, were among the most beautiful Renaissance buildings in Poland.

Cities and towns did not lag far behind. The main beneficiaries of the Renaissance art were Cracow and Gdańsk, which attracted many foreign artists. Because of its location, Cracow was influenced by new trends from Italy, Hungary, and Southern Germany, while Gdańsk from the Netherlands and Northern Germany. The Cloth Hall in Cracow Market Square was rebuilt in 1555 by Giovanni Maria Padovano, who constructed a raised decorative parapet along the top of its facades, a feature imitated in many buildings. In Gdańsk, a thriving commercial port city

I. Zygmunt's Chapel in Cracow, 1519-1533

II. Baranów palace courtyard, 1579-1602

on the Baltic coast, the Arsenal was designed by Antoni van Obbergen and Jan Strakowski in the style of the Flemish-Dutch Renaissance. The Red Room in the Town Hall was decorated with wood carvings by Simon Hoerle, its ceiling embellished with more than twenty painted allegorical compositions by Isaac van den Blocke.

Other towns, some of them quite small, were also able to express the artistic aspirations of their inhabitants. The Town Hall in Poznań was rebuilt by Giovanni Battista Quadro, gaining three-storied loggias and a tall parapet, and its walls were adorned in sgraffito. The Town Hall in Tarnów acquired a new parapet with mascarons, the work of Padovano. The same artist was engaged in remodelling the Town Hall in Sandomierz. Kazimierz Dolny, the bustling center of the grain trade was enriched by twenty five ornate granaries along the Vistula. The two arcaded houses in the Market Square which belonged to Mikołaj and Krzysztof Przybyła displayed an unusually high parapet and the facade covered fully with a mannerist decoration, featuring the owners' patron saints, narrative reliefs, and a profusion of ornaments.

In 1578, Jan Zamoyski, chancellor to three kings, conceived a bold plan of building the ideal Renaissance city. Designed by Bernardo Morando from Venice, Zamość was laid out along two axes. The large market square, dominated by the town hall, and the palace were located on the main east-west axis. Other major buildings included the academy, the library, the arsenal, and the Collegiate Church, all surrounded by modern fortifications flanked by seven bastions. Zamość grew quickly to become an important administrative, commercial, and educational center for the whole region.

In Tarnów, Jan Tarnowski, a powerful political and military leader, employed at his court Berrecci and Padovano. The sepulchers of Tarnowski, his father, brother, and his wife Barbara, placed in Tarnów Cathedral, are famous for their elegant composition, excellent proportions, and subtle lines. The same mastery of design and workmanship can be seen in the elaborate work of Jan Michałowicz, who sculpted the mausoleums of bishops Zebrzydowski and Padniewski in Cracow Cathedral. The bronze bas relief on the sarcophagus of Chancellor Krzysztof

Szydłowiecki in the Collegiate Church in Opatów, the work of Bernardino de Gianotis and Giovanni Cini, shows a group of courtiers lamenting the chancellor's death.

In painting, the Renaissance interest in man and the beauty of the world found its expression in many religious scenes and triptychs, located most often in the churches and monasteries of Little Poland. The pictures show realistic details and convey human emotions, e.g., in the figures of a suffering Christ or an expectant Mary. The art of portrait painting, practiced in Poland by such masters as Hans Süss, Hans Dürer, and Lucas Cranach, was cultivated by local painters, of whom Marcin Krober from Wrocław, a court painter of Stefan Batory and the author of his picture, was the most prominent. The portraitists left behind a splendid pictorial gallery of the noble and the wealthy, capturing characteristic features and social position of each person.

The miniatures in the Pontifical Book of Erazm Ciołek, featuring, for example, the king's coronation, show fine narrative details. Baltazar Behem's *Codex* (1505), a book of statutes and privileges presented by the author to the Cracow town council, contains twenty six color miniatures depicting with great realism various scenes from the life of local guilds. Stanisław Samostrzelnik gained recognition for his ornamental miniatures in the genealogical book of the Szydłowiecki family, polichrome painting in the Cistercian monastery in Mogiła, and portrait of Bishop Tomicki in Saint Francis Church in Cracow. Many of Samostrzelnik's religious miniatures are preserved in the collections of the British Museum, the Bodleian Library, and the Biblioteca Ambrosiana in Milan.

The center of musical culture was the royal residence in Cracow. The kings surrounded themselves with foreign and local composers and musicians. The players and singers of Zygmunt the Old performed during court festivities and followed him on his journeys and military expeditions. In 1540, the king also founded a choir of religious vocalists who sang in the Cathedral during the matins. The finest works of the period, many of them preserved in Cracow libraries, include vocal and instrumental compositions, dances, organ and polyphonic music as well as solemn oratorios and masses.

Especially popular were compositions for the organ and for the lute. The *Tablature* (c. 1540), compiled by Jan of

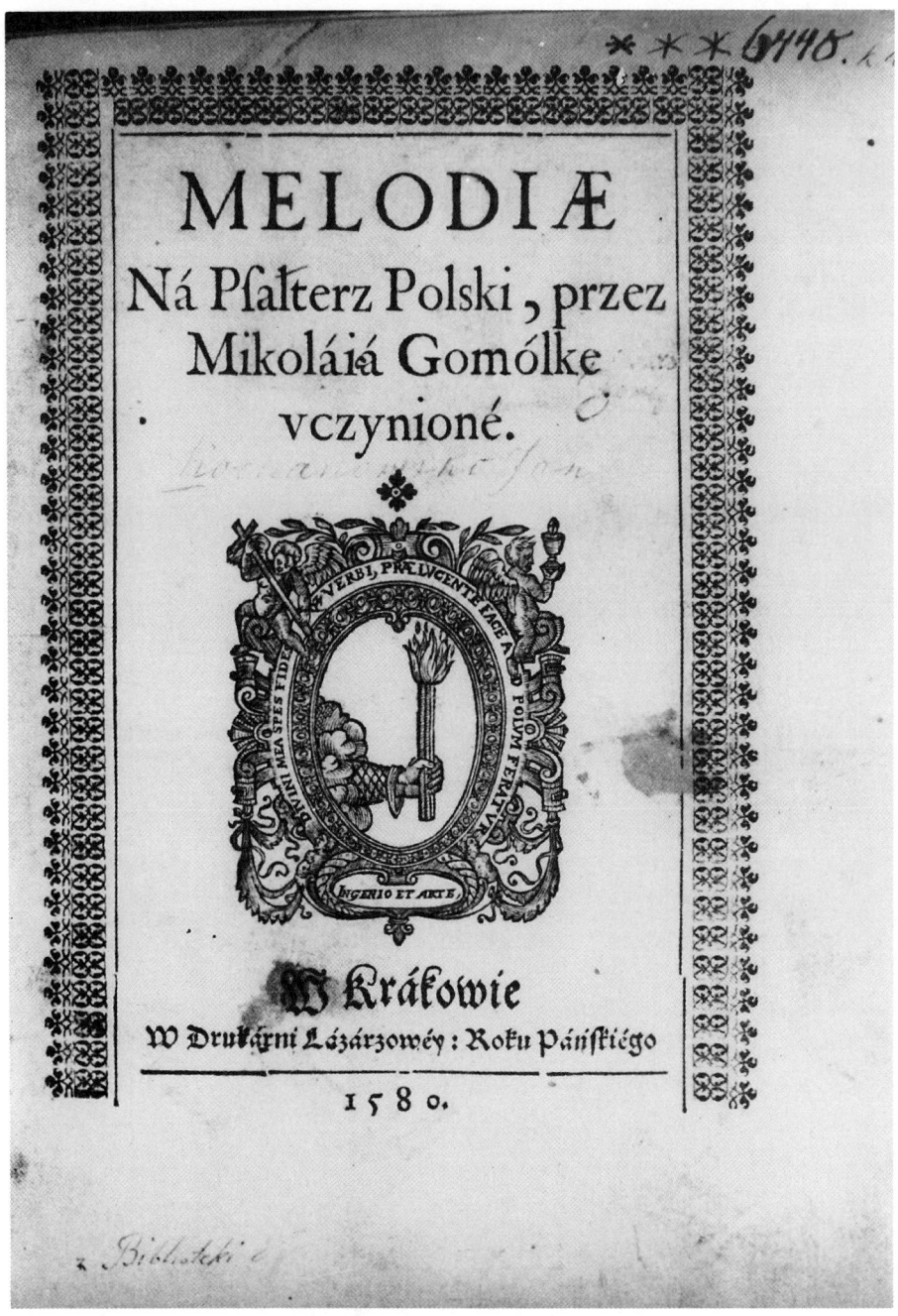

III. Title page of Mikołaj Gomółka's *Melodies for the Polish Psalter,* Cracow, 1580

IV. Title page of the Wujek *Bible*, Cracow, 1599

Lublin, was an extensive collection of all known European organ compositions. The recorded works were based on religious motifs as well as on lay dances and songs of Polish, French, Italian, and German origin. Mikołaj of Cracow composed more than forty elaborate works, among them Polish songs, dances, and fragments of the mass. Wacław of Szamotuły (c. 1526-1560), recognized as one of the outstanding Renaissance composers, was the author of the five-voice *Missa paschalis* and polyphonic motets, e.g., *In te Domine speravi* and *Ego sum pastor bonus*.

Mikołaj Gomółka (c. 1535 - after 1591) from Sandomierz spent many years of his youth at King Zygmunt's court, first singing in the royal choir, then as a trumpet and pipe player. In 1580, he published his only known work, the *Melodies for the Polish Psalter*, a musical rendition of one hundred and fifty poems translated from the Latin by Jan Kochanowski. Since Kochanowski's masterly interpretation of the psalms was published in Cracow in 1579, it is most certain that he had trusted Gomółka with his manuscripts before they were published.

Effectively using rhythm, melody, and harmony, Gomółka found a perfect idiom for expressing the lofty poetic language and spirit of the psalms. Penitential psalms were rendered in slow and sombre tones, while the psalms of joy were conveyed by lively melodies, resembling at times vivacious folk dances. The *Melodies for the Polish Psalter*, a combined effort of the two great artists, became one of the most sublime accomplishments of the High Renaissance culture in Poland.

## LITERARY BACKGROUND

The most efficient medium for disseminating Renaissance ideas was the printed word. In 1473, Kasper Straube from Bavaria set up the first workshop in Cracow and by 1477 published four texts, beginning with the almanac for 1474. Szwajpolt Fiol established between 1483 and 1486 a printing house, where after obtaining 230 Cyrillic molds, he published by 1491 the first four Cyrillic books in the world: two collections of Easter prayers and songs, a breviary, and a collection of hymns. Jan Haller, a prominent Cracow merchant who owned the first regular printing house, released between 1505 and 1525 about 250 texts, mostly liturgical. Other printers, among them Marek Szarffenberg, Florian Ungler and Hieronim Wietor, issued a variety of new titles including prayer books, Bibles, popular calendars, medical treatises, political and historical tracts, as well as textbooks, translations from the ancient authors, and works of Polish poets and prose writers. Łazarz Andrysowicz, who took over Wietor's printing house, published Frycz Modrzewski's treatise *De Republica emendanda* in 1551, his son Janusz Januszowski, was the publisher of nearly all books by Kochanowski and of Wujek's *Bible*, while Maciej Wierzbięta issued Rej's works and Górnicki's *Polish Courtier*. It is estimated that between 1561 and 1600, for example, seventeen printing houses in Poland published over 120 titles a year, that the average edition of a scholarly work in the sixteenth century was about 500 copies, and that the total number of printed books in that period was over two million volumes. Printers also contributed to the standardization of the language, as they regulated spelling rules and introduced diacritic marks to show phonemic differences.

The significance of the printed word grew with the advent of the Reformation. Half of the printing houses were in the hands of Protestants, as supporters of each creed realized the potential of this new form of communication in spreading their religious and social ideas. The Calvinist printers at Brześć and Wilno competed with the Arians at Pińczów and Raków, as well as with the Jesuit publishers in Poznań and Braniewo. What is more important, the Reformation movement, which spurred the growth of national culture, art, and learning, contributed to the increased popularity of the Polish language. Printed translations of the Bible proliferated following the 1561 publication of the first complete text in Polish by Jan Leopolita, while religious and social polemics were carried out more and more in the vernacular.

The gentry and the burghers, who played the leading role in the formation of the national culture, began to promote Polish as the language of state and literature. Numerous guilds of Cracow burghers recorded their statutes in Polish, and from the middle of the sixteenth century the courts and regional diets used the vernacular. The Church favored the Latin language, but in response to social demand most sermons were delivered in Polish. Even Frycz Modrzewski, who wrote exclusively in Latin, pointed out in his *Tractatus de sermone vernaculo* the advantages of propagating the Scriptures in the Polish language.

Polish Renaissance literature was essentially bilingual. Many writers, for example, Krzycki, Janiciusz, and Copernicus, wrote only in Latin. Some poets, most notably Kochanowski, Klonowic, and Szymonowic, used both Latin and Polish throughout their lives. But the majority of literary works of the period was written and published in the native language, for example, by Biernat, Rej, Górnicki, Kochanowski, Skarga, and Sęp Szarzyński, attracting many readers and popular acclaim. Their masterly use of various genres of poetry and prose led to the emergence of modern Polish literature and contributed to the consolidation of a national language.

Middle Polish, formed and developed mainly in the region of Little Poland with Cracow as its center, was influenced to a great degree by the dialect of Great Poland. Linguistic features characteristic of both dialects provided the foundation of an integrated idiom. The sound system underwent many changes of quality and quantity, affecting both vowels and consonants. The stress became fixed, falling on the penultimate syllable. The paradigms of certain declensions and conjugations became more uniform. The syntax underwent changes, allowing, for example, for a clear distinction between direct and indirect speech and greater regularity in the formation of compound sentences.

Lexical resources of Middle Polish more than tripled, reaching about 50,000 words. Borrowings from Latin, Czech, German, French, and Italian provided many new words for various semantic fields and for abstract concepts, allowing the language to function at many stylistic levels. Thus, the Middle Polish borrowed from Latin, e.g., *testament*, *aforyzm*, and *architekt*; from German, e.g., *burmistrz*, "Burgemeister"; *szpital*, "hospital"; and *druk*, "print"; and from Italian, e.g., *fontana*, "fountain"; *tulipan*, "tulip"; and *gracyja*, "grace."

Numerous dictionaries, some of them multilingual, for example, Joannes Murmelius's *Dictionarius* (1526), some bilingual, for example, Jan Mączyński's *Lexicon Latino-Polonicum* (1564), listing about 21,000 Polish words, recorded the Middle Polish lexical stock. The first practical orthography of the Polish language was prepared by Stanisław Murzynowski in 1551. Other authors, including Piotr Statorius-Stojeński in 1568 and Jan Januszowski in 1594, published grammar books. Linguistic polemics, concerning chiefly the importance of Polish and its relation to Latin, stimulated additional interest in the vernacular and in literature.

The dominant role of the nobility in political and cultural life was also reflected in literature. A great number of the most prominent writers belonged to the gentry, for example, Rej, Kochanowski, and Sęp Szarzyński. But the noblemen were not the only members of the literary elite, as it included many burghers, to mention only Biernat of Lublin, Klonowic, and Szymonowic, clergymen, among them Krzycki, Orzechowski, and Skarga, and even some men of humble origin, e.g., Janiciusz, Hussowski, and Jan of Kijany.

The literature they produced was just as varied. At the court, poets like Krzycki, Dantyszek, and Gąsiorek (also known as Kleryka) wrote occasional pieces to honor their patrons or to celebrate their weddings and victories. Religious literature was represented by theological treatises, by learned commentaries, and by collections of Protestant and Catholic hymns. The Catholic version of the Bible by Leopolita was followed by the Calvinist rendition (Brześć Bible of 1563), the Arian text (Nieświerz Bible of 1572,) and the most popular, authorised translation by the Jesuit Jakub Wujek (1599). Political writings, dealing with matters of State organization and the public weal, were disseminated in leaflets, pamphlets, and books, some of them authored by eminent writers, such as Orzechowski, Frycz Modrzewski, and Skarga. Burgher literature, including popular plebeian romances, satirical dialogues, and anonymous facetious stories, described with realism the lives and activities of craftsmen, journeymen, clerics, vagabonds, and even criminals.

The general tone, however, was set by the noblemen who propagated their own ideals of material and spiritual life. They lived upon their estates and occupied themselves with agricultural labors. The countryside and rural activities, measured by a peaceful flow of seasons, became their favorite artistic subject. Rej extolled the life and occupations of the ideal country squire, while Kochanowski celebrated in songs the beauty of the landscape and joys of rural life. Familiar with nature and inspired by its luxuriant manifestations, the poets painted original pictures of the world, presenting it with simplicity and sincere fascination.

They were able to do it by using a variety of new literary forms. Lyrical poetry was enriched by the Horatian ode, by the pastoral, and by the Italian sonnet. Other genres included elegy, romance, and satire. Among dramatic types, religious comedy and Jesuit school performances were staged next to popular morality plays. *The Dismissal of the Greek Envoys* by Kochanowski was the first Polish humanist drama. The new poetic devices, combined with originality and depth of thought, brought Renaissance literature to a high level of artistic expression.

Andrzej Krzycki, Mikołaj Hussowski, and Klemens Janiciusz belonged to the cosmopolitan fraternity of humanist poets who, like their predecessor Filippo Buonaccorsi (Kallimach), the celebrated poet from Tuscany, propagated the ideals of Renaissance culture in Poland. Krzycki chronicled major events at the royal court in his witty epigrams, e.g., *Four-line Poem on Queen Barbara* or *The Picture of Life at Court*, and delighted his readers with ingenious love conceits, e.g., *On a Girl Lidia*. Hussowski's *Poem on Bison*, modelled on Roman didactic poems, was known outside Poland for its original and vivid description of the majestic animal. Klemens Janiciusz, considered the most accomplished lyric poet before Kochanowski, was the author of polished epigrams, e.g., *Andrzej Krzycki, a Pole*, dedicated to his protector, and of moving elegies, e.g., *About Myself to Posterity*.

Many authors writing in the vernacular gained instant popularity. Some translated chivalrous romances and fantastic stories, others entertained broad masses of readers with amusing anecdotes and fables. One of the best known writers was Biernat of Lublin, whose moralistic poems, e.g., *He Who Holds the Sword Has the Peace* and *He Who Is Diligent Won't Go Wrong*, were based on versified renditions of Greek fables ascribed to Aesop, read throughout Europe in Latin translations. Marcin Bielski related in the first general history written in Polish some important local events, e.g., *Death and Funeral of Zygmunt the Old*. The anonymous stories of *Owlglass Facetious and Amusing*, derived from the German folk tales about Till Eulenspiegel, copious compilations of plebeian romances, including *Conversations Which Wise King Solomon Had with the Coarse and Vulgar Marcholt*, and bawdy epigrams by Jan of Kijany, e.g., *Hares* and *Wolves*, provided common people with an abundant supply of ribald entertainment.

The Latin prose works of Nicholas Copernicus constitute the paramount achievement of Renaissance science. Fully aware of the implications of his discovery for the accepted teachings of the Church, Copernicus tried to protect himself and his work from the attacks of hostile scholars and clergymen. When after a long delay he decided to have the new theory of the universe published, he dedicated the *De revolutionibus*, in a carefully worded letter of introduction, to Pope Paul III. In the field of historiography, Marcin Kromer's *De origine et rebus gestis Polonorum* (1555) and *Polonia* (1575) became a worthy continuation of Długosz's monumental *Annales*. Issued in many editions and adaptations abroad, Kromer's lively descriptions served for many years as a major source of information about Polish people, history, culture, economy, and political system.

Andrzej Frycz Modrzewski, a prominent political writer, was a utopian thinker and moralist who intended to enlighten and edify the nation. His bold ideas concerning a thorough reform of the state and the church, expressed in *Commentariorum de Republica emendanda* (1551-1554), won renown among European humanists, though they could not have been put into practice. Frycz considered Christian morality as the foundation of society and state, education and public duties as the most important obligations of citizens. He postulated the creation of a universal church, which would embrace the main teachings of Catholic and Protestant doctrines. He believed that the state should strive to preserve peace, be prepared to repel enemies, and engage only in just, defensive wars.

Stanisław Orzechowski, Frycz's adversary, was a gifted polemicist and ardent patriot who wrote with consummate skill on major religious issues. He also concerned himself with weighty problems of State reorganization, gaining immense popularity among the gentry whose causes he championed with fervent eloquence. Zealous and impassioned, he was unable, however, to rise above his changeable and, at times, narrow concerns.

Another prominent prose writer was Piotr Skarga, an inspired Jesuit preacher who became engaged in the debates and polemics stirred by the Reformation. Skarga, who dedicated his entire life to serve God and his fellow man, especially the poor and the unfortunates, believed that his principal mission was to promote a reform of the country. His major work was a series of eight eloquent *Sermons to the Diet* (1597), in which he depicted the moral and political degradation in Poland. Skarga called on all citizens to fulfil their duties not only towards God, Church, and their neighbors, but also towards the imperiled homeland. His appeal for moral regeneration, written in a vivid language that was inspired by the Bible, emerged as a model of lofty, classical Polish.

Łukasz Górnicki's *The Polish Courtier* (1566), an adaptation of Castiglione's *Il libro del cortegiano*, became the most elaborate affirmation of Renaissance values. Written in masterly prose, the *Courtier* offered a high-minded view of Renaissance civilization transposed to the Polish soil. In Górnicki's conception, the courtier's obligations extended beyond his palace duties, embracing education and art as well as chivalry and moral probity, all of them shaping a human being of refined culture and character. A picture of the ideal statesman was drawn by Wawrzyniec Goślicki in his *De optimo senatore libri duo* (1568). Goślicki was ahead of his time in advocating that kings should be held responsible for their deeds. Translated into English as *The Counsellor exactly portraited in two books* (1598), the first edition was promptly confiscated, but other translations and adaptations followed. They became popular among dissidents, who used excerpts from the book in political debates.

One of the most important Renaissance writers, called by many "the father of Polish literature," was Mikołaj Rej. This versatile and prolific author, keenly interested in political, religious and moralistic issues, was a staunch advocate of Calvinism and of the Polish language. His programmatic motto recorded in the collection of epigrams entitled the *Bestiary* declared:
>Among other nations let it always be known
>That the Poles are not geese, have a tongue
>of their own.

Rej's language was indeed his own; it was pithy and picturesque, at times chatty, but always lively and witty. His poems and prose works gained him immense popularity, a clear confirmation that literature could develop in the national language and that literary ability was appreciated by a great number of readers.

Rej excelled in a variety of genres. His *Short Conversation Between Three Persons, a Squire, a Bailif, and a Parson* is a mordant satire directed mostly against the gentry and the clergy, to some extent against the peasantry. Rej's views on education, military service, married life, as well as on farming and household activities, were contained in *The Life of an Honest Man*, a veritable encyclopedia of everyday life of the gentry in the countryside in sixteenth century Poland. His *Bestiary* was a collection of about seven hundred epigrams presenting portraits of outstanding personalities, including Luther and Kochanowski, and the *Trifles*, a book of short poems in ribald style. Rej also wrote verse plays, religious treatises, and translated the psalms.

Polish Renaissance literature reached its highest point with the poetry of Jan Kochanowski. He was steeped in the great traditions of the ancient world, namely Greek mythology, Greek and Latin literatures, and the Bible. He was familiar with the programs and achievements of Italian humanists and the poets of the French *Pléiade*, whose goals, including the propagation of national languages and literatures, were advanced by the Reformation. He also reached out to his native heritage and language. Out of these deep sources of inspiration Kochanowski created modern Polish poetry, widening its thematic range and setting a course for its growth. He also enriched its form and stylistic options.

Kochanowski was above all a lyric poet. His books of *Trifles* form a collection of about 300 epigrams, anecdotes, and light poems, a real compendium of the poet's experiences and observations. Some of them, to mention only *On Health* and *On the Linden Tree*, perceived as samples of national wisdom and pictures of the bygone beauty of nature, are read by every child in Poland. Others, including *On Human Life* and *To Sleep*, address in a few lines the essential topics of the Renaissance worldview. Still others, for example, *On a Spanish Doctor* and *To a Maid*, entertain the readers with good natured humor.

Kochanowski's major lyric form was the song. His songs were modelled on Horatian odes and Petrarchan *canzoni*, and dealt with the themes of friendship, love, religion, and philosophy. One of them, published in 1562 and known as *Song* or *Hymn to God*, a thanksgiving prayer expressing some of the most characteristic ideas of Renaissance philosophy, is full of serene optimism and joyful fascination with God's creation. The poem praises the beauty and harmony of the world and man's secure place in it. The poems from a cycle entitled *Saint John's Eve Song* attest to Kochanowski's interest in Polish country life, folk culture and customs. The songs were written in novel poetic patterns, varying in the length of lines, number of verses, and sequence of rhymes.

The poet's mastery of the vernacular and profound knowledge of the Renaissance ideas were displayed in his adaptation of the *Book of Psalms*, in which he used fifteen syllabic types of verse and thirty two types of stanzas. In *The Dismissal of the Greek Envoys*, an original Renaissance drama filled with the classical spirit, Kochanowski introduced unrhymed blank verse into Polish poetry. The *Laments*, the most mature and personal of Kochanowski's poems, form a cycle of nineteen elegies, written after the loss of his daughter. They are considered one of the most poignant expressions of a father's sorrow in world literature.

In 1584, when Kochanowski died suddenly, Sebastian Klonowic wrote in his honor thirteen *Funeral Laments*. A burgher from Lublin, Klonowic excelled in long descriptive poems based on keen observation of country and city life. In *Sailing, that is Navigating Boats*, Klonowic described the raftsmen's customs and activities during their annual voyages along the Vistula River to Gdańsk, while in *Judas's Bag*, he painted in fine detail many realistic scenes, featuring thieves, crooks, and tramps, frequent visitors in the town hall courts and jails.

The spiritual character of Polish poetry is visible in the elaborate sonnets of Mikołaj Sęp Szarzyński, a fervent Catholic, who often saw the human condition in tragic dimensions. Sęp Szarzyński struggled with an overwhelming sense of the vanity of life and with his own weaknesses, achieving in many a poem a dramatic tension which would subside in an emotional climax. A mood of religious reflection, colored by melancholy and pessimism, permeated the poems of Sebastian Grabowiecki, the author of *Spiritual Rhymes*, who found inspiration in Spanish and Italian mystical poetry. Kasper Miaskowski, who was influenced by the Bible and symbolical writings, concerned himself with questions of man's fleeting existence in the universe.

Kasper Miaskowski, Szymon Szymonowic, and Szymon Zimorowic occupy the borderline between the Renaissance and the Baroque. Although Szymonowic wrote mostly Latin verses, it was his *Idylls*, a genre he introduced into Polish literature, that became his major poetic accomplishment. The provenance of the *Idylls* is classical, their form imitates conventional eclogues, yet the best of them, including *The Reapers*, are realistic and true. Szymonowic was able to describe the beauty of nature and paint delicate scenes of rustic life, showing against this pastoral background the hard, sometimes brutal reality of the peasant's lot. Zimorowic's *Roxolans, or the Ruthenian Maidens* is a collection of melodious love poems, inspired by folk songs, a gentle echo of Renaissance harmony.

# SELECT BIBLIOGRAPHY

## ENGLISH ANTHOLOGIES AND TRANSLATIONS

Bloch, Alfred. *The Real Poland: An Anthology of National Self-perception.* New York: Continuum Publishing Co., 1982.

Bowring, John. *Wybór Poezyi Polskiey. Specimens of the Polish Poets; With Notes and Observations on the Literature of Poland.* London: Baldwin, Craddock and Joy, and Rowland Hunter, 1828.

Carpenter, Bogdana. *Monumenta Polonica. The First Four Centuries of Polish Poetry. A Bilingual Anthology.* Ann Arbor: Michigan Slavic Publications, 1989.

Kirkconnell, Watson. *A Golden Treasury of Polish Lyrics.* Winnipeg: The Polish Press Ltd., 1936.

Klonowicz, Sebastjan. *The Boatman. A Voyage Down the Vistula River from Warsaw to the Green Gate of Danzig.* Tr. by Marion M. Coleman. Cambridge Springs: Alliance College, 1958.

Kopernik, Mikołaj. *Complete Works.* Vol. II. *On the Revolutions.* Ed. by Jerzy Dobrzycki. Tr. and com. by Edward Rosen. Warsaw: PWN, 1978.

Kridl, Manfred, Józef Wittlin, and Władysław Malinowski. *For Your Freedom and Ours. The Democratic Heritage of Poland. An Anthology.* London: George Allen and Unwin Ltd., 1944. (First Polish edition in New York: Polish Labor Group, 1945).

Noyes, George R. (ed.). *Poems by Jan Kochanowski.* Tr. by Dorothy Prall Radin et al. Berkeley: University of California Press, 1928. Reprint: New York: AMS, 1978.

Olszer, Krystyna E. (ed.). *For Your Freedom and Ours:*

*Polish Progressive Spirit from the 14th Century to the Present.* 2nd Enlarged Edition. New York: Frederick Ungar Publishing Company, 1981.

Peterkiewicz, Jerzy and Burns Singer. *Five Centuries of Polish Poetry 1450-1970.* 2nd ed. Westport: Greenwood Press, 1979.

Segel, Harold B. *The baroque poem: a comparative survey, together with 150 illustration texts from English, American, Dutch, German, French, Italian, Spanish, Mexican, Portuguese, Polish, Modern Latin, Czech, Croatian, and Russian poetry.* New York: Dutton, 1974.

Soboleski, Paul. *Poets and Poetry of Poland. A Collection of Polish Verse.* 3rd ed. Milwaukee: The Paul Soboleski Society, 1929. (Nearly all Renaissance poems in this volume were reprinted from Bowring's *Specimens*).

Sokoloski, Richard. *The Poetry of Mikołaj Sęp Szarzyński (c.1550-1581).* Wiesbaden: Otto Harrassowitz, 1990.

Strzetelski, Jerzy. *An Introduction to Polish Literature. An Anthology.* Kraków: Uniwersytet Jagielloński, 1977.

## POLISH ANTHOLOGIES

Badecki, Karol. *Polska fraszka mieszczańska. Minucje sowiźrzalskie.* Kraków: Biblioteka Pisarzów Polskich 88, 1948.

Badecki, Karol. *Polska komedia rybałtowska.* Lwów: Ossolineum, 1931.

Badecki, Karol. *Polska liryka mieszczańska. Pieśni, tańce, padwany.* Vol. VII. Lwów: Zabytki Piśmiennictwa Polskiego, 1936.

Badecki, Karol. *Polska satyra mieszczańska. Nowiny*

*sowiźrzalskie.* Kraków: Biblioteka Pisarzów Polskich 91, 1950.

Baumfeld, Gustaw B. *Klejnoty poezji staropolskiej. Nowa antologia.* Warszawa: Towarzystwo Wydawnicze w Warszawie, 1919.

Bełza, Władysław. *Antologia polska. Wybór najcelniejszych utworów ze stu poetów polskich.* 4th ed. Lwów: H. Altenberg, 1906.

Bełza, Władysław. *Złote ziarna zebrane z dzieł pisarzy polskich.* Poznań: K. Kozłowski, 1907.

Bobowski, Mikołaj. *Polskie pieśni katolickie od najdawniejszych czasów do końca XVI wieku.* Kraków: Akademia Umiejętności, 1893.

Borowy, Wacław. *Od Kochanowskiego do Staffa. Antologia liryki polskiej.* 4th ed. Warszawa: PIW, 1981.

Brückner, Aleksander. *Ezopy polskie.* Kraków: Akademia Umiejętności, 1902.

Brückner, Aleksander. *Sielanka polska XVII wieku.* Kraków: Krakowska Spółka Wydawnicza, Biblioteka Narodowa I 48, 1922.

Budzyk, Kazimierz, Hanna Budzykowa, and Juljan Lewański. *Literatura mieszczańska w Polsce od końca XVI do końca XVII wieku.* 2 vols. Warszawa: PIW, 1954.

Bukowski, Kazimierz. *Biblia a literatura polska. Antologia.* Warszawa: Wydawnictwa Szkolne i Pedagogiczne, 1984.

Chmielewski, Piotr. *Obraz literatury polskiej w streszczeniach i celniejszych wyjątkach.* Vol. III. Warszawa: Gebethner i Wolff, 1898.

Chróścielewski, Tadeusz et al. *Księgi humoru polskiego.*

Vol. I. *Od Reja do Niemcewicza.* Ed. by Stanisław Czernik et al. Łódź: Wydawnictwo Łódzkie, 1958-68.

Chrzanowski, Ignacy. *Wybór staropolskich bajek ezopowych od Biernata Lubelczyka do Mickiewicza.* Kraków: Biblioteka Pisarzów Polskich 55, 1910.

Drewniak, Stanisław and Marian Kaczmarek. *Antologia pamiętników polskich XVI w.* Wrocław: Ossolineum, 1966.

Duralska-Macheta, Teresa. *O edukacji dawnych Polaków. Materiały z XVI-XVII wieku.* Warszawa: Nasza Księgarnia, 1982.

Dürr-Durski, Jan. *Arianie polscy w świetle własnej poezji. Zarys ideologii i wybór wierszy.* Warszawa: PZWS, 1948.

Folkierski, Władysław. *Sonet polski. Wybór tekstów.* Kraków: Biblioteka Narodowa, 1925.

Gloger Zygmunt (ed.). *Nieznany śpiewnik historyczny polski z końca wieku XVI-ego.* Warszawa: W.L. Anczyc, 1905.

Gruchała, Janusz and Stanisław Grzeszczuk. *Staropolska poezja ziemiańska.* Warszawa: PIW, 1988.

Grydzewski, Mieczysław. *Wiersze polskie wybrane.* 2nd ed. London: Orbis, 1948.

Grzeszczuk, Stanisław and Anna Niewolak-Krzywda. *Literatura polska do końca XVIII wieku.* 3rd ed. Rzeszów: Wydawnictwo Uczelniane WSP, 1982.

Grzeszczuk, Stanisław and Anna Niewolak-Krzywda. *Literatura polska. Średniowiecze-Renesans-Barok. Wybór tekstów.* 2 vols. 5th ed. Rzeszów: Wydawnictwo Uczelniane WSP, 1990.

Grzeszczuk, Stanisław. *Antologia literatury sowizdrzalskiej*

*XVI i XVII wieku.* 2nd ed. Wrocław: Ossolineum, 1985.

Grzeszczuk, Stanisław. *Staropolskie frywolności plebejskie.* Białystok: KAW, 1989.

Hertz, Benedykt. *Antologia bajki polskiej.* Warszawa: PIW, 1958.

Hertz, Paweł and Władysław Kopaliński. *Księga cytatów z polskiej literatury pięknej od XIV do XX w.* 2nd ed. Warszawa: PIW, 1959-1975.

Jelicz, Antonina. *Antologia poezji polsko-łacińskiej 1470-1543.* 2nd ed. Szczecin: Wydawnictwo "Glob", 1985.

Kamieńska, Anna. *Od Czarnolasu. Najpiękniejsze wiersze polskie.* Warszawa: Iskry, 1971.

Kapuścik, Janusz and Wojciech Podgórski. *Poeci żołnierzom 1410-1945. Antologia wierszy i pieśni żołnierskich.* Warszawa: MON, 1970.

Kijas, Juliusz. *Facecje staropolskie.* Kraków: M. Kot, 1951.

Kolbuszewski, Jacek. *Najpiękniejsze epitafia polskie.* Warszawa: SiT, 1989.

Kot, Stanisław. *Urok wsi i życia ziemiańskiego w poezji staropolskiej.* Warszawa: Osobne odbicie z *Księgi pamiątkowej na 75-lecie "Gazety Rolniczej",* 1937.

Kridl, Manfred. *An Anthology of Polish Literature.* New York: Columbia University Press, 1957.

Krzyżanowski, Julian and Kazimiera Żukowska-Bilip. *Dawna facecja polska (XVI-XVIII w.).* Warszawa: PIW, 1960.

Krzyżanowski, Julian et al. *Nowa księga przysłów i wyrażeń przysłowiowych polskich. W oparciu o dzieło Samuela Adalberga.* 4 vols. Warszawa:

PIW, 1969-1978.

Krzyżanowski, Julian. *Mądrej głowie dość dwie słowie. Pięć centuryj przysłów polskich i diabelski tuzin.* 3 vols. 3rd ed. Warszawa: PIW, 1975.

Krzyżanowski, Julian. *Proza polska wczesnego Renesansu. 1510-1550. Wybór.* Warszawa: PIW, 1975.

Lemański, Jan. *Satyra polska. Antologia.* Warszawa: M. Orgelbrand, 1914.

Lewański, Julian. *Dramaty staropolskie. Antologia.* 6 vols. Warszawa: PIW, 1959-1963.

Lewański, Julian. *Teatr polskiego Renesansu. Antologia.* Warszawa: PIW, 1988.

Lichański, Jakub Z. *Apophthegmata. Myśli pisarzy staropolskich, leki na choroby duszy.* Warszawa: LSW, 1985.

Marx, Jan. *Staropolska poezja erotyczna.* Warszawa: WAiF, 1989.

Mecherzyński, Karol. *Przykłady i wzory najcelniejszych poetów i prozaików polskich zebrane i zastosowane do historyi literatury polskiej opowiedzianej w krótkości dla młodzieży.* 2nd ed. Kraków: J.M. Himmelblau, 1877.

Merwin, Bertold. *Polskie listy miłosne od XV do XIX wieku.* Lwów: Wydawnictwo Polskie, 1922.

Michalski, Waldemar. *Pod Twoją obronę. Matka Boża w poezji polskiej.* Lublin: Wydawnictwo Kurii Biskupiej, 1986.

Miłaszewska, Wanda, Jan Rembiński and Stanisław Miłaszewski. *Chór wieków. Antologia poetycka.* Poznań: Księgarnia św. Wojciecha, 1936.

Mitzner, Zbigniew (Szeląg, Jan). *Wybór satyr z literatury polskiej XV-XX w.* Warszawa: LSW, 1953.

Nadolski, Bronisław. *Poezja renesansowa na Pomorzu.* Gdańsk: Wydawnictwo Morskie, 1976.

Nadolski, Bronisław. *Wybór mów staropolskich.* Wrocław: Ossolineum, Biblioteka Narodowa I 175, 1961.

Nieznanowski, Stefan and Juliusz Nowak-Dłużewski. *Kolędy polskie. Średniowiecze i wiek XVI.* 2 vols. Vol. I. *Teksty.* Warszawa: PAX, 1966.

Nowak-Dłużewski, Juliusz. *Polskie pieśni pasyjne. Średniowiecze i wiek XVI.* 2 vols. Vol. I. *Teksty i komentarze.* Ed. by Mirosław Korolko with Jadwiga Puzynina and Teresa Dobrzyńska. Warszawa: PIW, 1977.

Okoń, Jan. *Staropolskie pastorałki dramatyczne. Antologia.* Wrocław: Ossolineum, 1989.

Prosnak, Jan. *Siedem wieków pieśni polskiej. Śpiewnik dla młodzieży z komentarzem historycznym.* 2nd ed. Warszawa: Wydawnictwa Szkolne i Pedagogiczne, 1986.

Rębowski, Wojciech. *Wokół Bożego Narodzenia [Drukowane dramaty Bożonarodzeniowe z XVI i XVIII wieku].* Warszawa: PAX, 1983.

Rożej, Stefan J. *Bogiem sławiena Maryja. Antologia twórczości poetyckiej o Matce Boskiej Jasnogórskiej.* Rzym: Abilgraf, 1981.

Siomkajło, Alina. *Mała muza: od Reja do Leca. Antologia epigramatyki polskiej.* Warszawa: PIW, 1986.

*Skarbczyk Poezyi Polskiej. Poezye najsławniejszych naszych poetów, stósowne do deklamacyi i zabaw w kółkach towarzyskich i familijnych.* Chicago: Wł. Dyniewicz, 1896.

Sokołowska, Jadwiga. *I w odmianach czasu smak jest. Antologia polskiej poezji epoki baroku.* Warszawa: PIW, 1991.

Sokołowska, Jadwiga. *Patrząc na rozmaite świata tego sprawy. Antologia polskiej poezji renesansowej.* Warszawa: PIW, 1984.

Sokołowska, Jadwiga. *Poeci Renesansu. Antologia.* Warszawa: PIW, 1959.

Szczucki, Lech. *700 lat myśli polskiej.* Vol. II. *Filozofia i myśl społeczna XVI wieku.* Warszawa: PAN, 1978.

Szczucki, Lech and Janusz Tazbir. *Literatura ariańska w Polsce XVI wieku. Antologia.* Warszawa: Książka i Wiedza, 1959.

Taszycki, Witold. *Obrońcy języka polskiego. Wiek XV-XVIII.* Wrocław: Ossolineum, Biblioteka Narodowa I 146, 1953.

Taszycki, Witold. *Wybór tekstów staropolskich XVI-XVIII w.* 3rd ed. Warszawa: PWN, 1969.

Tazbir, Janusz. *Literatura antyjezuicka w Polsce 1578-1625. Antologia.* Warszawa: LSW, 1963.

Tuwim, Julian. *Cztery wieki fraszki polskiej.* Warszawa: Czytelnik, 1957.

Tuwim, Julian. *Polski słownik pijacki i antologia bachiczna.* Warszawa: Czytelnik, 1959.

W.B. *Antologia polska. Wybór najcelniejszych utworów poetów polskich.* 3rd ed. Lwów: H. Altenberg, 1887.

Woźnowski, Wacław. *Antologia bajki polskiej.* 2nd ed. Wrocław: Ossolineum, 1983.

Wójcicki, Kazimierz W. *Biblioteka starożytna pisarzy polskich.* Vol. VI. 2nd ed. Warszawa: S. Orgelbrand, 1843-1854.

Wydra, Wiesław and Wojciech Rzepka. *Chrestomatia staropolska. Teksty do roku 1543.* Wrocław: Ossolineum, 1984.

Zawiliński, Roman. *Wyjątki z pomników języka polskiego wieku XIV-XVI.* Kraków: Spółka Wydawnicza Polska, 1892.

Żukowska, Kazimiera. *Poeci polscy od średniowiecza do baroku.* Warszawa: PIW, 1977.

Żurakowski, Bogusław. *Antologia bajki polskiej.* 2 vols. Kraków: WL, 1986.

## GENERAL SURVEYS AND CRITICAL STUDIES

Ameisenowa, Zofia. *Kodeks Baltazara Behema.* Warszawa: Auriga, 1961.

Backvis, Claude. *Renesans i barok w Polsce: studia o kulturze.* Warszawa: PWN, 1993.

Bardach, Artur and Stanisław Herbst. *Kultura polska w źródłach i opracowaniach.* Warszawa: LSW, 1961.

Białostocki, Jan. *The Art of the Renaissance in the Eastern Europe: Hungary, Bohemia, Poland.* Ithaca, N.Y.: Cornell University Press, 1976.

Błoński, Jan (ed.). *Jan Kochanowski. Interpretacje.* Kraków: Wydawnictwo Literackie, 1989.

Bochnak, Adam. *Kaplica Zygmuntowska.* Warszawa: PIW, 1953.

Bogucka, Maria. *Dzieje kultury polskiej do 1918 roku.*
2nd ed. Wrocław: Ossolineum, 1991.

Borowski, Andrzej. *Renesans.* Warszawa: Wydawnictwa
Szkolne i Pedagogiczne, 1992.

Brückner, Aleksander. *Dzieje kultury polskiej.* Vol. II. 2nd
ed. Warszawa: Wydawnictwo J. Przeworskiego, 1939.

Budzyk, Kazimierz. *Szkice i materiały do dziejów literatury
staropolskiej.* Warszawa: PIW, 1955.

Budzyk, Kazimierz, Roman Pollak and Stanisław
Stupkiewicz. *Bibliografia literatury polskiej okresu
odrodzenia. Materiały.* Warszawa: PIW, 1954.

Chomiński, Józef and Zofia Lissa (eds.). *Music of the Polish
Renaissance; a selection of works from the XVIth and
the beginning of the XVIIth century.* Translation of the
Polish songs by Przemysław Mroczkowski. Kraków:
PWM, 1955.

Chrzanowski, Ignacy. *Historia literatury niepodległej Polski
(965-1795) (z wypisami).* 13th ed. Warszawa: PWN,
1983.

Davies, Norman. *God's Playground. A History of Poland.* 2
vols. New York: Columbia University Press, 1982.

Dobrowolski, Tadeusz and Władysław Tatarkiewicz (eds.).
*Historia sztuki polskiej w zarysie.* Vol. II. Kraków:
Wydawnictwo Literackie, 1962.

Dobrzycki, Stanislas. *History of Polish Literature.* In: *Polish
Encyclopaedia.* Vol. I. Geneva: Committee for the
Polish Encyclopaedic Publication, 1926.

Durling, Robert M. (ed. and tr.). *Petrarch's Lyric Poems.*
Cambridge: Harvard University Press, 1976.

Dziechcińska, Hanna (ed.). *Literary Studies in Poland.* Vol.
III. *Renaissance. Baroque.* Wrocław: Ossolineum,

1979.

Fiszman, Samuel (ed.). *The Polish Renaissance in Its European Context.* Bloomington: Indiana University Press, 1988.

Fiszman, Samuel. "Jan Kochanowski w krajach języka angielskiego." In: *Jan Kochanowski 1584-1984. Epoka -Twórczość-Recepcja.* 2 vols. Ed. by Janusz Pelc. Lublin: Wydawnictwo Lubelskie, 1989.

Fiszman, Samuel. "Złota też, wiem, nie pragniesz, bo to wszystko Twoje". In: *Necessitas et ars. Studia staropolskie dedykowane Profesorowi Januszowi Pelcowi.* Vol. I. Ed. by Barbara Otwinowska et al. Warszawa: Semper, 1993.

Frick, David A. *Polish Sacred Philology in the Reformation and the Counter-Reformation: Chapters in the History of the Controversies (1551-1632).* Berkeley: University of California Press, 1989.

Guerquin, Bohdan. *Zamki w Polsce.* Warszawa: Arkady, 1974.

Grzeszczuk, Stanisław (ed.). *Pisarze staropolscy. Sylwetki.* Vol. I. Warszawa: Wiedza Powszechna, 1991.

Grzybowski, Stanisław. *Król i kanclerz.* Kraków: KAW, 1988.

Halecki, Oscar. *A History of Poland.* New York: David McKay Company, Inc., 1976.

Ichnatowicz, Ireneusz, Antoni Mączak, Benedykt Zientara and Janusz Zarnowski. *Społeczeństwo polskie od X do XX wieku.* 2nd ed. Warszawa: Książka i Wiedza, 1988.

Iłowiecki, Maciej. *Dzieje nauki polskiej.* Warszawa: Interpress, 1981.

Kawecka, Alodja. *Kancjonały protestanckie na Litwie w w. XVI.* Kraków: Drukarnia Literacka, 1926.

Kębłowski, Janusz. *Dzieje sztuki polskiej. Panorama zjawisk od zarania do współczesności.* Warszawa: Arkady, 1987.

Kieniewicz, Stefan et al. *History of Poland.* 2nd ed. Warszawa: PWN, 1979.

Kiryk, Feliks. *Nauk przemożnych perła.* Kraków: KAW, 1986.

Klemensiewicz, Zenon. *Historia języka polskiego.* Warszawa: PWN, 1981.

Klimaszewski, Bolesław (ed.): *An Outline History of Polish Culture.* Warszawa: Interpress, 1984.

Kłoczowski, Jerzy et al. (eds.). *Chrześcijaństwo w Polsce.* Lublin: Wydawnictwo Towarzystwa Naukowego KUL, 1980.

Korolko, Mirosław. *Klejnot swobodnego sumienia. Polemika wokół Konfederacji Warszawskiej w latach 1573-1658.* Warszawa: PAX, 1974.

Kozakiewiczowa, Helena. *Renesans i manieryzm w Polsce.* Warszawa: Auriga, 1978.

Kridl, Manfred. *A Survey of Polish Literature and Culture.* New York: Columbia University Press, 1957.

Krzyżanowski, Julian et al. (eds.). *Literatura polska. Przewodnik encyklopedyczny.* 2 vols. Warszawa: PWN, 1986.

Krzyżanowski, Julian. *A History of Polish Literature.* Warszawa: PWN, 1978.

Krzyżanowski, Julian. *Tradycje literackie polszczyzny. Od Galla do Staffa.* Ed. by Maria Bokszczanin.

Warszawa: PWN, 1992.

Krzyżanowski, Julian. *W wieku Reja i Stańczyka. Szkice z dziejów Odrodzenia w Polsce.* Warszawa: PWN, 1958.

Kucała, Marian (ed.). *O języku poetyckim Jana Kochanowskiego.* Kraków: Towarzystwo Miłośników Języka Polskiego, 1984.

Kuraszkiewicz, Władysław. *Polski język literacki. Studia nad historią i strukturą.* Warszawa-Poznań: PWN, 1986.

Lewański, Julian. *Dramat i teatr średniowiecza i renesansu w Polsce.* Warszawa: PWN, 1981.

Libera, Zdzisław, Jadwiga Pietrusiewiczowa, and Jadwiga Rytel. *Literatura polska. Od średniowiecza do oświecenia.* Warszawa: PWN, 1988.

Michalski, Grzegorz et al. *Dzieje muzyki polskiej w zarysie.* 2nd ed. Warszawa: Interpress, 1983.

Michałowska, Teresa with Barbara Otwinowska and Elżbieta Sarnowska-Temeriusz (eds.). *Słownik literatury staropolskiej. Średniowiecze. Renesans. Barok.* Wrocław: Ossolineum, 1990.

Miłosz, Czesław. *The History of Polish Literature.* 2nd ed. Berkeley: University of California Press, 1983.

Misiąg-Bocheńska, Anna. *Głowy Wawelskie.* Warszawa: PIW, 1953.

Morawińska, Agnieszka. *Polish Painting 15th to 20th Centuries.* Warszawa: Auriga, 1984.

Nieznanowski, Stefan. *Studia i wizerunki. O poezji staropolskiej i jej badaczach.* Warszawa: PAX, 1989.

Nieznanowski, Stefan and Jerzy Święch (eds.). *Jan Kochanowski. W czterechsetlecie śmierci.* Lublin:

Wydawnictwo Uniwersytetu Marii Curie-Skłodowskiej, 1991.

Nowak-Dłużewski, Juliusz. *Okolicznościowa poezja polityczna w Polsce. Czasy Zygmuntowskie.* Warszawa: PAX, 1966.

Pelc, Janusz. *Jan Kochanowski. Szczyt renesansu w literaturze polskiej.* 2nd ed. Warszawa: PWN, 1987.

Pelc, Janusz. *Europejskość i polskość literatury naszego renesansu.* Warszawa: Czytelnik, 1984.

Pelc, Janusz (ed.). *Problemy literatury staropolskiej.* 2 vols. Wrocław: Ossolineum, 1972.

Piszczykowski, Mieczysław. *Obrońcy chłopów w literaturze polskiej.* Kraków: M. Kot, 1948.

Płaza, Stanisław. *Wielkie bezkrólewie.* Kraków: KAW, 1988.

Pollak, Roman et al. (eds.) *Bibliografia literatury polskiej "Nowy Korbut". Piśmiennictwo staropolskie.* 3 vols. Warszawa: PIW, 1963-1965.

*Polski Słownik Biograficzny.* Kraków: Polska Akademia Umiejętności, 1935-.

Rożek, Michał. *Złoty wiek. Szkice o sztuce renesansowej.* Kraków: KAW, 1991.

Saintsbury, George. *A History of English Prosody. From the Twelfth Century to the Present Day.* 3 vols. New York: Russell and Russell, 1961.

Segel, Harold B. *Renaissance Culture in Poland: The Rise of Humanism, 1470-1542.* Ithaca, N.Y. and London: Cornell University Press, 1989.

*Słownik polszczyzny XVI wieku.* Wrocław: Ossolineum, 1966-.

Sowiński, Janusz. *Polskie drukarstwo.* Wrocław: Ossolineum, 1988.

Sucheni-Grabowska, Anna. *Spory królów ze szlachtą w złotym wieku.* Kraków: KAW, 1988.

Suchodolski, Bogdan. *A History of Polish Culture.* Warszawa: Interpress, 1986.

Szwejkowska, Helena. *Książka drukowana XV-XVIII wieku. Zarys historyczny.* 5th ed. Wrocław-Warszawa: PWN, 1987.

Tazbir, Janusz. *A State Without Stakes: Polish Religious Toleration in the Sixteenth and Seventeenth Centuries.* New York: Kosciuszko Foundation, 1973.

Tazbir, Janusz. *Szlaki kultury polskiej.* Warszawa: PIW, 1986.

Trzeciak, Przemysław. "Renesans i manieryzm w Polsce." In: *Sztuka świata.* Vol. VI. Ed. by Jose Pijoan et al. Warszawa: Arkady, 1991, 329-353.

Urban, Wacław. *Epizod reformacyjny.* Kraków: KAW, 1988.

Weintraub, Wiktor. *Nowe studia o Janie Kochanowskim.* Foreword by Tadeusz Ulewicz. Kraków: Wydawnictwo Literackie, 1991.

Weintraub, Wiktor. *Rzecz czarnoleska.* Kraków: Wydawnictwo Literackie, 1977.

Wisner, Henryk. *Rokosz Zebrzydowskiego.* Kraków: KAW, 1989.

Wójcik, Zbigniew. *Wojny kozackie w dawnej Polsce.* Kraków: KAW, 1989.

Wyczyński, Andrzej. *Dogonić Europę czyli Polska w czasach*

*Zygmunta.* Kraków: KAW, 1987.

Zachwatowicz, Jan. *Architektura polska.* Warszawa: Arkady, 1966.

Zamoyski, Adam. *The Polish Way. A Thousand-Year History of the Poles and Their Culture.* New York: Franklin Watts, 1988.

Zimmer, Szczepan K. *The Beginning of Cyrillic Printing.* New York: University of Columbia Press, 1983.

Ziomek, Jerzy. *Literatura Odrodzenia.* Warszawa: PWN, 1987.

Ziomek, Jerzy (ed.). *Odrodzenie w Polsce.* Vol. IV. *Historia literatury.* Warszawa: PIW, 1956.

Ziomek, Jerzy. *Renesans.* Warszawa: PIW, 1973.

# ANDRZEJ KRZYCKI (1482-1537)

A humanist poet writing in Latin, Krzycki received an excellent education in Cracow and Bologna, and was well known in Poland and abroad. In his brilliant career, Krzycki served as a senator, diplomat, and secretary to Barbara Zapolyi, King Zygmunt's first wife, and then as the royal secretary. In 1522 he became the bishop of Przemyśl, then of Płock, finally reaching the position of archbishop of Gniezno and Primate of Poland.

A gifted poet, Krzycki chronicled major events at the royal court in Cracow, attacked his political adversaries, and wrote ingenious, sometimes bawdy, love poems that foreshadowed baroque conceits. He attacked the teachings of Luther and defended the Catholic Church, but at the same time criticized his compatriots' abuses in social and religious matters.

### Four-line Poem on Queen Barbara[1]

Nobody in the whole world, revered Barbara,
    Has been above you and above your progeny.
But because great fortune quickly changes its course,
    You were taken too soon, yet to the better world.

### Notes

1. Barbara Zapolyi, the first wife of King Zygmunt the Old, was married in 1512, died in 1515, leaving behind two daughters.

### On the Armory of King Zygmunt I

Zygmunt's greatness--castle, the Lord's glory--churches,
    While this house of Mars[1] testifies to achievements.
If you love peace--tremble before war! It goes round:
    Arms give birth to peace, while peace has to hammer arms.

Notes

1. The armory was established in 1533.

## On the Picture of Life at Court

What picture is that? The picture of life at court.
   Who is entering the door? This is a new man.
Who sits up on the throne? Ruling Prosperity.
   Who greets the visitor here? Hope, strengthening him.
5 And now who took him? Intrigue and servility.
   Who do they send him to? To toil, who is waiting.
What will he do with him? Between worry and hope
   He will be passing him along until old age.
Did anyone leave him? Hope, that unfaithful friend.
10   And who smashes him with his fist? Despair. In grief
Did anyone remain with him? Yes, vain sorrow after
   seeing through.
Only few can flee from here, when Prosperity
Looks at them, granting what it took from other hands.

## On Jan Zambocki

That you praise Luther's teachings which muddle the faith,
   Although you yourself no religion would embrace,
It's not because you want to get and guard the truth,
   But so you don't perform the deeds in God's service
5 And can indulge in voluble talk, giving vent
   To your anger against churches, priests, and heaven.

## How a Girl Answered a Priest

A priest who mowed a field called his flock to make hay
   By blowing a horn. A girl was just passing by.
He asked her if she wanted to go to the hay.
   "It can be done--she said--on the chuff as well."

### On a Girl Lidia

    Lidia tossed a snowball at me. I always thought
        That there was no fire in snow--but this snow was fire.
    What can be colder than snow? And yet it could burn
        My bosom, when it was thrown, maiden, by your hand.
5  Where is a safe place for me against the love snare,
        If fire is lurking in depths of frozen water?
    Only you, Lidia, can put out the fire in me
        Not with snow or ice, but with this very same heat.

*Text*: Jelicz, Antonina. *Antologia poezji polsko-łacińskiej 1470-1543*. Translated into Polish by Edwin Jędrkiewicz. Szczecin: Glob, 1985, 153, 167, 171, 175, 184, 190.

# MIKOŁAJ HUSSOWSKI (c. 1480-1533)

Mikołaj Hussowski, born in a poor family in Hussów, was the author of panegyrical works and of *A Poem on Bison* (1523). This poem is a detailed descriptions of the bison, its life and habits. Written in Latin for Pope Leo X, an avid hunter, it stems from Hussowski's experience in hunting and observing bison, and contains no literary comparisons with ancient legendary creatures.

*A Poem on Bison*
(selections)

This wildest beast is born in Lithuanian woods
    And is well known for such an enormous body,
That when it bends down its defeated head, dying,
    Three big men can place themselves right between its horns.
5  But its gigantic neck may appear far too small,
    If you would like to compare it with other limbs.
The large beard sticks out, hanging from terrible long mane,
    The fiery eyes glare with horrible anger,
Monstrous hair of the mane falls down on its shoulders,
10  Covering fully the knees, front, and the whole chest.
But if I am to combine great matters with small,
    If it is permitted to use the hunting words,
It appears from its figure like a goat with horns,
    Although from all limbs one can see it's a born bull.
15 It is of darksome hue; from the yellow and black
    It is blended, forming an intermediate shade.
    (...)

I will try briefly to describe the animal
    And its practices, going along with this tale.
It's more fierce than other animals or equal,
20  Dangerous to man only when wounded hy him.
With the greatest caution it protects its own life,
    It's hard for anyone to imagine greater.
It casts its eyes around, looks in all directions

And can perceive the most distant points of its path:
25 It can detect a swift twitch of a man's eyelid
    Even if one kept his movements under control.
It'll catch with its ears the faintest rustle behind,
    Watchful to be guarded carefully from the rear.
Quite often it promenades with a solemn stride,
30  If arrows do not glimmer and arms do not shine.
When the cow sets her eyes on you with a long look,
    She halts, as human gaze captivates her so much.
But if she is leading, watchful, her little ones,
    She gets rabid at once, struck by the clang of arms.
35 She announces with dreadful roar her awful rage,
    This is a sign not to come up too close to her.
But won't charge anyone needlessly, save a foe,
    When safe, she will not harm those trying to escape.
An agile tribe of calves plays merrily, set free,
40  They do not bring on their fathers any worry.
And they are so able that with effortless leaps
    They make their way, following mother's every step!
Before long they skip over the broken down logs
    Or race along the plain, as if chased by someone,
45 They know how to jump over wide ditches in swift run,
    Shake their little horns with threatening appearance.
In endless wrestling they exercise soft bodies,
    Using only rare moments to take a rest.
It is a steadfast creature, ready for great toils,
50  It's hard to imagine this, looking at its shape!
An when in a tight place it begins to circle,
    From mere movement it passes into rapid pace.
It turns around, and snatches manure thrown high up
    And before it falls, it strews on its horns this dung.


*Text*: Jelicz, *Antologia poezji*, 136-137, 139-140. Translated into Polish by Jan Kasprowicz.

# KLEMENS JANICIUSZ (1516-1543)

Klemens Janiciusz (Ianicius) came from a peasant family. His father sent him to the local school at Żnin and then to the *gymnasium* in Poznań, where he distinguished himself in the study of the classics and showed great promise as a Latin poet. In 1536, he obtained the patronage of Andrzej Krzycki, Archbishop of Gniezno, and after his death, of Piotr Kmita, a wealthy nobleman, who sent him to study in Padua. Although he suffered from poor health and did not write much, his talent was recognized and he was crowned with poetic laurels in 1540, before returning to Poland.

In the last two years of his life, Janiciusz published his major works, *Elegiae (Tristia* and *Variae Elegiae)* and *Epigrammata*. He is best known for the autobiographical poem *About Myself to Posterity*, a moving description of his short life. Janiciusz's Latin poetry shows the influence of the classics and of the Italian culture on Polish literature in the sixteenth century.

### *Amo*

Three small letters bring me ruin and return to life ...
Oh, how can this little word possess such great might?

### *Andrzej Krzycki, a Pole*

Krzycki alone was everything: the highest gifts
   Were bestowed on him by God and fate with great zeal,
But fate couldn't bear that Krzycki held it in disdain,
   And took him away from us, before his time came.

*Text*: Jelicz, *Antologia poezji*, 269, 296. Translated into Polish by Edwin Jędrkiewicz.

## Elegy VII
### About Myself to Posterity

You that will think of me and wish some time
In the future to learn about my life,
Read the lines hurriedly dictated, when
Hydropsy[1] was pushing me to Lethe.

5   High above the Żnin marsh[2] lies a village,
Named after the name of one Januszek[3];
Along that route, reportedly, our kings
Traveled from Gniezno to their Prussian lands.[4]
My father turned over that soil with his plough,
10  A noble man in his humble station.
While he cried over the children he lost
In the fierce plague, he saw me being born
At a time of mourning; he was childless
Only for ten months. The light gleamed for me
15  The fourth day past the Ides of November,[5]
On Sunday, at noon, on the same day, when
Our king was taking off the mourning clothes
He'd worn a year after his spouse's death,
Barbara, from the clan of the Trencin wolf[6]
20  (Her death saddened everyone profoundly).

I was just five years old, when I was sent
Before the first threshold of the Muses,
Because my father loved me so deeply
That he did not desire that a hard plough
25  Hurt my feeble hands during heavy toil,
And the heat burn my face. When I received
Learning rudiments from unskilled masters,
(I owe you nothing more, my town of Żnin!)
I went on to the school which Lubrański[7]
30  Had established by the Warta's current,
There I met someone who excellently
Taught the knowledge of the Romans and Greeks.
Having prepared the new soil, he[8] began
To cultivate it most conscientiously.
35  At long last, I heard the name of Maro[9]
And also your name, my beloved Naso![10]
As I read, I began to worship. Oh,

The poets became nearly gods to me.
To Apollo, their patron, how many
40  Supplications I offered tearfully,
So he would admit me to his chorus
And his retinue even as a squire.
He beckoned, I rushed, he stretched out his hand
And gave me a lute.  How I fondled it,
45  I trained my fingers with resolve, with joy,
A day or night wouldn't pass without the lute--
I remember it well.  I spared no toil,
So as to make what progress my years permitted.

When for the first time I read a poem
50  Before an audience, I wasn't yet sixteen,
The subject of the poem was Lubrański--
To him were offered my earliest efforts.
People applauded--not for my merit,
But because they set their hopes on the boy.
55  I had the first place among the equals
And from that time on my master loved me.
Having tasted fame, object of desire,
I admired it so greatly in my soul,
That every day I dreamed of grander plans
60  And kept searching for all roads to it.
But along this route, gloomy poverty
Stood up in my way, constraining my feet:
My father said he did not have money,
To pay the costs of my farther studies.
65  Ready to bid farewell to the Muses,
I was saved by an unexpected fate.

Krzycki[11] was then bishop, dear to Phoebus[12]
As only few men.  He opened for me
A magnificent gate that led to his court,
70  Promising good fortune to my Muses,
And he would have likely kept his promise,
If premature death had not taken him.
After this loss, so distressing to me,
Kmita[13] gave me shelter in his home,
75  Not sparing costs, he sent me to the lands
Of Latins.  Like a merchant for jewels
I hurried on to Euganean Pallas,[14]

To acquire priceless knowledge from her.
Fortune was jealous of me: she ordered
80   I return in sickness to the home fires
Earlier than I wished and Kmita desired.
What could I do--fate rules over us all.
So I'll die at home; the only comfort:
I will not be covered by foreign soil.
85   So then you, Kromer,15 or you, Rotundus,16
Who will cry over your departed friend,
If a headstone is laid down on the grave,
Write out with capital letters these words:
HERE I REST WITHOUT ANY HOPE AND FEAR,
90   TRULY ALIVE.  FAREWELL, DEPARTED LIFE!

Enough of that.  Now I return to you,
My reader, to weave again a story
Of my life.  I was very sickly,
The smallest hardships would soon make me tired.
95   I was good looking and full of good cheer
(Though you could detect shyness in my eyes),
Articulate, with a clear voice, white skin,
I was quite shapely and tall in stature;
Sensitive, quick to anger; now and then
100  For many days I was irritated
And never did I hide hostility,
But ever did I give reason for it.
In friendship I was fastidious and firm,
Knowing it was the most precious treasure.
105  Had fate brought me great riches, I believe
No one would have lived more grandly than I,
Nor would have been more giving.  I admired
These Roman words, so truly imperial:
"I haven't given out anything today,
110  O, shame, I have lost a day, lived in vain!"17
I had a compassionate heart--but such
As beats in the timid chest of a deer;
I detested all arms and always was
An enemy of the warlike Pallas.
115  The elegance of manners, costume, food
I loved too much, nearly like a woman.
From boyhood until the age of twenty
I drank only water; from this, I think,

My liver began to ail; that water
120 Once drunk, strangles my life at the present.

Judging by deceptive appearances,
Many contrymen thought me licentious--
Either because I much liked songs and jokes,
Or because while still a boy I praised love;
125 At first Leukorode, then more virtuous
Alfesibea lived in my elegies.[18]
Where are those works, you will ask? The same place
As the other works--gone into the fire,
Worthy of short life as everything else,
130 Which was hurried on by my youthful pride.
And today, with one score and five years passed,
When the time has arrived for greater works,
I hear the call and die prematurely,
Without glorifying you, as I wished,
135 My homeland, your past history and kings,
And that which deserves glory at present,
Specially the nuptials, which his father--
Our king--and Ferdinand prepared for
Augustus.[19] Others will do it later.
140 What I can, I do: pray he lives and reigns.

Live, friends, remembering your Ianicius,
Even now be prepared to follow me
One day along the same road. So farewell,
My Antoninus,[20] let fortune favor you
145 And your loved ones. I am sad that never
Will I be able to prove how I love you.
It is not my fate to tell the living
About your care for me. But when I go
To that country where the blessed spirits
150 Will accept me gaily to their circle,
Then I will talk about you. If, looking
At my shadow someone will inquire how
With this lethal water in my body,
Sick liver and spleen, I could live longer
155 Than the severity of such sickness
Usually allows for, I will answer:
There is among people a physician,
Who surpassed the might of Apollo's son,[21]

>That brought Hippolitus once from the depth,
160 But the other extracted me many times
From the grave and deluded the Parcae,²²
Delayed the fateful moment many days.
If he did not restore my former health,
It is not his fault, but that of tireless
165 Sickness. Many a weakness can be cured.
Who, save for Christ, could defeat hydropsy?
Montanus and Cassanus,²³ who brightened
The Euganean land with highest glory,
Could not destroy the Hydra,²⁴ even though
170 It then was just barely hatching in me.
Antoninus had to fight a full grown
And already victorious monster.
He would have surely overpowered it,
If victory could have been in man's might.
175 But this death seems to be the destiny
Of my family; my father before
Died the same way. So many blows and foes
Everywhere! And the doctors' hands fell faint.

>This I will retell about you, my life--
180 I give you this name as you kept me live!--
You'll hear it yourself, when you come to me
Much later. You will come with the others
I leave behind. Because the fates offered
No human being an eternal home here.

### Notes

    1. Hydropsy, an accumulation of fluid within an organ or tissue.
    2. Żnin, a town in Poznań voivodship.
    3. Januszkowo, district Szubin, Janiciusz's home village.
    4. Gniezno was the first Polish capital and archbishopric in Poland. Prussia was the part of the Polish kingdom, situated north of Masovia.
    5. The seventeenth of November.
    6. Barbara, daughter of Stephanus Zapolya, voivod of Transylvania, the first wife of Zygmunt the Old; she died in October 1515. That family of powerful Hungarian noblemen

had a wolf in their coat of arms and their family castle was situated in Trencin on the river Wag.

7. Bishop Lubrański founded in Poznań, situated on the River Warta, one of the best schools in Poland in the sixteenth century.

8. Christophor Hegendorfinus, German humanist, taught six years in the school.

9. Maro--Virgil.

10. Naso--Ovid.

11. Andrzej Krzycki--poet and archbishop of Gniezno, one of the luminaries of the Polish Renaissance.

12. Phoebus--Apollo as the god of the sun.

13. Piotr Kmita--a nobleman, politician, protector of writers and scholars.

14. The University of Padua. South west of Padua there are the Euganean Mountains.

15. Marcin Kromer, a famous writer, royal secretrary, bishop of Warmia, author of *Polonia*.

16. Augustus Rotundus, a humanist and lawyer.

17. The words of the Roman emperor, Titus.

18. Elegy--in Latin humanist poetry a lyric poem.

19. The wedding of Zygmunt August with Elizabeth, daughter of Ferdinand I Habsburg, the king of Bohemia and Hungary, was planned for May 1543.

20. Joannes Antoninus--a famous humanist and physician, a friend of Erasmus and royal physician in Cracow.

21. Aesculapius, son of Apollo, and god of medicine.

22. Parcae or the fates were supposed to decide upon the course of the child's life.

23. Famous Italian physicians.

24. Hydra was the monster slain by Hercules.

*Text:* Janiciusz, Klemens. *Poezje wybrane.* Edited and translated into Polish by Zygmunt Kubiak. Warszawa: PIW, 1975, 42-47.

# BIERNAT OF LUBLIN (c. 1465 - c.1529)

A burgher and scribe who took holy orders, Biernat was a popular poet and translator who wrote in his native language. His prayer book *Raj duszny* (*Paradise of the Soul*), translated from Latin and published in Cracow in 1513, was one of the first printed books in Polish. His major work, *The Life of Aesop the Phrygian, a Virtuous Sage, Together with His Fables*, containing over two hundred short moral stories, each of them with a proverb, was published in 1522, and gained great popularity.

### *A Short Description of Aesop's Life and Also of His Other Affairs*
(selection)

    There was one quite unusual man,
In his life truly provident,
He was born in captivity,
Yet his mind showed nobility.
5      In Ammonium his life began,
Phrygian village in Trojan land,
His face was disagreeable,
And his speech was most pitiable.
    His head was immensely swollen,
10 His skin was dark, his eyes sunken,
His neck short, his jaws enormous,
His teeth black and his mouth monstrous.
    He was stocky and of small size,
With bulky legs and fleshy thighs,
15 At the back he had a big hump,
In the front his belly was plump.
    Even worse, to put it blunter,
Aesop had a nasty stutter:
Yet in spite of these flaws so plain,
20 Every riddle he could explain.

V. Title page of Biernat's *A Short Description of Aesop's Life*, Cracow, 1578

## Fables

### He Who Holds the Sword Has Peace

The eel had asked the snake one day,
What of this matter he would say:
"Since we have a like appearance
Why then in luck such difference?

5 With you all people suffer fear
And feel threatened when you are near;
But I just whet their appetite,
In catching me they all delight."

Said the snake: "I am left alone,
10 Because I can bite with venom;
If one wished to harm me in strife,
Then he would have to risk his life;

But you are a defenseless man,
The strain from all sides must withstand.
15 If you could only have my teeth,
Then all would leave you just in peace."

So if you want to live in peace,
You should be ready to resist;
No one will want to launch attack,
20 If you at once can fight him back.

Text: Biernat z Lublina. *Wybór pism.* Ed. by Jerzy Ziomek. Wrocław: Ossolineum, Biblioteka Narodowa I 149, 1954, 3-4, 162-163.

### He Who Loves Books Is Not Bored

A farm hand, who had a master,
A very diligent reader,
Into his study went one day,
Where, reading books, he'd always stay.

5   When he saw the master alone,
    Leaning over another tome,
    He asked these words to make it clear:
    "How can you stay so lonesome here?"

    Master said: "I'm never alone:
10  Always have a feast of my own;
    Only now I've become lonely,
    When I see you in front of me."

    He who is sitting with a book,
    Can never suffer solitude,
    But when he sits down in a throng,
    Then he truly feels forlorn.

*Text*: Sokołowska, Jadwiga. *Patrząc na rozmaite świata tego sprawy. Antologia polskiej poezji renesansowej.* Warszawa: PIW, 1984, 25.

### He Who Is Diligent Won't Go Wrong

    The hare laughed at the turtle once,
    That he could not too fast advance.
    The turtle said: "You want a test,
    Let's have a race, find who runs best."

5   The hare said: "Turtle, my brother!
    I wouldn't like to lose a wager:
    Haven't you heard yet someone tell
    That I can scurry pretty well?"

    The turtle said: "No more these talks!
10  We want to call upon the fox;
    And let's ask him to draw the line,
    How each can run let him define."

    The fox then drew the finish line,
    As in such things he acted fine,
15  He gave them time to run the course
    And also test their mental force.

The hare moved slowly to the start;
He paid the turtle no regard,
And as he trusted in his feet,
20   He sat down and soon fell asleep.

But the turtle, without delay,
Went along, skipping on his way,
And did not take a rest at all,
Until at last he reached his goal.

25   At that point the hare awakened,
Made a rush towards the course end;
He swiftly covered lots of ground,
But on the line the turtle found.

So the fox called the race order,
30   To the turtle gave the wager,
Saying: "Hare, you lost this event;
Because you were not diligent."

Not only those achieve their ends,
Who have been blessed with great talents;
35   A diligent man is better,
Especially when he doesn't err.

*Text*: Chrzanowski, Ignacy. *Historia literatury niepodległej Polski (965-1795) (z wypisami)*. 13th ed. Warszawa: PIW, 1983, 87.

# MARCIN BIELSKI (1495-1575)

Marcin Bielski was born into a nobleman's family and educated at the courts of influential magnates. He fought against the Tartars in 1524 and 1534. In 1540, he settled in his native village of Biała and devoted himself to writing.

Bielski was the author of *A Chronicle of the Whole World* (1551), a morality play entitled the *Comedy of Justin and Constance* (1557), and numerous satirical works, among them the *Parliament of Women*.

His *Chronicle*, the first comprehensive textbook on general history written in Polish, gained enormous popularity. It presented to the public basic facts of world events and geography, mixing myth and historical truth. Bielski devoted a separate part of the *Chronicle* to the history of Poland and although he was not an original writer, he related some events he had witnessed. *Death and Funeral of Zygmunt the Old* was based on Bielski's personal recollection.

## *A Chronicle of the Whole World* (1551)
### (selection)

### *Death and Funeral of Zygmunt the Old*

In the year of 1547, Zygmunt, the King of Poland, convened by letters the noblemen and knights of the Polish crown to a general session of the Sejm, which according to tradition was held on Saint Martin's day.[1] Having made decisions on all matters of the Republic pertaining to laws, defense and other things which the republic of this crown always needs, and being in the advanced years of his life, he fell gravely ill, and during this time, already half dead, he was moved from Piotrków to Cracow in the month of February in the year of our Lord 1548. On the glorious holiday of Easter, Resurrection of our Lord, having received God's rites like a true Christian, he separated himself from this world with great contrition and humility at the royal castle.[2] It does not seem necessary for me to describe his behavior or the morals of his nearly saintly life, which he displayed on the royal throne, because they appear clearly as upright in the chronicle of his life. Additionally, the learned men described it quite well and widely in their orations and sermons and clearly presented it to the general public, especially Stanisław Orzechowski, who praised him nearly to the skies in his writing. That is why his death saddened not only us, citizens of this land, but also other Christian people. He was 81 years, 2 months, 7 days old. His funeral was splendid, as is our custom for kings. Each district standard-bearer carrying his banner beneath the coat-of-arms was on a fully arrayed horse. There were about one hundred and thirty of them, and also many biers covered with variously colored cloth of gold. Just behind the biers went thirty royal horses covered with silk of various colors with royal coats of arms. After them came each district's standard-bearer, in the cuirasses of mourning, having on their banners various regional coats of arms. (...)

Before the bier with the royal body rode Jan Tarło in full cuirass, given to the king by Emperor Maximilian when they were together in Vienna, holding in his hand an unsheathed sword. He was followed by a servant with a spear. In front of the bier walked district deputies. The royal insignia were also carried in front of the bier; Zygmunt Wolski carried the sword, Tęczyński, court marechal, carried the orb, Jan of Tarnów, Cracow castellan--the sceptre. Behind them, the courtiers carried the body with many cast candles. Behind the body walked the king between the envoys of the Emperor and of Ferdinand, King of Rome. Behind them walked the queen, his mother, between a Prussian duke and a margrave. They escorted the body to the chapel, and placed the insignia on the bier. Having committed the body to the earth under the chapel, they went back to the castle in the same order.

The next day, on Friday, they all went to six churches with processions, having put the insignia on the bier, first to the church of All the Saints, where the bishop of Kamieniec celebrated the mass, second to Saint Francis's, where the bishop of Chełm sang the mass, third to Saint Anne's, where the bishop of Przemyśl sang the mass, fourth to Saint Szczepan's, where the bishop of Płock sang, fifth to the market square, at Saint Mary's, where the bishop of Poznań sang the mass, and sixth to the Holy Trinity, where the suffragan sang the mass.

And on Saturday, the archbishop of Gniezno held mass in the castle, co-celebrated by a bishop and all the abbots. Af-

VI. King Zygmunt August, engraved portrait from Kromer's *De origine et rebus gestis Polonorum*, Basilea, 1555

ter the gospel, Samuel Maciejewski, the bishop of Cracow had a very good and long sermon about the king's saintly life. And when the prayer in the mass was sung, Jan Tarło in armor, and the servant who carried the spear, rode into the church with candles in his helmet and armor. When Agnus Dei was sung, the noblemen placed on the altar the insignia or ornaments, whichever they carried; King August carried the helmet, the duke--the shield, the margrave--the sword, the duke of Cieszyn--the spear: this they struck on the floor and broke. Then this cuirassier fell off his horse by the bier; the chancellor and his deputy smashed the seals of the deceased king and received the new ones in their place from the young king. After taking care of these matters, they left the church in the same order. The next day, on Sunday, the Cracow burghers observed the event at Saint Mary's in the market square mournfully and religiously during the mass, the bishop of Przemyśl serving God. This funeral took place a day after Saint James, on Thursday, in the year 1548 after our Lord's birth, on the 26th of July.

Notes

1. Saint Martin day is on 11 of November.
2. Zygmunt I died on Easter Sunday, on April 1, 1548.

*Text*: Chrzanowski, *Historia literatury*, 137-138.

*Parliament of Women*
(selection)

Prologue by Fair Ladies to Men

    Why are you laughing at us, gentlemen with beards,
    Did not God give us ahead of you many gifts?
    Take a good look at us, this beauty so cultured,
    Like a winter wedding, like May in the orchard:
5   Fluent speech, smooth complection, delightful features,
    Which He did not give to any other creatures.
    Restraint in drink and food, that's how we live longer,
    We are better, more tolerant, and more sober.

>     If in these we excel, then why shouldn't we counsel
> 10  On our common good, specially since we know well
>     You, our lazy husbands. So, if you do not know,
>     Whatever our government is, please do not crow.

*Text*: Sokołowska, *Patrząc na rozmaite świata tego sprawy*, 37.

# ANONYMOUS

## *Owlglass, Facetious and Amusing* (1540)

Modelled on the popular German folk stories about Till Eulenspiegel, the Owlglass writings became quickly adapted in Poland. Owlglass, the irreverant hero of these stories, was a patron saint of rascals and criminals. A clever and impudent vagabond, he made fun of the powerful and learned, not sparing with his mordant wit emperors, bishops, philosophers, and high officials. The owlglass stories and poems, side by side with Aesop fables and Marcholt romances, enjoyed great popularity among common people, providing them with an abundant supply of facetious tales and ribald humor.

2. How all the peasants with their wives complained about a young Owlglass saying what kind of a pert fellow and slanderer he was; Owlglass, sitting on a horse behind his father, was sticking out his butt at people

Now when Owlglass grew up, leaving behind his infancy, he was making strange and diverse pranks among children and would roll over on the grass as if he were a monkey until he was four years old. So he was growing up in his natural wickedness, the older he was, the worse; until all the neighbors grumbled about him and complained to his father that he was a great rogue. Having listened to their complaints, the father began to scold his son, saying: "What is going on, dear son, that all the neighbors complain about you? They are saying you are a perfidious and thorough rogue." Owlglass responded to that: "My dear father! I don't disturb anybody at all; and if this is true, I will show it at once: sit on your own horse, I will sit behind you and we will ride quietly along this street, and yet they will be complaining about me, though I don't care about it at all."

So his father did just that. He put Owlglass behind on the horse and Owlglass pulled up his robes high and stuck out his butt at the people. Having seen this foul deed of his, all the neighbors with their wives ran behind him, scolding and cursing him for being so malicious.

His father, to test him, put him in front on the horse so that they would not complain about him. And although his little son was sitting quietly, he could not contain his natural wickedness; he was making faces at the people and sticking out his tongue. The people were quite astonished and scolded him a lot. His father said: "Indeed, my son, you were born in an unhappy hour. I can see you are quiet and yet the people accuse you and disgrace you together with me."

Then, to avoid shame, he moved from that place because he loved his son very much; and he moved to the Magdeburg land where his wife had come from. The poor old man did not live long there; he left his wife and children in great poverty.

And Owlglass, though he did not know any craft nor had any wish to learn one, being in his sixteenth year, had, however, with his trickery and clowning, a place everywhere and good food, according to an old saying: the clowns have it best.

28. How Owlglass in Prague, in Bohemia, disputed with learned doctors at the university

Traveling to Marburg, Owlglass went to the Czech land and to Prague. He presented himself there as an illustrious master who could reportedly answer difficult questions and riddles which not every master could cope with. And he had announcements and notices made and, attempting to gain notoriety, he had them posted on all church doors, especially on the university. It made the rector and all masters unhappy.

The doctors and masters, when they heard about it, began to take counsel how they could entrap and catch Owlglass with some difficult questions so that he would be disgraced and they agreed, conveying it to the rector, what question or riddle to ask him. So they let Owlglass know through their messenger to come the next day, and since he himself had challenged them, to answer questions. If he could not do it, then he would have no place among them.

Owlglass told the messenger to respond saying: "Tell your masters there that I won't do otherwise but as I resolved. I trust in God that as it is appropriate for a virtuous person, I will satisfy everyone, as I always do."

Next day all the doctors and masters came together. Owlglass came as well. He brought with him his host, together with burghers and also quite a group of people in case of violence and disarray from students. When they saw him, they told him to take a place at the desk and to answer their questions. First was the rector's question to tell them and prove truthfully how many drops there are in the sea. If he did not know this, they would consider him a fool and an importunator of all sciences and would, on top of this, punish him. To this question, not thinking much, he answered promptly: "Order first all the waters that flow to the sea to stand still; then I will tell you and prove truthfully, and it will be quite obvious." The rector did not see it possible to stop the waters so he dropped this matter and was embarassed.

He gave him the second riddle saying: "Tell me how many days have passed since the times of Adam until today?" Owlglass answered him in short words: "Only seven; and when they pass or are gone, the other ones begin, and it will last until the end of the world."

The rector said: "Explain the third riddle! Where is the middle of the world?" Owlglass answered: "The middle of the world is right here. If you want to find out truly, have it measured with a cord." The rector answered: "If I have to do it, I prefer to give up and not to dispute this matter with you any more."

Being already quite angry, the rector asked the fourth one: "Tell me, is heaven far from earth?" Owlglass answered: "Very near. When someone is talking or speaking in heaven, then it can be heard well here on earth. Go to heaven and I will talk softly here so that you can hear it being in heaven; and if it does not happen, I will be guilty."

He gave him still the fifth riddle: "How big is heaven?" Owlglass answered immediately: "Six thousand feet wide, one thousand elbows high, this cannot be wrong. If you do not want to believe this, take the sun and the moon, also all the stars from heaven and measure them; then you will find it is what I say."

They were all astounded that he was so cleverly learned; they had to give up. Then they all got mad at him that he had defeated them with his deceitful knowledge; they had heavy hearts that they could not entrap him and prove his levity.

So Owlglass having left them took off his gown and wandered to Erfurt.

*Text*: Krzyżanowski, Julian. *Proza polska wczesnego Renesansu 1510-1550*. Warszawa: PIW, 1954, 194-195, 203-205.

## JAN OF KIJANY
(turn of the sixteenth century)

Jan of Kijany (his real name is unknown) was the leading practitioner of the plebeian literature known as the 'owlglass literature.' A poet, author of several collections of humorous trifles and anecdotes, Jan of Kijany parodied also songs and carols in order to entertain his readers and to vent his anger against religious and secular authorities and institutions.

*New Owlglass or Rather Newglass* (1614)

### 4. *Wolves*

When a wolf showed and opened its muzzle,
I shoved my hand all way down its throttle.
Then I found the hole right under its tail,
And turned the wolf inside out straightaway.

### 5. *Hares*

For hares, I tossed onions on the roadway.
When they picked them up, they cried right away.
When the tears stopped flowing, their eyes froze tight,
Till they turned blind; I plucked them day and night.

*Text*: Grzeszczuk, Stanisław. *Antologia literatury sowizdrzalskiej*. 2nd ed. Wrocław: Ossolineum, 1985, 128.

# NICHOLAS COPERNICUS (1473-1543)

Nicholas Copernicus, whose Polish name is Mikołaj Kopernik, was an astronomer, economist, and physician. He was born in Toruń, a bustling city in Warmia, in the family of a prosperous burgher whose forbears came from Silesia. His father died in 1483 and Nicholas's uncle, Lucas Watzenrode, a learned and influential bishop of Warmia, became the guardian and patron of the family.

From 1491 to 1495 Copernicus studied astronomy and mathematics at the Cracow Academy and from 1496 to 1503 canon law, medicine, and astronomy in Bologna and Padua. In 1503 Copernicus returned to Warmia, where he spent the remaining forty years of his life. He served for over six years at the court of bishop Watzenrode in Lidzbark, where he was the bishop's secretary, personal physician, and inspector of the cities of Prussia and Warmia, entrusted with diplomatic and financial duties. In 1512, after Watzenrode's death, Copernicus settled in Frombork, devoting himself to his astronomical studies and to administrative activities.

In 1520-1521, during the war with the Knights of the Cross, Copernicus organized a successful defense of the city of Olsztyn. In recognition of his services, he was nominated commissioner of Warmia in 1521. In 1523 he became the general administrator of the Warmia diocese.

In 1522 Copernicus brought out his treatise on money, entitled *Tractatus de monetis, Modus cudendi monetam* (*The Manner of Minting Money*), in which he advocated the uniform currency for the whole country. The major work of his life, *De revolutionibus orbium coelestium libri VI* (*Six Books On the Revolutions of the Heavenly Spheres*), which Copernicus began to write already in the 1510's, was published in 1543 in Nüremberg, just before he died. He dedicated the book to Pope Paul III, expressing a hope that the Holy Father would shield him from slanderous voices with his authority and love of knowledge.

VII. Nicholas Copernicus, portrait from Frombork Museum

## On the Revolutions
(selection)

### To His Holiness Pope Paul III, Nicholas Copernicus's Foreword to His Books on the Revolutions

I am fully aware, Holy Father, that there will be some people who, as soon as they hear that I ascribe certain motions to the terrestial globe in these books about the revolutions of the spheres of the universe, will clamor immediately to condemn me together with this belief. For I am not so enamored of my own work as not to pay attention to what others will think about it. And although I know that the thoughts of the scholar are independent of the judgment of the general public--because the scholar's aspiration, provided that God permits it to human reason, is to seek the truth in everything--yet in spite of this I am of the opinion that one should refrain from views completely different from the accepted orthodoxy. So when I was deliberating how nonsensical it would sound to people if I advanced an assertion that the Earth moves, against their quite opposite belief confirmed by the verdicts of ages that it is motionless and lies in the middle of the heavens as its central point, I hesitated long whether to publish these books, which I have written to prove the motion of the Earth, or rather to follow the Pythagoreans and some other thinkers, who had a habit of transmitting the secrets of their philosophy not in writing but by word of mouth, just to their relatives and friends, as attested by Lysis's letter to Hipparchus. And they did so, in my opinion, not because they were in some way jealous about teaching others, as some suppose. They did it so that the most beautiful things, the fruit of long and laborious studies of great men, were not exposed to humiliation and contempt by those who either are reluctant to endeavour honest work in any pursuit that is not profitable or who, even when inspired and given example by others, having taken an interest in the noble study of philosophy, their minds being dull, they linger among philosophers as drones among bees. So when I weighed accurately all of this, the derision which I had to fear on account of the difficulty in understanding the novelty of my theory almost led me to abandon completely my intentions concerning this work.

But after a long hesitation, and even resistance, I was prevailed upon by my friends. Foremost among them was Nicholas Schoenberg, cardinal of Capua, widely known for his mastery of many fields of learning, and next to him my dear friend, Tiedemann Giese, bishop of Chełmno, full of enthusiasm for theological as well as all other noble branches of knowledge. For he encouraged me frequently and, at times with bitter reproaches, urgently insisted that I publish and finally permit to reveal to the world this work, deeply buried and concealed not merely nine years but by now the fourth period of nine years. Many an outstanding scholar told me to do the same, urging me no longer to refuse, on account of my fear, to make the work available for the common benefit of the people engaged in mathematical studies. They maintained that the more preposterous my doctrine about the Earth's motion appeared to the sizeable group of scholars, the more admiration and recognition it would bring, when they would see upon the publication of this work how the darkness of absurdity would be scattered by the lightness of the obvious proofs. Surrendering therefore to the persuasion of these people and led by this hope, in the end I allowed my friends to prepare an edition of this work, as they had long entreated me to do.

However, Your Holiness will be surprised not so much that I dared to publish the results of my labors, since I have put so much effort into working them out, or that I did not hesitate to write down my thoughts on the Earth's motion, but rather will be interested to find out how it occured to me that in spite of the generally accepted opinion of mathematicians and in spite of the nearly universal belief of the people, I had the courage to imagine any motion of the Earth. Therefore I desire that Your Holiness know well that I was prompted to start thinking about a different principle of calculating the motions of the universe's spheres by nothing else but the observation that mathematicians themselves contradict one another in their investigations. For, in the first place, they have so many doubts about the motion of the Sun and the Moon that they cannot even determine and calculate the constant length of the tropical year. Secondly, when they determine the motion of these two, as well as of the remaining five planets, they do not use the same principles, premises, and proofs in explaining the observed revolutions and motions. For some accept only homocentrics, while others accept eccentrics and epicycles, and yet are not able to reach the desired results. For although those who base their work on homocentrics showed that some nonuniform motions can be compounded in this way, they could not determine any results that would correspond exactly to the observed phenomena. On the other hand, those who conceived the eccentrics, even though it seems they determined with their help appropriate calculations for most observed motions, accepted with them many assumptions which stand in obvious contradiction to the first principles of uniform motion. They were not able either to discover or elicit from the eccentrics the most important thing, namely the structure of the universe and the established order of its parts. They did the same as if some one took from various places hands, legs, a head, and other parts of the body and drew them, it is true, very well, but in such a fashion that in relation to one and the same body they would not fit together at all and the result would be some sort of a monster, rather than a picture of a man. So the result is that in the process of their demonstration, that is what is called "method", they either have omitted something important or they have accepted something extraneous, which is wholly irrelevant. That would not have happened at all if they had resolutely observed certain principles. Because if the assumptions they accepted were not fallacious, all conclusions resulting from them would also have been proven true without any doubt. What I am saying may not be clear now, but it will become more comprehensible in the appropriate place.

So during long deliberations on this uncertainty of traditional mathematical approaches concerning calculation of the motions of the universe's spheres, I was seized by an unpleasant feeling that the philosophers, who otherwise have examined so thoroughly even the most insignificant phenomena, were not able to arrive at any satisfactory method to explain the movements of the world machine, created for us by the best and most perfect master. For this reason I set myself this task to reread all the available works of the philosophers in order to examine if by any chance anyone had ever expressed an opinion concerning the motions of the universe's spheres differing from the principles accepted by the teachers of mathematics. And indeed I found first in Cicero that Hicetas thought the earth moved. Later I also found in Plutarch some other names of people sharing the same opinion. I have decided to quote his words here so that they could be made available to everybody: "According to a general belief, the Earth remains at rest. But Philolaus the Pythagorean believes that it revolves around the fire in an oblique circle, like the Sun and the Moon. Heraclides of Pontus and Ecphantus the Pythagorean hold that the Earth moves not in a progressive motion, but like a wheel in a rotation from west to east about its own center."

Thus inspired, I too began to ponder over the mobility of the Earth. And although such an idea seemed absurd, nevertheless, as I knew that others before me had been granted the freedom to imagine any circles in order to explain the heavenly phenomena, I came to the conclusion that I too without any obstacles had a right to essay if by assuming some motion of the earth it would be possible to find a sounder method of explaining the revolutions of the celestial spheres.

Therefore in this way, having assumed the motions which I ascribe to Earth later in this work, after numerous and long observations I finally became convinced that if the motions of the other planets are correlated with the orbiting of the Earth and calculated in relation to the revolution of each separate planet, not only can their phenomena be deduced but they will also link together so precisely the order and size of all the planets and spheres, and even heaven, that in no part can anything be moved without confusion in the remaining parts and in the whole universe. Accordingly, in the arrangement of this work I have decided on the following order: in the first book I describe the positions of all the spheres together with the motions I attribute to the Earth, so that this book contains, as it were, the general structure of the universe. In turn in the remaining books I correlate the motions of the other planets and of all the spheres with the movement of the Earth, so that one can thereby understand to what extent the motions and the phenomena connected with the other planets and their spheres can be explained in relation to the motions of the Earth. I have no doubt that gifted and learned mathematicians will fully agree with me, provided that they will do what this discipline especially requires, namely they are willing to study and take under consideration, not superficially but thoroughly, what I adduce in this work to prove my propositions. However, to demonstrate to both the educated and uneducated alike that I do not evade at all anybody's criticism, I preferred to dedicate the fruit of my labors to Your Holiness rather than to anyone else, for in this distant corner of the earth where I live, you are considered the highest authority by virtue of the dignity of your office as well as your love for all branches of knowledge, including mathematics. It will be therefore easy for you, with your authority and judgment, to suppress the attacks of slanderous tongues although, as the proverb says, there is no remedy against the bite of a false accuser. Perhaps there will be those who like to talk nonsense and although they are completely ignorant of mathematics, claiming a right to express their opinion on the basis of some passage in the Scriptures, interpreted incorrectly and fallaciously to suit their purpose, they will dare to condemn and censure my theory. I completely ignore them, to the extent of despising their judgment as frivolous. It is not a secret, after all, that Lactantius, otherwise a famous writer but weak in mathematics, speaks about the Earth's shape just like a child, mocking those who declared that the Earth has the form of a globe. Therefore men of learning should not be surprised if any such persons will likewise ridicule me. Mathematical works are written for mathematicians, who--unless I am mistaken--will notice that my labors bring some benefits to the Church, over which Your Holiness has authority now. For not so long ago under Leo X, when during the Lateran Council a reform of the ecclesiastical calendar was debated, the matter was left undecided only because they did not have at their disposal the sufficiently exact measurements of years and months or of the motions of the Sun and the Moon. Since then, encouraged by the distinguished man, Father Paul, bishop of Fossombrone, who was then in charge of this matter, I began to try as hard as I could to examine these matters more thoroughly. But what I have managed to accomplish in this regard, I leave above all to the judgment of Your Holiness as well as all other learned mathematicians. And lest it appears that I promise Your Holiness more benefit from this work than I can indeed provide, I now turn to the discourse itself.

*Text*: Kopernik, Mikołaj. *O obrotach*. Ed. by Jerzy Dobrzycki. Translated into Polish by Mieczysław Brożek. Warszawa: PWN, 1976, 3-6.

# MARCIN KROMER (1512-1589)

Marcin Kromer came from an affluent burgher family in Biecz. In 1528 he enrolled in the Cracow Academy, receiving a bachelor's degree in 1530. He remained in Cracow, devoting himself to writing and translating. From 1533 to 1536 he worked in the royal chancellery in Wilno. In 1537 Kromer went to Padua, where he studied Latin and Greek, then to Bologna, where he received the doctorate in law and became acquainted with new trends in historiography. In 1540 he visited Rome and returned to Cracow. Kromer worked in the chancellery of Archbishop Piotr Gamrat and from 1545 to 1558 as royal secretary, became the bishop of Warmia, and accumulated benefices. He was engaged in many diplomatic missions, staunchly defended Catholicism, and wrote extensively on religion and history.

Kromer's *Conversation Between a Courtier and a Monk* (1551-1554), was the first example of humanist prose written in Polish. His other major works were *De origine et rebus gestis Polonorum*, a history of Poland published in Basel in 1555, which had five Latin editions and was translated into German and Polish, and its supplement *Polonia* (1575), which described the geography and structure of the state, its people, and their ways of life.

*Polonia or About the Geography, Population, Customs, Offices, and Public Matters of the Polish Kingdom in Two Volumes*

Book I
(selections)

People here are usually of light complexion, fair-haired or even verging on white; they are of average height or somewhat taller, of robust body build, and only women, especially from the most distinguished noble or burgher homes take great care so that by appropriate endeavors they make themselves look like slim reeds, as the famous poet says.[1] Besides this, they do not pay much attention to good looks, for making up one's face and dying one's hair is generally considered a shameful thing. But on the other hand, both for men and for women, a genuine color is their natural adornment.

The Poles have an open and sincere disposition, they are more likely deceived than they would deceive someone else; they are not so much inclined towards quarreling as towards harmony; one cannot see in them impudence and arrogance, on the contrary--they are even submissive, so long as they are treated politely and gently. They are most impressed by personal example and in general they listen to their rulers and officers. They are inclined to bestow upon others acts of kindness, courtesy, friendliness, and hospitality to such a degree that they not only willingly receive and entertain strangers and vistors from other lands, but they even invite them and offer all their help; they easily form social acquaintances and friendships with everyone; what is more, they eagerly imitate the customs of those they deal with, especially the foreign ones.

The upbringing of youth is somewhat too free and perhaps too little attention is given to it, but the good inborn features of character compensate for these failings. All people, both poor and rich, both nobility and common folk, especially burghers, endeavor to send young boys to schools and for practical instruction, to accustom them to Latin from the earliest childhood. Many keep tutors. Therefore even in the very center of Italy it is difficult to find so many people of all kinds with whom one could communicate in Latin as here. Also the girls learn either at home or in convents to read and write in Polish, and even in Latin; when they become more mature, they begin to get accustomed to household duties, especially pertaining to the kitchen and tending flock, and to spinning flax or wool as well as to weaving and embroidery. The young men learn to work in the fields or in some craft or trade and to hold office and prepare themselves to assume ecclesiastical or lay positions which fall to more affluent people. Many live at home with their parents and help them in estate matters, and after their parents' death fulfill their duties as the heads of family.

There are many people who, disregarding the expenses, deprivations, and all the troubles that accompany travelers abroad, go readily to far-off countries, bearing well the lack of conveniences as they find more attractions in those things which are abroad than in those in their own country. That is why they diligently and easily learn the languages of those nations which they visit, and also try to bring back from abroad something new pertaining to food, clothing, and customs, perceiving in it some reason for distinction on account of refinement. This plague has crept even into religion.

The Poles have quick minds capable of overcoming any difficulties, but they are more likely inclined to accurately master foreign ideas instead of managing to independently invent something new and gain a decisive superiority in some field. Maybe it happens because they are not very eager to devote themselves to one art or skill, but want to learn many disciplines or maybe because of carelessness, tardiness, and unwillingness to make an effort, characteristic of them in many a field, especially since the people, who on account of their functions occupy themselves with both liberal arts and mechanics, satisfied with average results, do not look too hard for accomplished craftsmen and the highest quality of work. Finally, maybe it is so because more affluent people succumb to careless inactivity and pleasant amusements, leaving to the poorer people the intellectual work and improvement of inventiveness. Those in turn, according to the words of the philosopher[2] who says that it is difficult to expect good work from a pauper, must look around everywhere for earnings that would secure their upkeep and fathom the studies and occupations which are at times foreign to their interests and not in the range of their abilities; additionally, when they achieve enough to be satisfied and when they conform to the way of life of the more affluent, they immediately begin to be distracted by matters connected with securing their possession by suits and legal tricks or by supporting the policy of the rich. And they do all this either because they cannot be left alone by their own ambition or because they want to find for themselves and their kin some absolute defense against the harm and insults from others that threaten them. Because I do not know how it happens that especially now, in the epoch we are living in, the goodness of mind and heart as well as the decrees and civil law do not effectively guarantee the acquisition of values that serve life and its adornment, let alone their essential defense.

## Notes

1. Terence.
2. Aristotle.


*Text*: Kromer, Marcin. *Polska, czyli o położeniu, ludności, obyczajach, urzędach i sprawach publicznych Królestwa Polskiego księgi dwie*. Translated into Polish by Stefan Kazikowski. Olsztyn: Pojezierze, 1984, 68-72.

# ANDRZEJ FRYCZ MODRZEWSKI (c.1503-1572)

Andrzej Frycz was from a nobleman's family in Wolborz. He attended a parish school in his native town and later in Cracow. In 1517 Frycz entered the Cracow Academy, two years later received a baccalaureate (with distinction), and continued his studies. In 1523 he entered the court of Jan Łaski, primate of Poland, and worked as notary to the bishop of Poznań.

From 1531 to 1535 Frycz studied in Wittenberg, where he became acquainted with Philip Melanchthon, Luther's associate, and then, until 1540, lived in Germany. In 1537 he was engaged in making arrangements to transport Erasmus's library, purchased by Jan Łaski, a nephew of the primate, from Basel to Poland. After returning to Poland, Frycz was supporting himself by the income from his prebends. In about 1547, he became a royal secretary, serving also as a diplomatic envoy. He returned to his native Wolborz in 1553 and devoted himself to writing. Criticized and threatened for his ideas, Frycz had to leave his home for some time. His writings were placed on the church index.

In *De poena homicidii* (*Punishment for Homicide*) (1543), Frycz advocated, well ahead of his time, a uniform penal code for the gentry and the plebeian, as he considered all citizens equal before the law. In his major work *Commentariorum de Republica emendanda libri quinque* (1551-1554), translated into Polish as *On the Reform of the Commonwealth*, Frycz Modrzewski was mainly concerned with the mores, considered as a set of ethical motivations of each citizen. He also discussed laws, war, church, and school, drawing up a blueprint for the ideal state.

Many sections of Frycz's work speak to our current concerns. In Chapter VI Frycz discussed the role of parents in bringing up children, while in the section *On guardians of the poor*, he analyzed a welfare system that would be fair and acceptable to society.

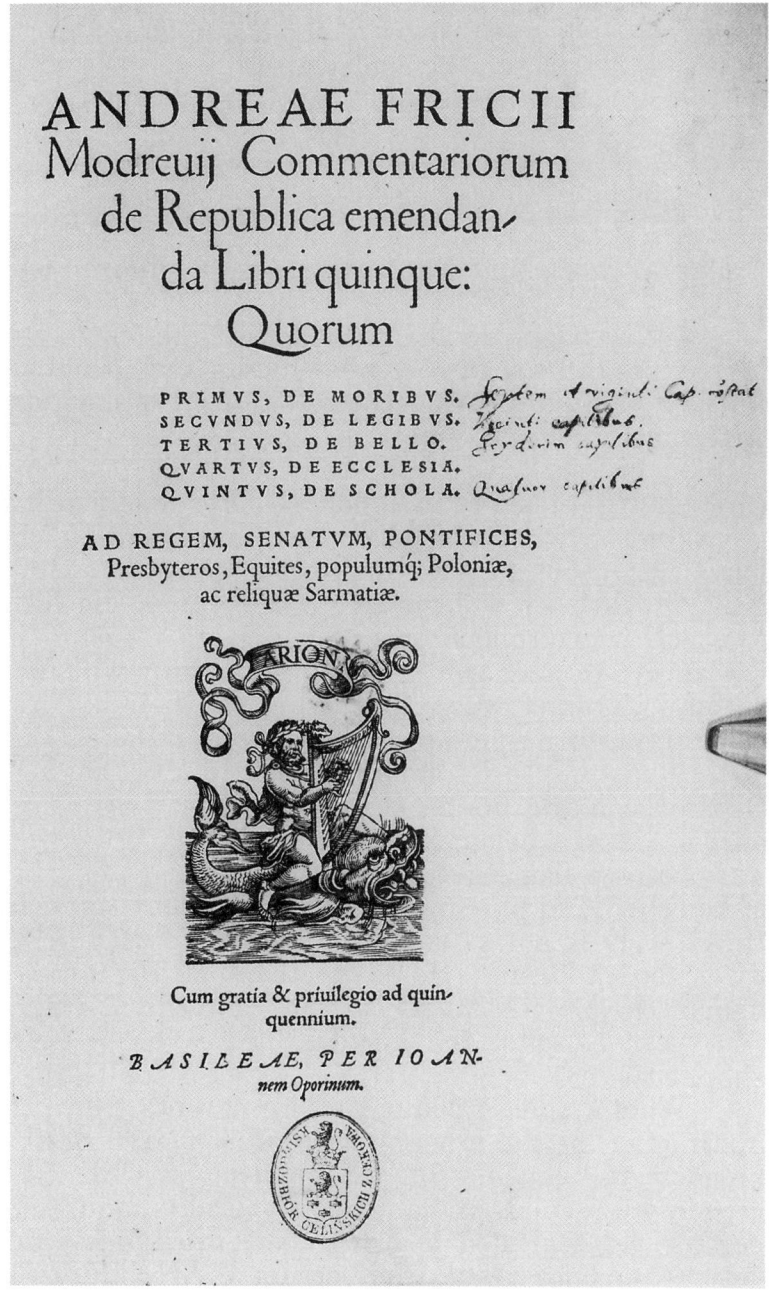

VIII. Title page of Andrzej Frycz Modrzewski's *Commentariorum de Republica emendanda*, Basilea, 1554

## On the Reform of the Commonwealth
(selections)

### Book I

### Chapter VI

*How to care about good upbringing of children and youth*

Let us begin this discussion with childhood, about which I have just talked, namely what habits and thoughts it should be filled with so that it becomes like a strong foundation for a forthcoming honest, spotless, and praiseworthy life. For nothing is instilled in the souls of people more firmly than what they got used to in childhood. For if something harmful is grafted on when they are young and yielding, then it will stay with them forever, as if you saturated with poison a graft which later will grow into a big tree; the fruits of that tree will be poisonous and will in large measure pass down the ability to do harm to the seeds, which will not be much better. Parents, when they bring up their children, should bear in mind the picture of Christ who rebuked His disciples for not wishing to let children come to Him, saying: "Let the children come to me for it is to such as these that the kingdom of heaven belongs. Truly I tell you, unless you change and become like children, you will never enter the kingdom of heaven. And putting His hands on their heads, He blessed them."[1] Is it not evident from these words how much God cares for children? He takes them in His arms, He commends them with prayer to the Heavenly Father, calls all who want to enter the kingdom of heaven to emulate their simplicity.

What crime is committed by parents who neglect good upbringing for the progeny born of them and destined to the kingdom of heaven? For what reason was Eli the priest together with children punished by God's hand?[2] Was it not because he neglected to bring them up properly and to lead them? And for those who corrupt their children and are a stumbling block for them, would it not be better if they, as Christ says, had a millstone fastened to their necks and were drowned in the depths of the sea?[3]

So parents should take care to instill in children such teachings and bring them up in such a way that from the earliest years they would learn to understand what is honest, and what is shameful, what to strive for, and what to avoid.

They should strongly lead them away from pleasures, because wherever they rule, there is no room for virtues.

They should prescribe for them moderation in food, which should be light, plain, and not inflaming the insides. This age burns with an inborn heat and there is no need to add fire to fire. This will help not only in restrainig the bodily desire but also in maintaining a strong and healthy body and soberness of mind.

They should make them get used not only to moderation in food and drink, but also to bearing of cold and heat, and to hard bedding (so long as this would not be a detriment to their strength and good body condition, which should be taken care of, in order for the mind to be in good form and active).

They should not allow them to associate with bad people.

They should form their language and all deeds after a model of beauty, justice, mildness, kindness and human civility.

And they should tell them to avoid ugliness, abuse, anger, envy, pride, and cruelty.

They should restrain their chatter, because immeasurable garrulity and empty talk are born of it, disgusting at any age. Just as they do not allow wicked deeds, they should not permit them indecent talk. They should demand that they are aware of what they say and do. Parents would do a useful thing if they encouraged the young, by insisting on virtue and citing examples of it, and if they praised them even more than was true, because as Ovid says:

Excellence grows with praise
And applause is its immense stimulus.[4]

Commonly known sayings about virtue and fulfilment of one's duties, numerous in every language, have great influence on a child's soul, so long as it is still pure and not stained by evil thoughts. Those sayings are, for example: "One should eat to live, not live to eat." Or: "Improperly gained, improperly lost." Or: "A hand washes a hand, a city lives for a city." Or: "Strive for offices with virtue, not through supporters; he who acts beneficially has enough friends." Or: "It is hard to be victorious over others, but it is even greater to be victorious over one's own soul and restrain one's impetuosity." Or: "Just as one bridles the wildness of the horse by tiring it and taking away its oats, one tames excessive desires by work and fasting." Or: "What is not proper to do is improper to think and talk about"--which is truly correct, because honest deeds must stem from honest will and thought.

This is why parents who want to open the way to righteousness in everything for their children should firmly lead them away, as much as they can, not only from evil deeds and unpleasant words, but also from thinking about bad things. They will not achieve it in any way more easily than by not allowing them to be idle.

They should therefore be careful that boys and girls do not spend their first years in idleness; they should always attempt to give them some work, and should also demand that they account for it. There is no wrong in combining work and play, so long as the play is not disagreeable. One can choose fables or riddles or stories, which would encourage the children to work; if they are too listless and slow, it is proper to reprimand them, and those who avoid chores even more to punish with a rod. King Solomon, great sage, says: "Do not allow the child to shun discipline. He will not die from a rod. You beat him, and save the soul from hell."

Since it is the inborn human nature to seek rest, recreation, and a breathing spell after work, parents should make sure that the children's games are appropriate. It will be easier to do, if parents themselves are present while they play or entrust the task to someone older and honest, whom children respect and in whose presence they will not dare to say or do anything unpleasant or disagreeable. One should try as hard as possible not to have boys take part in girls' pastimes, especially when they become adolescent, because this age in itself spurs them to desire. These habits of play, youthful loves and frenzies which inflame them at the age when they do not recognize yet what is right cannot but be immoral; with years they get stronger and it rarely happens that they can be rooted out.

Boys should not neglect horseback riding or foot exercises, such as running or jumping, or throwing stones, or playing with a ball or discus and other such sports, provided they are done moderately. For moderate activity and exercise invigorate, fortify and improve health, strength, and robustness of the body; if, however, they are too intense and violent, they weaken and injure it. Doctors teach that exercises of this kind should be done either before meals or not soon after, so that food, when the body is full, does not spoil on account of exertion and does not create harmful moistures or even grave diseases in the body.

But as I said all pastimes should be appropriate; they should not be effeminate, licentious, foolish, shameless. Children should also be taught what they are due others, what is due their parents, countrymen, commonwealth, also how they should keep peace and company with other people, how to behave towards their superiors, inferiors, and equals, towards companions, friends, family and relatives, towards public servants, noblemen, and attendants, and even towards enemies and opponents, both in private as well as in public life.

The most important, however, is to fill the youth with respect for immortal God, just as Christ indicates in the words quoted above, when he tells children to come to Him and blesses them. Children should be shown Christ and imbued with knowledge of God, so they would know from whom they could expect all that is good, with whose nod everything happens, who punishes evil and rewards good. They should be taken to churches and services so they would learn holy rites and ceremonies, worship sacraments, have opportunities to pray and become devoted to this which merits Almighty God's grace and people's affection. In this way they prepare for themselves remedies against all solicitations of the devil, body, and this world.

When parents recognize and observe a young man's talents, they should direct him towards the subjects to which, in their belief, he is naturally inclined, so that he can begin to learn and love the rudiments of those works that he will later be occupied with during his whole life. And if by any chance they want to send the young man to foreign lands, they should very carefully prepare him for this experience and instill in his heart to strive not so much to get to know as many people as possible in each country nor to become close to many, but to learn what is just in customs, law, and discipline in neighboring countries, so that he would observe everything and after his return could explain them in order to reform these matters in his homeland.

Since the young learn how to behave from older people, especially from parents, not only with their ears but also with their eyes, parents should make every effort to appear in their children's eyes much the same as they would like them to be. Surely a father who is a drunkard will not manage to arouse in his son a love of temperance; a squanderer and fancy dresser will not recommend thrift to children; nor will a violent man, who in anger becomes cruel, bloodthirsty, and homicidal, be able to prescribe to his children the laws of gentleness or conciliation and humaneness, because the young are attracted to follow in the footsteps of their parents and to be like them. I would be pleased to see all parents examine themselves if they did not corrupt most the morals of their children.

Sons of great lords are brought up for the most part too leniently and in too much freedom: they spend time dancing with girls, playing lutes and singing indecent songs, surrounded by ingratiating courtiers and teachers. From the earliest years they absorb pride and haughtiness and get to know silk garments before they begin to speak; they admire gold chains and numerous servants, since childhood they think of nothing but ruling, pomp, various feasts, vindictive irritability. Because of excessive leniency, they completely lose common sense and although they were never taught to listen, they would like to command.

They are laughable dunces who flatter the children of rich people and bedazzle them with wealth, power, splendor of their family house, and who first instill in them pride and haughtiness before they gain some understanding of honesty and moderation. Would it not be much better if children did not know about it, and learned from teachers what is more helpful to virtue and solid work, rather than what fills them with puffed up pride? Because if they develop such habits and absorb such instruction, no teacher will be able to remake, no Mercury to change, no Vulcan[5] to recast them, and their whole lives they will hold to that which they in a way have sucked with their mother's milk. To be sure such people have usually the name of virtue on their lips, but they rarely know anything about virtue, which must be acquired in utmost toil, and even more rarely approach it in their actions. To put it briefly: forbearance of fortune and a way of life full of corruption do not allow them to reach anything good either in childhood or when they are growing up or when they reach manhood or when they become old, because the charms of vice stand in their way.

For it is not easy to get used to good behavior, if one has been accustomed to evil (similarly it is not easy for the Ethiopian to change black skin for a different one), and that cannot happen at all, unless, as the Holy Scriptures bear witness, by some exceptional grace of God.

It would then be necessary to reform bad habits in young hearts and to instill the true concepts of things since, as I have already said and will frequently talk about, there is nothing more destructive to good habits than false understanding and ignorance of the truth. And there is nobody who would not know, as I said, how limited parents are in this respect. How many are there who would properly bring up their children or, even if they wanted, know how to do it?

Our laws have not decreed anything about this matter and there is only a custom that the one who wants his children to gain glory owing to virtues sends them either to the masters at school or to the courts of great lords or to someone whose company could provide, in his opinion, a good education.

## Chapter XVIII
### On guardians of the poor

Just as the people able to work should not be allowed to beg, so an effort should be made to supply for the truly poor, that is those who are weak and without means of support, communal shelters and everything which they need to live. There are some poor people who live in hospices, where they are fed and taken care of; others roam the roads, begging; still others, hiding in their four walls, attempt to provide for their own needs as well as they can. An office should have them all under supervision so they would not deceive anyone by simulating either sickness or destitution. Those who seem able should be compelled to work, and if they would refuse, they should be driven out of town.

The same pertains to migrant beggars, who should be sent back to their community. For it is proper that each settlement take care of those who were either born in it or lived there a long time, so that they would not die on account of a shortage of food or other necessities.

The cause of poverty of each poor person should be determined. Even though those who became impoverished because of their own wrongdoing should also be placed among the poor and assisted so that they would not die of hunger, they should be given less food and tested with hard work, so that they would serve as a deterrent to others and keep away from committing a bigger offence. More consideration should be given to those who sank into poverty because of sickness or some other mishap. Those who provide for themselves and family as well as they can at home ought to be leased a piece of land at a low price or given a job that they could do or offered other means of earning a livelihood.

Poor girls should be provided with a dowry and married, so that their modesty would not be put out for sale on account of poverty. I believe migrant beggars should not be tolerated because under the guise of begging they do a lot of harm, committing thefts and murders and other crimes. They should rather be locked up in hospices, but only those among them who cannot work any more.

Nearly each town has some annual revenues allocated for supporting the poor. If these revenues are too small to support all, they should be increased in the following way: first, everyone could limit somewhat his expenditures, both for necessities and above all for those purchases which are made for luxury, pride, and vanity. Christ truly wants us to use the dishonest riches of this world to acquire friends, who would want one day to admit us into their tents. So we should share earthly goods with those by whose intercession we will one day be admitted to eternal life.[6] And most of all it is proper for those who are already moving from this life to the other to act like that; let them too leave a portion of their possessions for those friends. There are some who allocate great expenses for the splendors of their funerals, but in truth those who are at the end of their lives should expect praise and glory from God, not from people. It is also becoming their progeny to conduct them to the future life not with the signs of wealth and pride, but with deeds born of love, leading to the heavenly kingdom.

In the past, after all, bishops were granted possessions so that they would give one fourth to the poor. Let the office remind them of this obligation. God will punish those who do not give and do not do what they should.

There is a custom that either in churches or in town some boxes are placed for gifts to the poor. Let everyone put in as much as his pious desire prompts him. God will multiply these alms for those who give them, so that they will always have enough to continue giving, and for those who receive them, provided they ask modestly, take them piously, and use them moderately. These are God's benefactions, and when He opens His hand, blessing comes to each creature. But He demands from us that those who give, do it willingly, and those who receive, recognize God's blessings and are grateful for them, praying earnestly for themselves and for their benefactors.

The food of the poor should be neither sumptuous, as this might easily produce an inclination to commit bad deeds, nor too meager as this would only partially appease their hunger. For the maladies of both body and soul grow from a want of food. We should watch that the poor do not sink into degradation on account of idleness, but that each of them does what he can and as much as he can, that he has some decent occupation and shares its fruits with others. And those who have already regained their physical strength should be sent to work so that they do not profit like drones from the sweat of the others.

The office should also care for those who lack physical or mental strength and cannot take care of themselves alone. We are all brothers, children of the one Father in heaven. Also no one is free from human adversities. And if it is the duty of mankind to hasten to help those whose life is threatened, to save them from fire or from enemy or from another disaster, then it is the most just thing to assist all the hungry, thirsty, naked, cold, so they would not die on account of a shortage of that which is most needed. So we should strive to satisfy their needs either from public funds or by some other means. Kings, bishops, great lords, religious orders, towns, and those who live in riches have the most power to do so. This is true and sincere generosity: to be charitable to those who cannot at all repay. For the most benign Father in heaven, who promised to reward even a cup of cold water given in His name, will not deprive us of award.

Apostle Paul admonishes the Romans to assist, according to their means, the poor in Jerusalem. How much more it is proper for us to piously collect for those who live here with us, who gnawed by old age, sickness, or another misfortune lead hopeless lives among us.

So there should be an office that would care for the poor and sensibly give out what is set aside for their use. It seems it is necessary for me to talk in this place about those civil servants who would care for people's condition, who would punish wicked habits, and restore the good ones, and who would examine bad deeds not only according to legal regulations, but according to how they appear in life. About those who should judge according to law, I will speak somewhere else.

After this explanation, it is time to talk about all high offices.

## Notes

1. Matthew 19:14-15, 18:3. All biblical references in this volume are to *The New Oxford Annotated Bible. New Revised Standard Version* (Ed. by Bruce Metzger and Roland Murphy. New York: Oxford University Press, 1989), unless stated otherwise.

2. "Now the sons of Eli were scoundrels; they had no regard for the LORD or for the duties of the priests or the poeple." (1 Samuel 2:12-13)

3. "If any of you put a stumbling block before one of these little ones who believe in me, it would be better for you if a great millstone were fastened around your neck and you were drowned in the depth of sea." (Matthew 18:6)

4. "(...) excellence, when approved of, still increases.
    Applause, too, gives an immense stimulus." *The Pontic Epistles of Ovid*, tr. by Henry T. Riley. London: George Bell and Sons, 1903, 4, 2, 35, 444.

In the notes I quote the classical authors following the usage of *The Oxford Latin Dictionary*.

5. Mercury was the Roman god of trade, commerce, and travel. Vulcan was the god of fire and metalworking.

6. "And I tell you, make friends for yourselves by means of dishonest wealth so that when it is gone, they may welcome you into the eternal homes." (Luke 16:9).


*Text*: Frycz Modrzewski, Andrzej. *O poprawie Rzeczypospolitej*. Ed. by Stanisław Bodniak. Translated by Edwin Jędrkiewicz. Warszawa: PIW, 1953, 110-115, 167-170.

# STANISŁAW ORZECHOWSKI (1513-1566)

Orzechowski was born into a nobleman's family in or near Przemyśl. He studied briefly at the Cracow Academy, then went to Vienna and in 1529 to Wittenberg. He was a student of Luther and Melanchthon, under whose influence he became a Protestant. In 1531 or 1532 Orzechowski went to Italy to continue his studies in Bologna and Padua. In 1543 he returned to Poland, reluctantly became a priest, and derived benefits from a number of prebends. He rejected celibacy, took a wife in 1551, and engaged in a prolonged, notorious dispute with his bishop and the Roman Curia.

A demagogic and popular polemicist, Orzechowski wrote equally well in Latin and in Polish. He often changed his opinions and fiercely attacked various institutions and individuals, among them Andrzej Frycz Modrzewski. A staunch defender of the freedoms of the gentry, he looked down on other social groups. He advocated the dominant role of the Church, yet attacked the immorality of the clergy. He praised the role of Poland in opposing the religious influences of Islam, Orthodoxy, and Protestantism. In his *Chimera* (1560), Orzechowski warned against the dangers of heresy and formulated a theocratical model of the state.

### *Chimera or On the Shameful Heresy in the Kingdom of Poland*

#### Book III
(selection)

Take a look at Gniezno, capital of your metropolitan see, at Cracow, also at Włocławek and Płock, as well as at the remaining capitals of bishoprics in Poland. Look closely which tribe, which nation flourishes more with its bishopric capitals, which nation between the great oceans[1] is richer? And the clergymen in Poland acquired so much money not by stealing or cheating, but received it by our common will from shared patrimony. For we were taught that our Lord Jesus had his purses and a treasurer at His service. We were instructed that those purses constituted the treasury of the Church. So when in equal proportions a part of this land became the property of the king, another part of the clergyman, another part of the people, everyone having his assured and safe part from a general division, then we all lived a secure life and maintained this way of life in the happy Republic, so that we could live as happily and virtuously as if at home, in mutual love, and also outside we were always the glorious victors everywhere. We never fought with any other nations if we were not attacked; our sages made us aware that the royal sword which together with the crown and the sceptre we received from pope Benedict VII[2] was granted to us not to wage war, but to repel it. That is why Bolesław the Brave, our first king, forced by Kievan Ruś to fight a war, expanded his kingdom up to the River Dniepr. The same king, when the Germans inflicted many damages upon him, marked the borders of Poland on the River Elbe.[3] Forced by the knavery of Prussia and Livonia, he set his borders on the Atlantic ocean.[4] He did not pacify Hungary until he set the border against the attacking Hungarians at the Carpathian Mountains. We lived in the same way in this land during the reign of other kings. We believed that our Polish Kingdom was situated so far up north, north of the other Christian kingdoms, in order for our nation to fight for the Christian faith, for Peter's see against the Scythians,[5] against Moscow, against Wallachia, and against Turkey. There is no place or region around Poland that would not be moistened with the blood of our knights fighting against schismatic or Tartar people. We went to the most dangerous battle for the Christian faith, for Peter's see, we went there where we had no hope of returning. At Warna, a Hungarian town, in the battle against Murad of Turkey we lost our King Władysław.[6] From that war, out of forty thousand Poles only three survivors returned to Poland as the messengers of such great defeat. Polish blood is flowing again. Did not King Louis who died at Mochacs in the war against Turkey lose the regiments which he had received from our King Sigismund, his uncle?[7] And the slaughter of Bukowina?[8] And does not the defeat suffered at Sokal[9] prove too how steadfast we were in devoutedness, in battle? What kind of devoutedness did we embrace so strongly that when the Gospels are read, we stand with sabers drawn and do not sheathe them until the priest conludes reading? By this truly solemn custom we demonstrate that we are ready to die for the Christian faith. We have proved this often but most of all on that day, when with a handful of men and with a small force under Hetman Jan Tarnowski, castellan of Cracow, who loathful of your heresy came here when you were not alive but dead, we chased away the Wallachians, threatening us with a mighty army at Obertyn[10] in Ruthenia, then broke and subjugated them. Then under the same hetman, we forced Moscow, with great efforts and losses, after taking Starodub to sue for peace with the Polish king. Just as Wallachia in Ruthenia, so Moscow in Lithuania desired to take away from us the Roman faith and the rule of Peter's see. We proved to be braver than not only the outside enemies but also the local ones when some challenged the faith we received from Rome during the rule of Mieszko. That is why when the neighboring Czechs, related to us, were burning in the Hussite heresy,[11] and when the progeny of Mieszko came to an end with King Casimir, we were given Władysław Jagiełło from Lithuania, a famous war commander. We did not give Poland to him until he swore he would go with us against the Czech heretics. There were also other important reasons for summoning Władysław to Poland, because Prussia renewed an old war against us and supported by Germany, by the might of the Roman empire, attempted to detach itself from us. But those misfortunes seemed to us lighter than heresy. For it is easier to repel arms with arms, while heresy, once it creeps in and plants its roots, can be but barely, barely rooted out without destroying the common good. The reason for inviting Jagiełło was that Czech heresy. This brave king, to make Poland safe from that heresy, not only by arms but also by law, kept the laws against heretics that were prepared to be proclaimed. There are also other statutes clearly formulated.[12] What was his outstanding devoutedness like, his zeal in the defense of the faith? Our union teaches us with what harmony and with what dedication we followed him in that faith; all this is written down word for word in the statutes of the Kingdom.

## Notes

1. Orzechowski means Europe, situated between the Baltic and the Mediterranean 'oceans'.

2. It was Benedict VIII (1012-1024), who approved the coronation of Bolesław the Brave, which took place in 1025.
3. It should be on the Odra.
4. On the Baltic Sea.
5. The Tartars.
6. Władysław of Warna, king of Poland and Hungary, perished in 1444 in the battle against Turkey. Warna was in Turkey.
7. In 1526, the Hungarian army supported by Polish units was defeated at Mohacs by the forces of Suleiman the Magnificent.
8. King Albert's forces against Turkey suffered a defeat in Bukowina in 1497.
9. In 1519 at Sokal the Tartars deafeated Polish forces.
10. In the battle of Obertyn (22 August 1531), the Polish forces under Hetman Jan Tarnowski defeated the Wallachian army.
11. Jan Huss was a Bohemian religious reformer, burnt at the stake in 1415. The Hussites advocated clerical purity and poverty, supremacy of the Bible, and communion in both bread and wine for the laity. The Polish delegation to the synod of Constance in 1415 protested against the sentence.
12. According to the union of Horodło (1413), Jagiełło accepted the Polish crown in order to propagate Christian religion. In 1424, he implemented in Wieluń the statute against heretics.

*Text*: Orzechowski, Stanisław. *Wybór pism.* Ed. by Jerzy Starnawski. Wrocław: Ossolineum, 1972, 300-303.

# ŁUKASZ GÓRNICKI (1527-1603)

Górnicki was born in Oświęcim in a burgher's family. At the age of eleven he was sent to his uncle, Stanisław Gąsiorek of Bochnia, a court poet, to study in Saint John's parish school in Cracow. In 1545, Górnicki entered the court of Bishop Maciejowski in Prądnik, and then went to Padua, where he lived for many years.

In 1559 Górnicki was admitted to the court of King Zygmunt August, where as librarian and secretary in the royal chancellery he joined the luminaries of Renaissance Poland, including Kochanowski, Nidecki, Frycz Modrzewski, Kromer, and Zamoyski. In 1561 he was raised to the rank of a nobleman and gradually accrued possessions and offices.

It was during his years at the court that he translated, encouraged by the King, Baldassare Castiglione's *Il libro del cortegiano*. The fruit of several years work, *The Polish Courtier* (1566) was not a mere translation. Górnicki adapted the Italian text, transplanting its main ideas into the mainstream of Polish court culture. His major achievement was to produce in Polish the rich, reflective language characteristic of the original.

Even though Górnicki was not a writer of great originality, he is recognized as a master of Polish Renaissance prose. His other works include *History of the Polish Crown (...) from 1538 to 1572* (1637) and *A Conversation Between a Pole and an Italian on Polish Freedoms and Laws* (1587). Following in the footsteps of Jakub Parkosz, the author of *Treatise on Polish Orthography* (1440), Górnicki expressed in *The Polish Courtier* his thoughts on the language. The passage that follows differs in many points from the original Italian.

*The Polish Courtier*
(selection)
Book I
[*On Language*]

[Sir Wojciech Kryski]: So this courtier of mine will be exceptional beyond all expression and will be graceful in everything, especially in speech, if he avoids showing off; this vice appears everywhere but apparently more so here in Poland than anywhere else. For our Pole has barely been away from home, when he wants to speak nothing but the language where he lived briefly: if he was in Italy, every other word is 'signor', if in France, 'per ma foi', if in Spain, 'nos otro cavaglieros',[1] and at times, though he was not in Bohemia, but barely crossed the Silesian border, he will not want to speak any other language but Czech, and yet this Czech, God knows what it is like. And when you tell him to speak his own language, he will say he has forgotten or that his native language seems truly coarse, so to prove it, he will pick up some Old Polish word from *Mother of God*[2] and will compare it with some pretty word in Czech, to show the coarseness of his language and the beauty of the foreign one; finally, he will suggest that nearly every orator in Polish uses Czech words instead of Polish, as if this were exceedingly proper.

Here Sir Aleksander Myszkowski said: So Your Grace does not like it when a Pole puts Czech words into the Polish language?

Sir Wojciech Kryski answered: There is nothing to like when someone having his own Polish word gives it up and borrows in its place from a foreign tongue, and instead of 'crown states' says 'crown estates',[3] because it is as if someone chased the Poles away from their land and let the Czechs in; and everyone can see what kind of sense it makes. It is true that if there were no Polish word for this object which the Pole would like to name or if in translating from one language into another he needed a foreign word, not only would I not reproach him for taking a word from a tongue as similar as Czech, but I would even permit him to take it from Latin, especially if the word is easy to understand or is already somewhat popular. This is what our famous orators apparently did. People nowadays, however, not understanding it, on account of this showing off which does not become one at all, reached the point that they shamelessly began to put strange foreign words into their own language, and instead of excellent Polish words they put Czech words, much inferior to ours. From this it follows that we understand little of what those new Ciceros say, and practically nothing when they put it in writing. And they believe that it would be most wise to speak or write in such fashion that only a few people or none would understand them. In this they are wrong, as Your Grace knows very well.

To this Sir Aleksander Myszkowski responded: I suppose that if someone spoke in such a way that it would be difficult to understand him, it would be a serious fault, but in writing, it seems to me, it creates some solemnity if someone writes in a more elaborate way, and not too simply.

Sir Wojciech Kryski answered: I do not know why writing should differ from speech, since writing is nothing more than a certain form and picture of speech which endures after it has been expressed, as if it were an image of what was said. To put it simply, writing is this thing which gives life to words. So this difficulty which comes from foreign words would be more passable in speech than in writing because when we speak, those who listen to us can ask how to understand certain things. When I read someone else's writing, however, and the one who has written it is not there, it is hard to know what it is which I cannot understand. So if speech should not be difficult to understand, writing should be even less so, especially since the learned people say that the most wonderful speech is that which is similar to beautiful writing. So if this is the case (and it seems Your Grace does not doubt it), it is not proper for writing to be difficult, if speech should be easily understood by everyone.

Sir Aleksander responded: I agree, Sir Wojciech, that writing is like speech, but I still stand by what I said, namely that speech should be easy. Because if one's speech is difficult and complicated, so that it cannot get at once into our mind and understanding, then this speech is useless, just as if one did not speak at all. In writing it is otherwise, for when writing takes the form of speech (I am not saying difficult speech, but speech of a higher degree, not like that which is usual and commonly spoken), then this writing has greater importance and makes the one who reads it advance with better understanding of things, see everything clearer and, wondering at the intelligence and learning of the one who wrote it, gain more respect for himself when he understands on his own that precise statement over which he had to spend some time. But if the one who is reading is of such coarse mind that he cannot understand it, then it is not the fault of the writing but of the reader who could not overcome such a minor difficulty.

His Grace from Lublin said then: It is interesting to listen to this conversation about which writing we should praise more: the truly easy or the one which is somewhat complicated. But let us leave it for another time, and tell us now, Your Grace Sir Wojciech: since our Polish language is not quite perfect (I remember at court they praised the speaker who put the most Czech borrowings into his speech), with what language should the courtier supplement it? Should it be Czech or Russian or Croatian or Slavonic,[4] or is he allowed to revive an ancient and nearly dead Polish word, if it could be useful? Additionally, since the Latin tongue is very common here, is the courtier sometimes allowed to use a Latin word, instead of a Polish one? I would also like to know which of those languages related to ours is the most beautiful.

Sir Wojciech responded: It seems to me that I have said all I know. And yet to comply with your request, I will say what I think about these other languages. But I have to begin further back.

To begin with, if Your Grace would like to know, our language is not old, though the Poles have been speaking it for a long time, but was born quite recently from the Slavonic. For all these languages: Polish, Czech, Russian, Croatian, Bosnian, Serbian, Rassian,[5] Bulgarian, and others were in the past one language, also one people, that is Slavonic. There are others who say that both the Russian people and language might be the oldest, and that it was in Russia that the Slavs originated, from the word 'slava',[6] because they carried themselves courageously. But because it was in the remote past, this cannot be considered certain, nor do I find it necessary to discuss it now. It is enough to state that a majority of chroniclers agree that the Slavonic people are the oldest among those I have mentioned. It is from those people, when some moved their settlements here and the others there, that from one language many others were born. At that time, when they did not know writing or learning, there was great coarseness in people as well as in languages. And when the Bulgarians, having borrowed letters from the Greeks, adjusting some and changing others, began somehow to write, thanks to their intelligence they in time succeeded in translating a lot of the Word of God from Latin and Greek into their own language. So their language must be much richer than ours, because they have been writing longer than we. From the Bulgarians, writing was taken up by the Rassians, Serbs, Russians, and others. Czech writing, on the other hand, originated from Latin letters, somewhat more polished, apparently because the Czechs are neighbors with nations of higher culture. They soon began to speak more beautifully, neatly, with more flourish, keeping the length of the words close to the Latin meter, and from this grew the fame among us that their language was more beautiful than ours. It may be richer than ours, and this is because writing and learning came to them earlier than to us--but as for its beauty let us leave it undecided for the time being.

So coming to the point: when the Polish courtier is short of words, he will do right if he borrows from the Czech language, rather than from other languages, and that is because it is recognized and considered the most beautiful here. This common belief, which must be accepted after all, will add some dignity to Polish speech. But if there happened to be a word in the Czech language that would be quite difficult, and in its place there would be a Russian, Croatian or Serbian word, easy for a Pole to understand, then it would be better for a courtier in this case to take, according to his opinion, the easier and more obvious word from those other languages and leave the Czech out. But it is all up to his judgment to weigh which word serves the Polish ear better, which is clearer, which more expressive, which describes the thing more accurately. As for the old Polish words and how to use them, if we want to revive them, I say this: if one would like to throw away those words we are using now and choose the old ones in their place, he would be doing nothing different from a person who would scorn bread and eat acorns instead, as people did in bygone years. We should use words like coins, because people do not accept those they do not know; nor do they understand other words than those which are in common use. But if there is no current word for the thing the courtier wants to describe, not only will I not be insulted by an old word, but I would prefer it to the foreign one. Finally, the courtier should not despise Prussian or Kashubian words,[7] which we laugh at, because he will find there some words that describe a thing so accurately that they cannot be more proper. I also like it quite a lot when he coins a new word or makes one word out of two Polish ones.

Since Your Grace mentioned the Latin tongue, I can see this habit in some of our countrymen who want to show they know a lot and say every third word in Latin. They can be compared to a vat in which there is little wine or to a bag in which there are only a few peas: because if you knock at an empty vat, it responds with a loud sound, while the full one, like a bag full of peas, does not. The same goes for those who know only a few words and use them eagerly, showing off in this fashion, while others do not understand them. Therefore when there is a good Polish word, it is wrong to use a Latin word in its place, unless the word is so common, so usual that all will understand it or it cannot be translated properly from Latin to Polish (...).

### Notes

1. 'signor' (Italian), 'sir'; 'par ma foi' (French), 'word of honor'; 'nos otros caballeros' (Spanish), 'we, noblemen.'
2. *Mother of God*, written probably in the thirteenth century, is the oldest Polish religious poem.
3. 'estates' is given as a Czech word for the Polish 'states'.
4. This is Old Church Slavonic, mother tongue of Slavic languages.
5. Rassian was a dialect of Serbian. Ras was a capital of Serbia in the twelfth and thirteenth centuries.
6. Górnicki's comment on the seniority of Russian and the derivation of the name 'Slavonic' from 'sława' (glory) was borrowed from some early chroniclers.
7. Kashubian dialect is still spoken, but Prussian became extinct at the end of the seventeenth century.

*Text*: Górnicki, Łukasz. *Pisma*. Ed. by Roman Pollak. Vol. I. Warszawa: PIW, 1961, 104-111.

# WAWRZYNIEC GOŚLICKI (ca. 1530-1607)

Born into a nobleman's family near Płock, Goślicki studied at the Cracow Academy from 1556 to 1562 and then in Padua, Bologna, and Rome. His most important work, *De optimo senatore libri duo*, was published in Venice in 1568. After his return to Poland, Goślicki became a secretary of King Zygmunt August and took part in numerous diplomatic missions. In 1568 he was appointed the Bishop of Kamieniec, in 1590 of Chełm, in 1591 of Przemyśl, and finally in 1601 of Poznań.

*De optimo senatore*, dedicated to King Zygmunt August, shows the ideal statesman who is well versed in the humanities as well as in economy, politics, and law. This theoretical treatise on the art of ruling postulated the importance of the senate as a body mediating between the monarch's absolute tendencies and noblemen's attempts to acquire more power.

*The Accomplished Senator*
Book One
(selection)

Three things are particularly necessary in each happy and ideal state--the magistrate, laws, and citizens' obedience towards them. For without them no state or human community can function properly.

The function of a magistrate is to lead citizens and to recommend to them everything which is just and beneficial, in conformity with laws and reason. Cicero expressed himself beautifully and learnedly on this subject: "For as the laws govern the magistrate, so the magistrate governs the people, and it can truly be said tha the magistrate is a speaking law, and the law a silent magistrate."[1] One can judge the political system and condition of the state by evaluating its magistrates. Just as a ship tossed by the waves in a storm at sea usually sinks, unless the sailors save it by their effort and skill, similarly the ship of state sailing across the stormy sea of troubles, rebellions, disturbances, and discords would crash--like a wave against a cliff--if it were not supported by the magistrates' foresight and prudence. Also, just as our body is ruled by the soul, which in turn is ruled by thought and reason, so each state organism and human community must possess a soul, that is law showing the way to a good and decent life, this law originating from thought and reason, that is from the counsel of a prudent and wise man. For where there are no laws and offices, there can be no God and people, and no state can exist.

For man, law is true reason, which the sage finds within himself, while the common people receive it from magistrates and legal decrees, keeping in mind that one should avoid no less that which is forbidden by written laws than that which is forbidden by reason. Therefore those who surpass others in wisdom and prudence (...), should take their place at the head of the state, because they can render better service to the human community than others. For the state strengthened by their counsels, as if by fortified walls, will repulse attacks of the enemies, resist dangers, enjoy a peaceful and happy life. It is therefore necessary that those people are endowed above all with the virtues capable of securing happiness for the state, that they respect the political system in which they live, and being satisfied with it, they do not introduce any new elements that seem to be contrary to it, and finally that they obtain from the citizens the power of doing what in their opinion brings benefit to the state. For as a result they will govern with greater usefulness and dignity, while the citizens will better obey their commands. The one who wishes to take office and a leading role in the state truly needs immense competence and wisdom. For he has to govern not only his house, family, wife, and children, but also bring the state, which is divided on account of a variety of aims, thoughts, and intentions, to such a unanimity and accord that it becomes a harmonious unity.

Because in the state people who are in authority are divided into three ranks: the king occupying the highest, the senate in the middle, and the citizens the lowest, it is necessary to consider which of them brings the greatest benefit to this state. Great virtue, supreme wisdom, and nearly divine prudence of the monarch usually shines in the state. Just as God is the master and ruler of the world, so the king is the ruler and master of the state. He should rule the state justly and divinely, because he is considered God's representative in the state. For the same reason the monarch's prudence and wisdom come not so much from him as much as from God, who instilled them in the king's mind and heart. In addition, since one man cannot administer all matters of the state with equal prudence and care, for it is rather in the power of God than of man to know thoroughly all these matters which pertain to the faculty of ruling, therefore it is usual for the state to assign wise men to the king so that he could rule better with their assistance. And because they occupy a rank between the king and the citizens, it is not difficult for them to perceive what bears upon the protection of the king's office and dignity and what on the preservation of the benefits won by the citizens and state. I believe therefore that this intermediary rank of people who are in authority, called optimates and senators, brings more advantage than the other ones to the state. For the king, being alone, cannot see everything and it often happens that either he yields to desires or his emotions disturb his ability of discretion. Also an ignorant crowd without a thought and head (as a proverb says) cannot by any means possess such prudence, while the senate, composed of men distinguished by virtue, prudence, and glory of accomplished deeds is capable from its middle position, as if from an observation point, of caring for the common weal of the state, perceiving those matters which are beneficial, and freeing it from disturbances, rebellions, and dangers.

For this reason nearly every state gives to the senate a large share of power. Those who once upon a time gathered people scattered in the fields and forests and made a state out of them were indeed called kings and initially ruled only by themselves, but they could not manage to rule alone for a long time the rudiments of new states. That is why kings had to choose co-rulers so that they could together, in common counsel and wisdom, rule the state better. We read that Romulus acted in this way, for believing that the rule of one man is either abhorred or dangerous or not worthy at all to be called a just rule, he chose one hundred fathers and called them senators and fathers on account of their age and wisdom.[2] Theopompus, king of Sparta, did the same, appointing the ephors[3] to whom he transferred a large share of royal power and the highest powers in ruling the country. When his wife reproached him for it, saying that in this way he left a diminished kingdom to their son, Theopompus answered that only then it became bigger and more lasting. From these statements it follows that from the most ancient times the senatorial rank was related to kings, and all states respected this rank so much that according to a general opinion no binding decree could be enacted in the state, which would not be supported by a prudent counsel of the senators.

We call the senate the highest office in the state established to offer counsel and to rule the country. It follows that one should call the senator a citizen who belongs legally to the rank which is entitled to offer counsel and to rule the state. It should be always kept in view that the senators' rank consisted of citizens who came from the most prudent, wise, and noble families. For no country is barbaric to such a degree as to be unwilling to entrust power to such people and unable to consider obeying them as a just and proper matter. For among all citizens nobody can be so prudent and so virtuous as the senator. Other people are drawn away from the best way of living either by age, or an unstable course of life, or inconstancy of mind, while the senator is not affected by any emotion, is not deluded by desire, is not absorbed by young age, but is directed by reason, restrained by reflection, perfected by old age. He is called senator after all, because of his as if senescent maturity,[4] his abilities, ideas, views, and opinions; as if his youthful outbursts and passions died out and reason came to the fore, having achieved its true perfection and maturity, making man similar to God.

## Notes

1. Cicero, *Laws*, 3,2,5. Translated by Clinton W. Keyes. London, William Heinemann, 1928, The Loeb Classical Library.

2. Romulus "created a hundred senators--fixing that number either because it was enough for his purpose, or because there were no more than a a hundred who were in a position to be made 'Fathers', as they were called, or Heads of Clans. The title of 'fathers' (*patres*) undoubtedly was derived from their rank, and their descendants were called 'patricians'." (Livy, *The Early History of Rome*, 1,9. Translated by Aubrey de Selincourt. Baltimore, Penguin Books, 1960.)

3. Ephors were magistrates in various Dorian states.

4. The Latin root of 'senator' is 'senex', an old man.

*Text*: Szczucki, Lech (ed.). *Filozofia i myśl społeczna XVI wieku*. Warszawa: PWN, 1978, 314-316.

# PIOTR SKARGA (1536-1612)

Piotr Skarga, born near Grójec, studied from 1552 to 1555 at the Cracow Academy. In 1564 he became a priest, and in 1569 during his stay in Rome entered the Jesuit Order. He was the first rector of the Jesuit Academy in Wilno, which became the Wilno Academy in 1579, the second university in Poland. Skarga was a founder of many new Jesuit schools. An excellent orator, Skarga was named royal preacher to Zygmunt III, and became the leader of the Counter Reformation movement. He advocated strong ties with the Vatican and championed the cause of Christian unity. Not limiting himself to religious matters, Skarga wrote about the topical issues of the day.

Skarga's *Lives of the Saints* (1579) gained enormous popularity already in his lifetime. Twelve editions of the book appeared before the middle of the seventeenth century, providing the Catholic church with a stock of inspirational stories for various groups of readers, including children. *The Lives of the Saints*, although derivative, played an important role in the religious controversies of the period, and strengthened the victorious movement of the counter Reformation in Poland.

In *Sermons to the Diet* (1597) Skarga dealt with political issues. He showed the weaknesses of the republic and dangers resulting from its citizens' disregard for moral and civic obligations. Although the *Sermons* were not popular during Skarga's life, they were widely read, especially after the partitions, as a prophetic vision of Poland.

*Sermons to the Diet*
*Eighth Sermon*

*On the Sixth Illness of the Commonwealth Which Comes From Open Sins and Lack of Punishment for Them*

> "Sovereignty passes from nation to nation on account of injustice and insolence and insult, and of various betrayals."[1]

Just before your departure,[2] I have to talk about the sixth and last illness, which destroys kingdoms. You can cure it not only at the Diet but also at home, if you only want to. These are the sins that call to God for vengeance, which stain the earth so that it wants to devour its people, as the prophet said: "The earth lies polluted under its inhabitants; for they have transgressed laws, violated the statutes, broken the everlasting covenant. Therefore a curse devours the earth, and the mirth of the timbrels is stilled, the noise of the jubilant has ceased. No longer do they drink wine with singing; strong drink is bitter to those who drink it. The city of chaos is broken down, every house is shut up so that no one can enter."[3] And there are many such warnings from the prophets, in which they tell about the fall of kingdoms. Just as the Sage said in the words which appear at the beginning. Also I, your unworthy prophet, will reveal to you injustices, wrongs, slanders, betrayals in which this kingdom and its inhabitants are entangled, unwilling to leave them behind or mend their ways. Because of them the earth will likely cast you out, and the Lord will settle it with other people, and He will take the earth away from you and your sons and will give it to your foreign foes, destroying you and your sons, if you do not come to your senses. Just as He did to the seven Canaan nations in the Holy Land, which, as the Scripture says, He uprooted from the Holy Land and destroyed for their sins and malice, and settled those kingdoms with others whom He had chosen.[4]

The major sin and most terrible injustice in this kingdom is blasphemy towards the Christian God, one in the Holy Trinity, which takes place and is allowed to grow. Whoever wants, not only in speech but also in writing and printing,[5] can blaspheme without fear against our Almighty God in the Trinity, brought to us by the light of the holy gospel and the Christian faith that was revealed to us from heaven. The sect of anabaptists,[6] or rather pagans, is spreading everywhere. Especially in Lithuania, in the Lublin region, in Great and Little Poland, in Prussia, they blaspheme the Christian God in the Holy Trinity. And they disseminate this blasphemy as they wish, without any ban or prohibition. And the whole kingdom is stained by such consent, leading it into sin and God's vengeance.

It was a sin of Achan alone that stood in the way of a victory for the whole army, and God did not bless them over their enemies until the sin was punished.[7] The many people who blaspheme God will bring a much greater vengeance of the Lord on those who do not restrain them and who do not say like Phinehas and his companions to the Reubenites and the Gadites: "You have turned away today from the Lord, He will be angry with the whole congregation of Israel tomorrow."[8] That means against those who would remain silent and let you do this. Isaiah threatens that the whole kingdom will fall on account of an injustice done to God and blasphemy to His name. He says: "Woe to the sinful nation, people laden with iniquity. They have forsaken the Lord, despised the Holy One of Israel."[9] And what will happen? "Your country lies desolate, your cities are burned with fire; in your very presence aliens devour your land. You will be like a booth in a vineyard, like a shelter in a field, like a besieged city."[10]

And what is said about the blasphemy against God, one in the Holy Trinity, and about anabaptists, is understood about all heretics, who--as in the Revelation[11]--blaspheme God's sanctuary, that is His holy Church and His holy servants who dwell in heaven. As the kingdom does not provide any appropriate resistance to them, legal and secular, it will not escape God's punishment. For not only the one who is practicing such things, but also the one who allows others to practice them--says the apostle[12]--deserves to die. The one who keeps silent, and does nothing, when he should do what he can, allows for and takes part in someone else's sin.

And plundering of God's churches and devastation of God's ministry in this kingdom in many places, and the corruption of simple human souls, and taking of properties, incomes and tithes granted to the Lord,[13] by what court is it punished? This is a great wrong, for which God's vengeance will befall the whole kingdom that does not defend it with the full harshness of its laws. "Woe--says the Prophet--to the one who destroys and robs, because he will be destroyed."[14]

This injustice done to God's glory and to the clergy, which damages ecclesiastical courts and clerical jurisdiction (giving rise to great devastation of God's churches and to the increase of sins, restrained up to then by ecclesiastical law) is strong enough to ruin, God forbid, this kingdom that is not disturbed over it, nor does it reform itself, and remains in this contempt of ecclesiastical courts and anathemas,15 like an infidel and pagan state. For the Lord established and set first and foremost the ecclesiastical court and religious jurisdiction over the secular one in his holy gospel and in Christianity all over the world.16

The neglect and delay of secular justice, and especially of those injustices, which are tried in the Sejm court,17 how can it take place without a great fear of God's vengeance? So many people are wronged and oppressed by the more powerful and then, wandering from one diet court to another,18 they lose whatever is left and suffer much poverty. Their voices reach the Lord in heaven and will be heard, the guilty punished. The Lord is more merciful than that judge who neither feared God nor had respect for people, but who had to try a bothersome widow. The Lord will surely grant justice to such orphans and widows, and others downtrodden and robbed, who cry to Him day and night,19 and He will not spare the kingdom. These words of Solomon may speak to this: "Again I saw all the oppressions that are practiced under the sun. Look, the tears of the oppressed--with no one to comfort them! On the side of their oppressors there was power--with no one to comfort them."20

Homicides alone and constant shedding of neighbors' blood without punishment may doom this kingdom. Here a murderer, robber, attacker, having killed the first, second, and tenth person, cannot be arrested and fears no law, until in ten, thirty or forty years. In that time he will either kill more, or will betray his homeland, having a dozen or more free years, and will keep running away. It happened that one who killed his own father was not sentenced at the last diet and had free time to hide away.21

And the Lord wrote in His law: "You shall accept no ransom for the life of a murderer; he must be put to death. You shall not pollute the land in which you live; for blood pollutes the land, and no expiation can be made for the land, for the blood that is shed in it, except by the blood of the one who shed it. You shall not defile the land in which you live, in which I also dwell."22 Look how innnocent blood which is unpunished befouls the whole land and the kingdom and provokes God's vengeance. O my God, how much blood of innocent Abels this land has absorbed and is absorbing, calling constantly to the Lord for vengeance.

And this blood or sweat of the present subjects and peasants, flowing constantly without any restraint, what punishment does it foretell for the whole kingdom? You say yourselves that there is no state in which the subjects and ploughmen were oppressed under such *absolutum dominium*,23 which the gentry is using over them without any legal obstacle. We can see ourselves the great oppression not only of the peasants who work for the lord but also for the king, from which no one can deliver and rescue them. An angry nobleman or a royal subprefect not only will plunder everything the poor man owns but also will kill him, whenever he wants and however he wants, and will not even suffer a bad word.

That is how the kingdom provides for its poor little subjects by whose work we all live. That is why the Lord threatens in Isaiah: "It is you who have devoured the vineyard; the spoil of the poor is in your houses. What do you mean by crushing my people, by grinding the face of the poor?"24 Like seeds under the millstone, so are these peasants under their masters. And the prophet speaks on, showing how from this plundering of the poor they dress up their wives and daughters at excessive and unnatural costs. At the end, he tells of the following vengeance: "Instead of perfume there will be a stench; and instead of a sash, a rope; and instead of well-set hair, baldness; and instead of a rich robe, a binding of sackcloth; instead of beauty, shame. Your men shall fall by the sword and your warriors in battle. And her gates shall lament and mourn; ravaged, she shall sit upon the ground."25

And how did usury and lawless acquisition of property spread? There are people who surpass all the Jews: they take ten, twenty, and thirty percent. They ruin the houses of those who need loans and nearly devour them, but will not do anything out of compassion for the poor. The Lord is very angry about it and strictly forbade such larcenous and rapacious profits.26

Everyone is greedy--says the Prophet--from the least to the greatest; all practice unjust gain and greedy acquisition.27 No one can appease his hunger for money, never more abundant in Poland than now. No one says: I have enough. Everyone wants more, although he shall want for nothing.

Some keep and treat money as if it were a god. Others gratify their pride and haughtiness with waste and vanities.

O my God, what luxuries came into this Kingdom, and chased away all compassion! From the least to the greatest, they all have abandoned holy moderation and simple use, and spurned that old Polish and martial life. Everyone wants to drink wine. Not only water, which used to satisfy us, but also beer is not healthy enough for the young and fit. For one quart of wine a day they will lose close to one hundred złotys[28] a year. It is a rare impoverished nobleman who will not travel without silk clothes, without six horses, without a dozen or so servants and liveries, without litters and richly decorated carriages. The only saddles remaining are for coachmen. Pulling the carriage, a horse for several hundred złotys. From the noblemen's cavalry they became coachmen, riders on the down and feather pillows, they travel with pillows, with eiderdowns. The armed, equestrian squire has disappeared, masculine strength is weakened by pleasures. The fair sex has been so extravagant in dresses and attire that there is no end to waste. You will not be able to calculate waste for silks, samite, trains, golden buckles, and carriages. There must be enough for plates and an unusual number of dishes, just to show off and acquire the vanities of glory and fame, which stand for nothing.

Compassion towards the Commonwealth disappeared as well. No one takes care properly of castles and walls. The whole Commonwealth is impoverished, only individual houses are rich. There is nothing with which to roof what our fathers have built for defense. There is no money for soldiers, for constructing ramparts, for cannons and gunpowder, for securing forts. There is nothing for churches, for the poor and destitute subjects, and for other godly and beneficial needs. Everything is squandered on luxuries and indecent waste and goes into pigsties. And that is how the roots for the fall of Sodom shall be fully grown here, about which the Prophet says: "This was the guilt of Sodom: pride, excess of food, and prosperous ease, but no hand extended to the poor and needy.[29] O lewd Sodom, with waste and idleness, and with your excess, and with your cruelty towards your subjects and the needy. How soon will you fall and perish in fire?

No one loves the Commonwealth with his whole heart. Such *peculatus*, that is thievery of common goods, has developed in this kingdom that people barely have any conscience about it. If there is something to be taken from common taxes and income, it becomes the most desirable theft, for which one does not need to fear any punishment at all. But when something is to be done for public good, then it is hard and difficult and there are no means. But for the pomp and diets, and soldiers, and Haiduks, and revenge against enemies, and for grandiosity and pride,[30] even if they are paid with villages, then the means must be found. When they take care of the public treasury, o my God, how they stain their hands, so that barely a half from the poor peasants and burghers' taxes goes to the public coffers. It has come to such a shameless and merciless robbery of our homeland and dear mother. There is no such unfortunate Commonwealth as ours, say those who know, that would experience less friendship from its children and sons.

And who will count our court accusations, in summons,[31] our treacheries in suits and in courts, our deceptions, dissimulation, and hypocrisy? Who will count shameless incests and open adultery, perjuries, false testimonies and other obscenities which do not even have a *forum* for punishment? I do not touch on wantonness and unchastity and shamelessness of the young, which infected the whole earth. I will not keep silent, however, about one new sin and injustice. A girl becomes an orphan: the relatives and foster parents take half or a sizeable part of her patrimony and dowry, they bargain with the future sons-in-law and will not let her marry until she and her husband give them what these good guardians and relatives want and what they have already plundered. There are other countless evils and injustices of this kingdom which cry for vengeance to heaven.

What can I do with you, unhappy kingdom? Whoever looks at you here, gathered from all parts of the kingdom, and at the heads of the people, and sees your customs and affairs, can guess what impieties and sins rule all over the Crown!

If I were Isaiah, I would walk nearly naked and barefoot, calling to you, men and women of pleasure, transgressors of God's law: "You shall be robbed and you shall flee in panic when the Lord shall bring your oppressors and put you to shame. Therefore this iniquity shall become to you like a break in a high wall, bulging out, and about to collapse, whose crash comes suddenly, in an instant; its breaking is like that of a potter's vessel that is smashed so ruthlessly that among its fragments not a sherd is found for taking fire from the hearth, or dipping water out of a cistern."[32] The walls of your Commonwealth are constantly breaking, and you say: No matter, no matter! Poland stands by unrule! But when you do not expect, it shall fall and shall crush you all!

If I were Jeremiah, I would put irons and fetters on my legs and a chain on my neck[33] and I would call to you, sinful, as he called: "That is how they will tie you and will drive you like stags into foreign lands."[34] And I would show you a rotten and putrid robe, beat it, and when it would be in pieces, I would tell you: "It will be ruined and will be good for nothing, and your pride and all your belongings and possessions will be reduced to ashes and charred ruins."[35] And having taken a clay jug, I would call all of you, and smash it hard against the wall in front of your eyes saying: "So will I break you, says the Lord, like this vessel, whose sherds cannot be glued and mended."[36]

And I would call like he did, crying: "O that my head were a spring of water, and my eyes a fountain of tears, so that I might weep day and night for the slain of my poor people! I would escape to the desert and go away from my people, for they are all corrupt (as if they were not the sons of those good fathers) and a band of malefactors. They bend their tongues like bows; they have grown strong in land for lies and falsehood. Beware of your neighbors and put not trust in them: they talk of peace, but inwardly are planning to lay an ambush."[37] That is why the Lord says: " 'I will feed them with wormwood, and give them poisonous water to drink.' Call for the mourning women to come, let them raise a dirge over us, saying: 'Let our eyes run down with tears, and our eyelids flow with water! How we are ruined and utterly shamed! Death has come up into our windows, it has entered our palaces, to cut off children and young men from the streets! Human corpses lie like dung upon the field, like sheaves behind the reaper, and no one shall gather them'."[38]

If I were Ezekiel, I would shave my head and beard, and divide my hair into three parts. I would burn one third of the hair, I would cut the second, and I would scatter the third to the wind. And I would call to you: "Some of you will die of famine, some by the sword, and some will scatter over the world."[39] And I would not leave my house through the door or window, but would dig through the wall as if to escape.[40] And I would call to you: "That's what will happen to you, no castles or forts will protect you! The enemy will smash them all and destroy you!"

If I were Jonah, I would walk in the streets crying out: "Forty days more, and Nineveh or this kingdom shall be overthrown."[41]

Fear these warnings. I do not have a special revelation from the Lord concerning you and your perdition. But I have a pronouncement from the Lord to you and this charge to show you your evil ways and tell you about the punishment if you do not reject them. All the kingdoms that were falling had such messengers and preachers from God, who reproached them openly for their sins and announced their fall. Just as the Jews had before the Babylonian captivity, about which the Scriptures say: "The Lord sent His messengers to them, rising in the morning and admonishing them every day, because He had compassion on His people and on His dwelling place. But they kept mocking the messengers of God and laughing (saying: you have been threatening us for a long time and, thanks to God, nothing has happened). And they took lightly the Lord's words, until the wrath of the Lord against His people became so great that there was no remedy."[42]

When the pagan Franks were to conquer at one time the whole of Gaul, settled with Christians, Sidonius, their bishop and preacher, wrote that there was such plundering and oppression of the poor by the Christian Roman officials, that the people were ready to accept the Aryan Goths for their masters, but did not dare to on account of religion. But they preferred to accept the pagan Franks, recognizing that they would be less harmful towards religion and would not tyrannize them as much as the Christians. And that is what happened. The Franks subdued the whole of Gaul and became Christians. And this wicked tribe of corrupted Christians was uprooted.

Salvianus and Victor Uticensis write this about Africa. When the Vandals were to settle there and to oppress and destroy all Christians, the bishops and prophetic preachers threatened them with God's vengeance for their terrible sins and lust, and for robbing the poor. When they did not want to change, this vengeance quickly fell on them.

When the Greek states were to fall, and the Turks were to seize Constantinople, pope Nicholas V was foretelling their fall for three years. He was thundering against their evil ways and apostasy, and threatened them with the ax and cutting down of the useless tree in the third year, according to the gospel.[43] And that is what happened when they did not want to do penance.

The Bible tells us that the first type of God's warnings can be moderated when people do penance and implore God to withhold His anger. So did the inhabitants of Nineveh who implored God not to destroy it and King Hezekiah who begged the Lord not to kill him, although he was told: "Set your house in order, for you shall die; you shall not recover."[44] He wept and prayed and the Lord deigned to change his judgment.

The second warnings of the Lord are not fulfilled swiftly, but they come to the descendants and to the sons who imitate their wicked fathers. So it was with the flood, which did not come to pass until one hundred and twenty years later. Also with the Babylonian captivity, when the same Hezekiah asked the Lord that the plunder of the royal house and enslaving of his sons would not happen during his days, saying to Isaiah: "What the Lord will do is good, although He will punish us so severely and bring us to destruction; but I implore for peace in my days so that I would not have to see it."[45]

The third warnings are those that cannot be altered at all. When the Lord sees that people are not ready or inclined to do penance, then He passes His irrevocable judgment for their doom. He did that against the Pharaoh, when He said: "I shall harden his heart so that he shall not listen nor will he do proper penance."[46] So the Lord knew (because it is difficult to deprive Him of this knowledge) that he would not use his free will for the good. And that is why He withdrew from him His grace and this withdrawal is called stubborness. And yet to demonstrate man's free will, He ordered Moses to reprimand and punish him, and often when he prayed to forgive him. And so He cared for him, like the most diligent physician. He knew, however, that no remedy could help him.

Jeremiah did the same with his people. He knew they were to perish and they would not do penance and that is why he was bringing them God's certain judgment of doom. And yet he was saying: "The Lord has sent me to tell you about your doom. But amend your evil ways and your doings, and listen to the voice of your God. The Lord will change this punishment He threatened you with."[47] He said that to show man's free will, which the Lord with His judgment and decision would not violate, but knew what was to happen, whether we would do penance or not.

With what warnings did the Almighty send me to you, my most respectable lords? If you ask me: with the first, second or third, I will answer: I do not know. I only know that you will not escape one of these three. And I wish you the first, my dearest brothers, my people, and my beloved homeland, so that the Lord would threaten you as if to give you help to rise and do penance to alter His judgments and warnings, so that we would not perish, but having become frightened, turned our whole heart and thoughts to appease the Lord's anger.

You, o Lord, said: "I may declare concerning a nation or a kingdom, that I will pluck up and break down and destroy it, but if that nation will do penance, turning from its evil, I will change my mind about the disaster that I intended to bring on it."[48] The Lord can alter His verdicts, if we alter our evil deeds. Let us do penance and turn to our Lord, who will cure us, as He gave us life. He will wound our hearts with true contrition and then He himself will heal these wounds, as the Prophet says: "After two days He will revive us; on the third day He will raise us up."[49] Let the first day be of mourning and true repentance, and of the confession of our sins. The second day of reform and of recompense, required for a true repentance. And the third day for our exculpation. "Who is a God like You, Lord (in goodness and mercy)? You pardon iniquity and pass over the transgression of the remnant of your people (Christians in the north) and your heritage."[50] You will appear to us in Your truth--for Your dearest Son, Jesus Christ, and the innocent spilling of His blood and death. He rules with You and the Holy Ghost, one God in eternity. Amen.

## Notes

1. Skarga's biblical quotations are sometimes taken from other sources or from memory, and do not always agree exactly with the original. When that happens, the reference is preceeded by 'Cf.', as for example in this case: Cf. Sirah 10:8. Short restatements of the main points on the margins of the text are omitted in the translation.
2. Even though Skarga did not deliver these sermons to the Diet (Sejm), he gives the impression that he is addressing the deputies before the end of the session.
3. Skarga condenses here various fragments of Isaiah's prophecies in 24:5, 6, 8-10.
4. Cf. Deuteronomy 9:4.
5. Skarga alludes to the printing houses, for example the Arian press in Cracow, propagating Reformation ideas.
6. Anabaptists belonged to a Protestant sect which rejected infant baptism and insited on believer's baptism. They advocated complete religious liberty, separation of church and state, and opposition to military service.
7. Cf. Joshua 7:18-26. Achan was a thief. Only after he was stoned, did God give victory to the Israelites.
8. Cf. Joshua 22:18.
9. Cf. Isaiah 1:4.
10. Cf. Isaiah 1:7-8.
11. Cf. Revelation 13:6.
12. Cf. Romans 1:32.
13. This pasage refers to the conversion of some Catholic churches into Protestant congregations, followed sometimes by destruction of pictures and statues.
14. Cf. Isaiah 33:1.
15. The gentry diregarded church anathemas as they did not have any legal consequences.
16. Cf. Matthew 16:18-19.
17. Skarga refers here to criminal cases litigated at a Sejm court, not at a tribunal, appelate court.
18. Many cases waited for years in the Sejm court.
19. Cf. Luke 18:2-8.
20. Ecclesiastes 4:1. The work was attributed to Solomon.
21. This case was recorded in 1597. The murderer was sentenced in absentia.

22. Cf. Numbers 34:31, 33-34.
23. 'absolutum dominium'--absolute domination.
24. Isaiah 3:14-15.
25. Cf. Isaiah 3:24-26.
26. Cf. Leviticus 25:36, Deuteronomy 23:19.
27. Cf. Jeremiah 6:13.
28. 'złoty'--monetary unit of Poland.
29. Cf. Ezekiel 16:49.
30. Skarga is talking here about private armies, used for parades and entrance to the diets, as well as for civil wars. Haiduks were originally the Hungarian infantry soldiers, later similarly attired servants.
31. Indictments were often formulated in an exaggerated manner.
32. Cf. Isaiah 20:2, 30:13-14.
33. Cf. Jeremiah 27:2.
34. Cf. Lamentations 1:6.
35. Cf. Jeremiah 13:1-12.
36. Cf. Jeremiah 19:11.
37. Cf. Jeremiah 9:1-4, 8.
38. Cf. Jeremiah 9:15, 18-19, 21-22.
39. Cf. Ezekiel 5:1, 2, 12.
40. Cf. Ezekiel 12:4,5.
41. Cf. Jonah 3:4.
42. Cf. 2 Chronicles 36:15-16.
43. Luke 13, 7-9.
44. Isaiah, 38:1.
45. Cf. Isaiah 38:9.
46. Cf. Exodus 10:1.
47. Cf. Jeremiah 18:11.
48. Cf. Jeremiah 18:7-8.
49. Hosea 6:2.
50. Cf. Micah 7:18. Skarga refers here to the notion that the Poles are the inhabitants of the last bastion of Catholicism in the north-east of Europe.

*Text*: Skarga, Piotr. *Kazania sejmowe*. Ed. by Janusz Tazbir with Mirosław Korolko. 4th ed. Wrocław: Ossolineum, 1984, 188-207.

# MIKOŁAJ REJ (1505-1569)

Mikołaj Rej was born in a well-off nobleman's family. His formal education was scanty; he attended parish schools in Skalmierz and Lwów and studied one year at the Cracow Academy. Between 1525 and 1530, he was secretary at the court of Andrzej Tęczyński, the voivode of Sandomierz. In 1530 he settled in the village of Topole. In 1541, Rej converted to Protestantism, participated actively in numerous synods and organized congregations and schools. He obtained a position at the court of Zygmunt I and later became a royal secretary to Zygmunt August. As a deputy to the diet, he led a busy public and social life, at the same time energetically managing and increasing his private estates. At the end of his life he owned two little towns, seventeen villages, land in six other villages, and a house in Cracow.

Rej was a prolific and popular writer. His major works of the earliest period include moralistic and satirical dialogues, religious songs, and translations of *David's Psalter* (1546). The *Short Conversation Between Three Persons, a Squire, a Bailiff, and a Parson* (1543) is a political treatise in which Rej showed deep conflicts among the three estates. He ridiculed the failings of noblemen, priests, and peasants, giving in 2134 lines of a versed conversation a realistic presentation of everyday life and of his contemporaries.

In *Postilla* (1557), a religious treatise in the form of sermons, Rej championed the teachings of Calvin, attacking Rome and Christian morals. His major works, *A Faithful Image of an Honest Man* (1568) and *The Mirror* (1568) were Rej's attempts to deal with the cultural and moral issues, then current in Europe.

The *Life of an Honest Man*, which constitutes a part of *The Mirror*, records Rej's views on education, military service, married life, as well as on farming and household activities. Three books (youth, middle age, and old age) describe in detail the biological cycle of life and major occupations of a Renaissance man.

Rej's *Bestiary* (1562), a collection of about seven hundred epigrams, presents portraits of outstanding personalities from antiquity and contemporaneous Poland, practical advice, and

IX. Mikołaj Rej, engraved portrait, Cracow, 1568

**Krotka rozpra-
wa miedzy trze-**
mi osobámi/ Pánem/Woytem/ á
Plebanem. Ktorzy y swe y innich
ludzi przygody wyczytáią. A
takież y zbytki y pozytki dzi-
sieyssego swiátá.

W Krákowie przez Mácieiá
Szarffenberká, Látá.
1 5 4 3.

X. Title page of Mikołaj Rej's *A Short Conversation*, Cracow, 1543 animal fables. In a lighter vein, Rej wrote satirical poems in a ribald style, called trifles or pranks.

### *A Short Conversation Between Three Persons, a Squire, a Bailiff, and a Parson*
(selections)

#### Squire

    My good bailiff, what's going on!
    Does this priest laugh at us with scorn?
    He doesn't sing much, but likes to toll,[1]
    Gave his last mass long time ago,
5   When it comes to our good vespers,
    Everyone minds his own matters:
    One will scream, another will sing;
    Still another rarely comes in.[2]
    The matins you will never hear:
10  Most likely he sleeps somewhere near;
    Sometimes the owl sings it loudly,[3]
    Since the parson's head is heavy.
    Yet the priests will scold while they preach,
    Though little will they ever teach.
15  Only God knows if as things go,
    We will reach the heavenly door:
    I hope that none of us will dwell
    Along with the parson in Hell!

#### Baillif

    Dear sir, we are just simple folks,
20  What can we ever know, poor souls?
    We believe it's full deliverance,
    What he tells us in his sermons:
    If I only pay him a tithe,
    A sinful man, I'll still survive,
25  If I give him for good carol,[4]
    I will reach heaven, legs and all.
    Or if he comes at dinner time
    And on the table bread can find,
    He will quickly polish it off,

30  And give to me a pinch of salt,
    As if I were struck by a fit![5]
    He thinks I do not need to eat.
    Then he'll sprinkle me with water,
    So I walk with God together.
35  However, what is truly worse,
    You must, poor baillif, use your purse!
    And still before he'll raise his hand,
    It seems he wants to see a grant.
    I believe when I pay up all,
40  Among the saints I'll be installed.

### Parson

    Is this the baillif cackling loud?
    With what could we fill up his mouth?
    If we had a jug of good beer,
    We could talk down the wise master.
45  Surely at the third libation
    He wouldn't insist on salvation.
    Does the priest obstruct your actions,
    When he gives you good directions?
    The Lord has taught us these lessons:
50  You want to take, give to others.
    These are foremost admonitions
    With the Lord, this kind of actions.
    To the whole world you have declared,
    That a crumb of this tithe you shared.
55  You must have heard about the Lord,
    That when He was here, in this world,
    Having confirmed all commandments,
    For the good of human beings,
    He called upon the clergymen
60  To announce Him to all through them.
    And we, the religious estates,
    Carry on as your delegates.
    He imposed on you this duty,[6]
    Without causing you poverty,
65  Though from His bountiful goodness
    Your hand is rarely generous,
    And you provide us with substance,
    Which came forth from His abundance.

Just consider, my dear brother,
70 What the priest does as a worker:
He has to give up everything,
To take care of your well-being,
And to forsake rich possession,
Just to patch up your salvation.
75 You surely know that each craftsman
Should always require payment.
And this is a holy outlay,
Which brings then a generous pay.
Talk softer, you insulted me,
80 You try to fly, but aren't ready.
Be careful not to lose your way,
Today to rule is not your day.

### Squire

It would be nice so, dear parson,
But it seems you read it all wrong[7];
85 You carry on quite stubbornly,
And call yourself God's deputy.
It is true, you are His shepherd,
His chancelor in some matter,
But at times after sheep you stalk,
90 When you move just behind this flock.
Even though the flock is not full,
When you put your hand on the wool,
In truth, nowadays all these sheep
Anyone can easily fleece.
95 Today, truly, simple creatures
Undertake quite futile ventures,
They indeed made fools of themselves,
Having put in it their whole faith,
That nothing will bring salvation,
100 If the priest won't give direction.
(...)

All the bushes[8] are trampled there,
When people come to the church fair.
The priest in church bellows and shrieks
At graveyard grounds a barrel creaks,
105 Someone is shaking a basket,

Another a drum and fife set.
Still another, his neck stretched out,
"Cantor, your health!", is heard to shout.
The hens cackle loud, the pigs grunt,
110 Eggs on the altar people count.
We surely gained an indulgence,
Because we sang with reverence!
King David did not do the same,[9]
When on his harp he praised God's name.
115 So they leave with deep conviction
That they won by this donation.
They also jointly take reward:
Each one of them fills up his throat;
Rarely with this compensation
120 Would they last till night oration.
Many a man by vespers time
Ploughs with his neck in earth a line.
Carried by the head to the fence;
He didn't digest his indulgence,
125 And as he did not take it in,
The other just escaped running.[10]
And so today these simple folks
Will dare commit a lot of wrongs,
They care little for the Lord's Son,
130 When they fall in with the parson:
He will not become indignant--
And the Lord will remain silent.
(...)

## The Republic
### (speaks complaining)

I'm just looking from a distance,
If a man is in existence,
135 Who would view me with affection,
As my state is near perdition.

## Notes

1. The priest is always eager to toll the bell but not to say mass.

2. It is not clear what 'another' refers to. It may refer to another parishoner or to a celebrant (the parson or cantor). A third reading of the line implies that the vespers rarely take place.

3. The owl hoots at dawn, when the parson should celebrate the mass.

4. At Christmas time, between December 24 and January 6, priests called upon parishoners and collected donations, usually in goods, called 'carol'.

5. Disease common to animals; to stimulate their appetite, they were given salt.

6. The duty refers to supporting the clergy.

7. The parson makes an error, as when he gives his sermon or reads a lesson.

8. The word 'chrost' in the original may also refer to the wicker fence, broken by revelers, or to the ornamental greenery put up by parishoners on holy days, especially on Corpus Christi Day, Whitsuntide, or the day of the patron saint, when the church fair was celebrated.

9. Another reading: 'And yet King David did the same'.

10. He did not retain the food and drinks consumed at the church fair and his neighbor had to move away quickly.

*Text*: Rej, Mikołaj. *Krótka rozprawa między trzema osobami, Panem, Wójtem a Plebanem.* Ed. by Konrad Górski and Wacław Taszycki. Wrocław: Ossolineum, Biblioteka Pisarzy Polskich S.B. 1, 1953, 38-44, 48-50, 180.

*Life of an Honest Man*
(selections)

Book I

III. 3. What children's clothes should be like and training of their manners

Do not put on him in childhood any small buttons, embroidered frills, colorful clothes, like a piglet, because if he learns this in youth, he will absorb it in his memory and will then always want it like that and from this later both wantonness and wickedness can easily grow and will not go away, when he is more capable of understanding. Later, when he is growing up, one should not bring him up in fear, because this youth of his, when his senses must be still frail in the weak body, may be easily deprived of resoluteness by perverse fear and worry, so that later it is always timorous, dull, and mindless. So without too much fear and without worry, by gentle admonition, one should nevertheless gradually reduce his daily comforts of upkeep so that he would not grow like a willow, which bent over will grow that way. He should also be kept away from stupid and wicked boys, from corrupt servants; because what he sees and hears in his youth, will be easily impressed in his early memory and will also be growing with him. We hear it from older people that they remember better what was happening around them in youth than what they did not a long time ago. The child can learn nicely while playing a prayer and Latin words; and also an a,b,c, while playing, can easily be impressed in his memory. Do not allow him either to chatter anything, as some are pleased to see and call it a "little starling"; because if it becomes his habit, then it will grow into a wickedness which he will find difficult to break himself from. Also mothers should take great care of their daughters as they are a weak human race and allow themselves to bend easily. Believe me, early prudent upbringing can add a lot of good habits for everybody in old age. We can see it too among the brothers that one, brought up poorly and wantonly, how unpleasant he is in his habits, how careless in his own matters, that he can more easily lose everything, and bring himself to ruin. And the other, who will be of good and honest upbringing, will follow his brother, picking up everything. At the same time, honest people will look at each of them with different pleasure and different assessment of their habits.

## Book II

### XVI. 5. When the summer comes, what to do

So when the hot summer comes, isn't it a great pleasure when all of what you did and dug in spring delightfully ripens and grows? Here they are carrying nice apples, pears, sour cherries, plums from your first grafting; from the gardens little cucumbers, melons, and other delights of the garden. Here fresh butter, cheeses will come, fresh eggs; here hens are poking about, here geese are gaggling, here lambs are bleating, here piglets running, here fish are jumping; you can just say to yourself: "Enjoy it, dear soul, you have enough of all that is good," yet fearing God and giving Him honest thanks. You will ride with a sparrow-hawk to harvest; here they are reaping nicely, girls are singing, others are shouting a bit, they are putting sheaves into stacks; it is nicer for them and they work faster when they see the master, but not when he runs across the field with a club or whips them on their backs. There you can also hunt a nice quail, but not in such a way as to trample on millet or grain of these poor folk. They, looking at this, would not be without sorrow and say quietly: "May he come across an evil spirit." Not in this way either, so that they would all stand, wondering, and shout: "Lord, it's down, it's down!" And the master swaggers in front of them, as he has hunted a corncrake, and they stand wondering, having abandoned their sickles. One should do everything in the right time and with moderation.

This also has to be supervised that they do not put wet sheaves into rickstacks, to take care of the rickstacks before the time to store grain in them comes, to thatch them in time, and to clean up everything under them. And what is to be used for seed, should be carried in time and put in rickstacks or in stables, as it can also dry in the barn, because in every matter it is wasteful to lose time.

Book III

X, 3. Reading--a great pleasure

Isn't it a pleasure, if you can read, having made yourself comfortable under a nice little tree, surrounded by many beautiful and fragrant little flowers or in winter on your delightful and pleasant bed, to hold a discourse with those ancient sages, with those numerous philosphers, from whom you will find great joys in your old age, in whom you will find a great lesson for each matter you consider? Or if you want to calm yourself or find comfort, won't you find those pleasant stories about unusual deeds of those knights and of important people, whom you marvel about and whose unusual deeds you can enjoy? And if you want to laugh, won't you find those amusing tales of those sage people, from which you can find joy and always learn something? And sometimes you will visit the prophets, the apostles, the evangelists, so that you would know your responsibility and not allow yourself to go astray by false information found in this world, bacause the Lord does not want to consider you His own sheep, if you do not listen to His own voice, but follow the voice of the ugly corrupt person, who will only bellow and roar like a bull for his own use. And this will be the most important matter on this road of your wandering to ask for the straightest road to your Lord and to this delightful place, where your responsibility leads you truly and you justly have assured yourself a promise to go to Him. It is a delightful thing for everyone who rides out or walks out on a road that he will not go by the wrong or erroneous roads but will ride or walk straight ahead and safely, by his well-known and clear highroad.

And if you yourself cannot read, you may tell someone else to read nicely to you and explain and from this your joy can grow in your every thought and your responsibility can be so confirmed that you will always stand like a wall, in which there is yet no crack, before the face of your Lord. And if you have the means, you can tell someone to sometimes play nicely for you either the lute or some string instrument and to comfort your worrried thought and heart. When a friend comes to you, isn't it a pleasure when you can talk and laugh with him to your heart's content? And he will tell you about people's actions and deeds, what has happened to them, and you will only ponder it and recall that all of this had also happened during your younger years.

*Text*: Rej, Mikołaj. *Żywot człowieka poczciwego*. Ed. by Julian Krzyżanowski. Wrocław: Ossolineum, Biblioteka Narodowa I 152, 1956, 34-36, 362-363, 542-543.

## The Bestiary

### Mikołaj Rej of Nagłowice

   You may stamp, as much as you wish, with a shod boot;
      And at the painted walls you can take a long look,[1]
   Obey the master's call and try to catch a meal,
      And whichever you can, try to patch up your weal.[2]
5  I, sitting at home, have already chosen peace
      And given all to God; you may deal as you please,
   As I hear this Lord excells in bringing fortune,
      No one will get more from any other suzerain.

#### Notes

1. Rej is talking about the decorated walls of the Wawel royal castle.
2. An echo of the proverb saying that it is better to patch up one's own things than to reach for those that belong to somebody else.

### Jan Kochanowski

   Observe what glorious learning can bring at an end,
      When it is combined with a generous talent,
   You can judge of this from the deeds and achievement
      Of this Kochanowski, a Polish nobleman:
5  How his talent and work in unity join hands
      Can be shown clearly in his numerous poems.
   Tibullus[1] could compose tuneful strophes with his quill,
      I don't know if he could paint virtue with such skill.

#### Notes

1. Tibullus was a Roman poet (c. 54-c.18 B.C.), author of bucolic love poems.

### Martin Luther, the Doctor

The Lord in heaven counts one day as thousand years

And waits a long time before showing His powers,
    But here His holy patience lasted much too long,
As among true gossips His glory barely shone.
5 At last His holy might couldn't suffer it longer
    And He inspired a man who thought in like manner:
Martin from Wittenberg, a virtuous doctor,
    Who brought into the light of day His famed splendor.


*The Republic or the General Sejm*[1]

They paint the Republic naked on a wagon,
    Various people treat her in all kinds of fashion:
Some pull her to the left, while others to the right,
    Because this lady's servants never take one side.
5 And if you do not believe it, look at it when
    You wonder at the matters of the glorious Sejm:
You'll see how awfully this poor soul is screaming,
    They pull at her so much that her skin is squeaking.


Notes

1. Polish *Sejm* or Diet.


*Text*: Rej, Mikołaj. *Pisma wierszem (Wybór)*. Ed. by Julian Krzyżanowski. Wrocław: Ossolineum, Biblioteka Narodowa I 151, 1954, 243-244, 264, 267.


Trifles

*Old Woman Who Cried During the Passion of Christ*

When a priest sang the Passion, an old woman cried,
    Does she know Latin, another one inquired.
"You weep but I am sure you don't understand why
    And this looks as if you were senseless when you cry."
5 The old woman said: "I don't cry because of that,
    But recall my dear little donkey which is dead,
It brayed with the voice which sounded just like the priest's,
    It whimpered from time to time and then was at peace.

### On an Uncertain Conciliation

They say that a rooster flew into a pear-tree,
  When he saw a lady fox running in the field.
The fox came: "Sir rooster! Don't you know what's happened?
  All of us have made friends with the ones we had feared".
5 The rooster kept climbing, saying a hound was near,
  The fox made for the forest, trembling with great fear.
The rooster called: "Wait right here, we still have friendship!"
  The fox: "I don't know, dear sir, if the hound knows it."

### A Parson Buried a Dog at a Graveyard

A parson, who lost the dog that he loved a lot,
  Buried it in a graveyard; he was called to court.
He took some ducats, gave them to the suffragan,
  Saying that "This dog passed away like a Christian.
5 It had willed to you all this money, Your Highness,
  As for me it requested I say just one mass."
The suffragan took the gold, absolved the preacher,
  And out of the dog he made a parishoner.

### The Blacksmith Who Lived Beside the Merchant

A blacksmith who was poor lived beside a merchant,
  He worked and was merry, never felt discontent.
But since he bothered the merchant with his singing,
  He showered him with money, ruined his good feeling.
5 The blacksmith seeing a change, returned the money:
  "This way I'll lose a few years of being healthy!
I prefer what I earn while singing merrily,
  Than to think of money, hoarding it greedily."

*Text*: Rej, Mikołaj. *Figliki.* Ed. by Maria Bokszczanin. Introduction by Julian Krzyżanowski. Warszawa: PIW, 1970, 55, 89, 145.

## JAN KOCHANOWSKI (1530-1584)

I climbed the mountain of beautiful Calliope,
Where not a trace of Polish foot was left before me.
(From *David's Psalter*)

  Jan Kochanowski was born in Sycyn, near Radom, in a family of a nobleman of average means. In 1544 he entered the Cracow Academy, beginning a fifteen-year period of studies. In 1551 Kochanowski went to Królewiec (Koenigsberg) and in 1552 to Italy, where he spent his formative years, studying under Robortello and Tomitano in Padua, and travelling. In 1559, after visiting France, where he probably met Ronsard, Kochanowski returned to Poland.
  The next fifteen-year period Kochanowski spent at the courts of influential magnates and bishops in Little Poland, securing in 1564 a position as secretary and courtier to King Zygmunt August. During those years, Kochanowski participated in major political and intellectual debates and was strongly influenced by the literary milieu of the royal court and of Cracow, capital of Renaissance Poland. In 1575, to celebrate the election of Stefan Batory, Kochanowski wrote several Latin panegyrics and later, to commemorate the King's victories, he composed a triumphal ode. His Latin elegies and epigrams appeared in the volume *Ioann. Cochanovi Elegiarum libri IIII, eiusdem Foricoenia sive Epigrammatum libellus* published posthumously in Cracow in 1584.
  In 1575 Kochanowski married Dorota Podlodowska, settled in his country estate in Czarnolas, and devoted himself to poetry. This most happy and productive period of his life was interrupted in 1579 by the death of his daughter Orszula (Ursula) and soon after of her sister Hanna. Five years later, at the age of fifty four, Kochanowski died suddenly in Lublin and was buried in Zwoleń.
  Kochanowski excelled in lyrical poetry. Throughout his life he wrote light poems called the *Trifles* (1584), in which he described his thoughts, impressions, and activities, transforming ordinary sentiments and experiences into poetry. In the *Songs* (1585), more profound and meditative, Kochanowski borrowed some formal devices and general ideas from Horace

XI. Jan Kochanowski, portrait from his tomb in Zwoleń

to proclaim his moral philosophy as well as to give artistic expression to feelings inspired by love, beauty of nature, and patriotic exultation.

The goal of enriching Polish poetry with new genres inspired Kochanowski to undertake other artistic challenges. His poetic adaptation of *David's Psalter* (1578) gave Polish literature the elevated language and diction which were capable of expressing deep religious emotions. A play in the classical mold, *The Dismissal of the Greek Envoys* (1578), was the first modern Polish drama, bringing to the stage numerous allusions to the political situation in the country.

The Renaissance harmony and serenity of Kochanowski's poetry was shattered when the poet lost his beloved daughter Ursula. An artistic account of this moral crisis and the painful struggle to overcome it was immortalized in the *Laments* (1580), nineteen moving poems which described a great human drama.

### Latin Epigrams

#### 7. On Petrarch's Writings

When you tell of your grief for Laura who died young,
You raise her and yourself above death that had stung.

#### 89. To Łukasz Górnicki[1]

When Górnicki arrived, the lyre trembled spellbound
And with melodious tones it burst into a song.
Graces[2] are rejoicing, the Muses' airs resound,
Spring has arrived. Where is the gray haired winter gone?

### Notes

1. Łukasz Górnicki, author of *The Polish Courtier*, befriended Kochanowski in Padua.
2. Graces were three sister goddesses represented as beautiful associates of the Muses.

### 109. On Homer

    Sooner darkness will eclipse the day and the night
    Will be flooded by sunshine and glow in the light,
    Sooner limitless sea waters will become sweet,
    The dead will leave their graves the rays of sun to greet,
 5  Than the name of Homer and his glory upheld
    By his divine writings will perish from his world.

*Text*: Kochanowski, Jan. *Dworzanki czyli książeczka epigramatów.* Edited and translated into Polish by Zygmunt Kubiak. Warszawa: PIW, 1989, 26, 54, 60.

### Book II
### Latin *Elegy VI*

    It was an unfortunate day and hour for me,
    When I saw you first time, Lidia one and only.
    I entered then on a long road of suffering,
    And my heart was torn out of my breast by longing.
 5  Alas, for dazzled by the image of your face,
    I did not heed at that time your thoughts and your ways.
    Blind love prevented me and yet it was not blind,
    When the victorious palm to you it assigned.
    Because I had chosen you from many thousands,
10  Of rare beauty, famed among men in many lands.
    O, if you only were as faithful as pretty.
    But your heart could not be compared to your beauty.
    The beauty which you were given deserved as well
    That constancy, faithfulness, and love with it dwell.
15  It's likely your beauty's fame owes something to me,
    If you just wished to keep it in your memory.
    You have forgotten, unworthy, but in due time
    You will recall faithfulness and favors of mine.
    And although one can never move your heart of stone,
20  On that day on your face uncontrolled tears will flow.
    Yet I'll flee from you across a watery way,
    Unworthy, even if the sea raged in dismay.

So long as my eyes do not see this loathsome shore,
Let stormy whirlwinds chase me anywhere and roar.
25 There, let great depths listen to my complaint and woe,
About your ignoble deeds and my great sorrow.
I will complain to the rocks and maybe my dole
Will move them though it could not move you, cruel soul.
Eolian winds of the sea, do not stop to churn,
30 Sink me to the bottom, if I try to return.

*Text*: Kochanowski, Jan. *Z łacińska śpiewa Słowian Muza. Elegie, foricenia, liryki w przekładzie Leopolda Staffa.* Preface by Zygmunt Kubiak. Warszawa: PIW, 1986, 76-77.

### The Muse[1]
(selection)

I sing to myself and the Muses! Who on earth
    Would like to please his heart with my melodious airs?
Who wouldn't rather use this time to look after gain,
    Grasping small change everywhere, perhaps not in vain.
5 For what profit from poems besides hollow ring?
    But he who has money, has hold of everything
His is power, his are laws, his are offices;
    He is handsome, well-spoken, he takes best places.
It is not strange that people chase after gold hence,
10     While the poet, sans listeners, plays behind the fence,
Competing with crickets, which over meadow grounds
    Bid welcome to the warm summer with their loud rounds.
And yet I have this hope that many years away
    My wakeful nights will not be left without repay;
15 And what the present time takes while I still live by,
    Later age will richly reward after I die.
For fair Latona's son[2] foresaw it long ago
    That the ashes of my bones would not be laid low.

## Notes

1. Steeped in the classical literary tradition and conscious of his artistic vocation, Kochanowski wrote *The Muse* with an eye to posterity, as he believed that future generations of readers would appreciate his poetry. He was particularly inspired by Horace's ode *Exegi monumentum*, in which the Roman poet claimed that he had created with his poetry a monument more lasting than bronze. More than two centuries after Kochanowski's death, the theme of the immortality of poetry gained great popularity among Romantic poets in England, Poland, and Russia.

2. Apollo, the son of beautiful Latona, was the Greek, in later times the Roman, god of prophecy, poetry, music, and sunlight.

*Text*: Kochanowski, Jan. *Dzieła polskie.* Ed. by Julian Krzyżanowski. Warszawa: PIW, 1978, 119.

## TRIFLES

### Book I

#### 3. *On Human Life*

    Everything we think is but a trifle,
        Everything we do is but a trifle.[1]
    In this world there's no dependable thing,
        In vain man cares here about anything.
5    Esteem, beauty, power, money, greatness,
        All this will pass away like the field grass.[2]
    We and our arrangements will be laughed at,
        And, treated like puppets, tossed in a sack.[3]

## Notes

1. "All is vanity." (Ecclesiastes 1:2)
2. "All people are grass,
    their constancy is like the flower
    of the field." (Isaiah 40:6)

3. Cf. "(...) they are to play their play, win heaven's favor for it, and so live out their lives as what they really are-- puppets in the main, though with some touch of reality about them, too." (Plato *Laws*, 804 B, *The Collected Dialogues of Plato*. Ed. by Edith Hamilton and Huntington Cairns. New York: Pantheon Books, 1961, 1375).

### 21. *On a Pious Woman*

If you don't sin, as you often mention,
    Why do you always go to confession?

### 53. *On a Mathematician*

He measured the earth and the depthless sea,
    He knows how the day lights rise and recede,
He discerns the winds, can also foreshow,
    But he doesn't see he has a whore at home.

### 57. *On Drunkards*

Earth, that drinks rain, is then drunk by the trees,
    Seas live off rivers, all stars live off seas.
We don't know what people should object to,
    They find it unusual we had a few.

### Notes

1. It was believed that stars get their nourishment from the sea. Cf. Book III, 72, 11-12.

### 79. *On a Spanish Doctor*

"Our good doctor leaves and goes to his bed,
    He won't even wait with us to break bread."
"Let him alone! Later we'll find him there,
    And let's all be joyful and free of care!"
5    "Our supper done, let's go to the Spaniard!"

"Let's be off, but not without a tankard."
"Let us in, doctor, our dear companion!"
The doctor would not, but the door gave in.
"One glass won't harm you, God your health restore!"
10     "If it were just one"--replied the doctor.
It started from one and came up to nine,
    And the doctor is fuddled in his mind.
"It is hard"--he says--"to deal with these men:
    I went to sleep sober, will rise drunken."

## 82. *On Youth*

They might as well want the year without spring season,
    If they expect the youth to act within reason.

## 83. *On Old Age*

O poor old age, all of us desire you,
    But when you arrive, soon after we rue.

## 87. *On Trifles*

You'll find here good trifles, also fair, and worthless,
    Walls are not always built with the finest substance.
They put redder brick and dressed stone on the outside,
    Broken pieces and cast off rubble go inside.

## 97. *To His Lady*

Your name, sweet lady, that I gladly cite,
    You will find often written in my lines.
    And when it's read by many people's eyes,
    You will surpass others, if I am right.
5   If I would sculpt you out of rich marble,
    If I would cast you in most pure gold
    (To give beauty and goodness fitting mold),
    I still would not bring you lasting laurel.
No monuments, no Egyptian cities

10    Can at the end be free from ravagement;
   Either the fire or the sudden waters
      Or jealous years will overpower them.
   Poetic talent brings eternal fame,
      It knows no ruin, nor fears it will wane.


### 98. *On Love*

In vain to run away, in vain to seek shelter,
   Would not the one who flies catch up with the walker?[1]

### Notes

1. Cupid, Eros, or Amor, who personified love, was depicted as a winged boy with bow and arrows.


### 101. *On Human Life*

   Eternal Thought,[1] existing longer than Time's span,
   If You are ever moved by the same thing as man,
   I believe in heaven You must have a true show,[2]
   Looking at various matters of this world below.
5  You barely toss something out, when we, like children,
   Will snatch up even scraps in this turmoil and din,
   One will have his sleeve torn off, one will lose his cap;
   While still another will lose some hair in this scrap.
   At the very end misfortune or death sets in,
10 And one will soon drop those trinkets, though unwilling.
   Lord, if I may, let me feel this pleasure with You,
   Let others fight on, while I wonder at the view.

### Notes

1. Eternal Thought is a philosophical description of God.
2. During the carnival festivities of Shrovetide sweets were often tossed to the crowd and many people fought for them.

## Book II

### 6. *On the Linden Tree*

Guest, sit beneath my leaves and rest at ease!
    The sun will not reach you here, I promise,
Even if it truly soars, and straight beams
    Draw the scattered shadows under the trees.
5    Here cool breezes always blow from the field,
    Here nightingales and starlings sweetly keen,
From my fragrant flower, industrious bees
    Take honey which graces nobleman's feast.
With my soft whisper I know by what means
10    To lull you with ease into sweetest dreams.
Though I do not bear apples, my lord prizes me
The most fruitful plant among the Hesperian trees.

### Notes

1. According to Greek legends, the garden of the Hesperides was located at the western extremity of the world. The Hesperides were the three daughters of Night, who passed their time in singing and guarding a tree, upon which grew golden apples.

### 19. *On a Chaplain*

The queen wished to hear mass, but they didn't find
    The chaplain home, he was watching the wine.
He came in later in a red vestment,
    The queen: "Dear chaplain, you sleep without end!"
5    My good chaplain said to this charge of wrong:
    "I haven't been to bed, is that sleeping long?"

### 37. *To Sleep*

O sleep, that teaches all people to die
    And shows them the taste of the future life,
Put down for a short rest this mortal part,
    And for a moment let the soul depart.

5    If it wants, where bright dawns come from the sea,
        If it wants, where at dusk late glows recede.
    Or where the snow and the ice dominate,
        Or where from heat waters evaporate.
    Let it wonder at the stars in the skies
10       And watch closely their diversified flights,
    Which like the spheres in communal passing
        Make music most lovely for our hearing.[1]
    Let it enjoy itself, poor thing, at will,
        And let the body, which wants to rest still,
15    Experience in the meantime no worry
        And mark anon what it means not to be.

### Notes

1. According to Pythagoras, a Greek philosopher, the universe consisted of nine spheres, located one above the other. They were turning, producing the harmony of spheres.

### 66. *To Hanna*

A diamond on your finger, in your heart hard flint,
    Why don't you change your heart, as you give me the ring.

### 87. *To a Doctor*

We can truly call you an arch-doctor,
    Not only can you cure body languor,
But also have some fine means for good cheer:
    Wine, a lute, a girl--that's the joy so dear.

### Book III

### 1. *To the Mountains and Forests*

High mountains and forests attired in leaves,
    How gladly I see you and reminisce

On my earlier years, left behind up there,
    When for a stable life one didn't much care.[1]
5   Where haven't I been then? What haven't I savored?
    Across the bottomless sea I have sailed,
    I've called on the French, Germans, Italians,
    I've visited the Sibylline caverns.[2]
    One day a quiet scholar, the next day
10      A sworded knight[3]; one day in court array
    In lord's palace, then a mute clergyman
    In the council,[4] though not with holy men
    In grey cowls, but in double scapular;
    And why not, if you could be a rector?[5]
15  Such was Proteus,[6] changing to a viper,
    Then rain, then fire, then feigned shape of vapor.
    What will happen next? My hair turns grey,
    I keep with the man, who seizes the day.[7]

### Notes

1. In this autobiographical poem, Kochanowski recalls his carefree days of childhood and youth.
2. A reference to Sibyl, a prophetess who lived at Cumae near Naples, famed for longevity and oracular gifts (see *Lament XIX*, footnote 12). The cave of Sibyl is to this day a tourist attraction.
3. Kochanowski took part in a military campaign of 1567. In the original, he calls himself 'a knight attached to the sword', echoing Cicero's joke about a short soldier.
4. As a lay parish priest in Poznań and Zwoleń, Kochanowski was a 'silent' clergyman who did not perform any religious duties, but had the right to sit in the bishop's council.
5. The author refers here most likely to his unsuccessful attempts to become an abbot of a monastery in Miechów. 'Scapular'--in a monk's habit, a sleeveless outer garment which falls from the shoulders, a badge of membership in an order. The Polish words 'dwojaki płat' may also refer to a double pay.
6. Proteus was in the *Odyssey* (IV, 363-570), an 'ancient one of the sea', who herds the seals, knows all things, and has the power of assuming different shapes in order to escape being questioned.

7. Cf. Horace's "carpe diem" in *Odes*, 1, 11, 12. (*The Complete Works of Horace*. Edited, with an Introduction by Casper J. Kraemer, Jr. New York: Modern Library, 1936).

### 17. *On My Poems*

I don't write counter to the way I live,
    My poems are drunk, as I gladly drink.
I don't shrink from a feast, nor from capers,
    Nor at times a skirt, they fill my pages.
5    What use sham? You want to teach me temperance,
    While you, priest, hide your devil's preference.

### 37. *On My House at Czarnolas*

Lord, this is my toil and Your endowment;
    Deign to give Your benison to the end.
Let others own the marble palace halls,
    With rich brocade let them cover their walls,
5    Let me, Lord, dwell in this ancestral nest,
    Grant to me health and conscience that is blest,
Ample provisions, man's benevolence,
    Friendly relations, pleasant senescence.

### 38. *To the Lord*

Deign to give us now all that is good, Lord,
    Whether You were asked or not yet implored.[1]
But at every step keep the harm away,
    Even if asked for in a careless way.

### Notes

1. God knows best, regardless of people's requests, what they should receive.

## 50. *To a Guest*

Guest, since you have begun, read on until the end,
    Do not ask me questions, if you don't understand.
This part of the sermon is indeed peculiar,
    Unclear to the listeners, hidden to the preacher.

## 54. *On Health*

O noble health
How good you taste,
Then a man truly
And he asserts:
5  Nothing is better,
Because possessions,
Also sweet youth,
A high position,
Are all good, but
10  When strength is missing,
O precious stone,
Loyal to you,
No one will learn,
Until you fail.
Sees it quite clearly
Nothing like health,
Nothing is dearer;
Pearls, even jewels,
Gift of good looks,
Vast domination
With health intact;
The world isn't pleasing.
My humble home
Make your own too!

## 72. *Prayer for Rain*

Giver of all that's good, Timeless Steward,
    To You, the earth by the sun's fire seared
And woeful, bowed plants are praying for rain,
    So is ploughmen's hope, the desired grain.
5  Squeeze the moistful clouds with Your holy hand,
    They will nourish the trees and the dry land
Afire; You that bring forth from the dry rock[1]
    Unheard of springs, show Your gifts to this flock!
You send down night dew, and with rich redress
10    Add living waters to streams in distress.
You sate the abyss and the greedy deep,
    From where stars and fiery dawns get their keep.
If You wish, the world will drown in flood mire,
    If You wish, it'll burn like a plume on fire.

## Notes

1. "Strike the rock, and water will come out of it, so that the people may drink." (Exodus 17:6)

### 82. *To a Maid*

Do not run away from me, pretty maid,
   With your rosy cheeks, my beard that has greyed
   Will match well; look, when a wreath is arrayed,
   A rose near a lily is often laid.

5  Do not run away from me, pretty maid,
   My heart is not old, though my beard has greyed;
   Though my beard is white, I am not yet stale,[1]
   Garlic has a white head but a green tail.

   Don't run, dear; you know: the older the cat,
10 The harder his tail, so they often chat.
   The oak, though dry in spots, though its leaves pale,
   Still stands mightily, since its root is hale.

## Notes

1. Another reading: "I am beyond reproach."

*Text*: Kochanowski, Jan. *Fraszki*. 2nd ed. Ed. by Janusz Pelc. Wrocław: Ossolineum, 1991, 4-5, 13, 22, 25-26, 27-28, 37-38, 39, 39, 45, 46-47, 51-52, 58, 67-68, 82, 92, 107-109, 121, 133-134, 139, 141, 157.

## SONGS

### Book I

#### *Song II*

The heart swells, when we look at this season:
   Not long ago the forests were barren,

          Snow was piled higher than a foot outside,
          And on the river heavy carts could ride.
5       Now a trim of leaves graces every tree,
          The wild meadows blossomed beautifully;
          The ice has gone and over clear waters
          Sail along the ships and the carved cutters.[1]
        Now the entire world is truly laughing:
10          The grain is up, the west wind is blowing,
          The birds again are fitting out their nests
          And burst into song before the dawn crests.
        But the root of a truly happy sense
          Is when a man enjoys a clear conscience
15          And in his heart suffers no blemished spots;
          Why should he feel ashamed of his own thoughts?
        No need to pour him wine and drink along,
          Nor play the lute, nor lift the voice in song;
          With water alone he will be happy,
20          As he truly feels free from all worry.
        But the one who's gnawed by a hidden moth,
          Will not delight in the rich dinner broth,
          No song, nor even a voice will move him,
          Everything goes past his ears with the wind.
25      Good cheer, which no one can ever enthrall,
          Even by putting rich silks on the wall,
          Do not look down upon my twigged arbor,
          And stay with me, if I'm drunk or sober.

### Notes

1. Barges and boats with grain sailing along the Vistula to Gdańsk were a characteristic sign of spring.

### Song VII

        There is no other way, it's time to go,
          And for a time the joy and lute forgo.
          All my peace of mind goes away with thee,
          And from this jail no one will set me free,
5         Until I see you, most lovely lady,
          Beyond compare from among so many.
        The faces near me are far from my sight;

        Your lovely visage is like morning light,
        That is shining red over a big sea,
10      And turns night shades into dawn gradually;
        The smaller stars by and by disappear
        And wait unseen till the next night draws near.
That's how I see you. Fortunate the route,
        Along which will travel this dainty foot.
15      I envy you, dense forests and high cliffs,
        That ahead of me you will taste such bliss:
        You will hear charming voice and pleasing words,
        For which my poor head so profoundly yearns.
O my dear delight, my dear discourses!
20      It seems I'll seek in vain other counsels,
        I will only sustain my heart with faith:
        People plough with faith and they sow with faith.
        And you, don't punish me, don't discourage,
        Not showing for so long your fair visage.

## Song IX

We want to make merry.
        Tell your men to hurry,
        Let them, lord, bring good wine to the table
        And play the lute or the golden fiddle.
5    Who is so wise to guess
        What tomorrow offers?
        God alone knows it and laughs from heaven,
        When man worries more than it is prudent.
Use your wealth with prudence.
10      It all starts where it ends,
        Let Fortune have sway: if it wants kindly,
        If it wants otherwise--it holds mastery.
It's easy for Fortune:
        One who stands, has fallen;
15      And the one who was just under its foot,
        Behold him now, down at us he will look.
All will strangely tangle
        In this world, so humble:
        He who'd like to grasp all things with his mind,
20      Will die before the answer he will find.
In vain the mortal cares

                For these timeless affairs:
                He will not escape, that much he should know,
                What God had ordained for him long ago.
25      No one will ever err,
                Who his mind will prepare,
                So he can endure grief and happiness:
                First, bravely bear, second, without smugness.
        I praise changeless good fate;
30              But if it goes away,
                I give up all, wrap myself in goodness
                And wish for decent means without excess.
        'Tis not my way, when gales
                Strike suddenly the sails,
35              To lie prostrate and win over the saints,
                So that the avaricious water gains
        No goods from Turkish stocks,[1]
                When they fall between rocks.
                I, my heart free from care and full of trust,
40              Will sail a small boat through a stormy gust.

                           Notes

    1. Imported goods from Turkey were considered luxury items in Poland.


                        *Song XXIV*

        I hear the clock striking,
                Away, profound mourning.
                Staidness is for the day,
                Eve and night to be gay.
5       We are fools in God's eyes,
                Though among men blameless,
                And the more we labor,
                The greater our error.
        If one tried on this earth
10              To find out what takes place,
                This truth I likely think,
                Man is but God's plaything.
        High places and stations
                Are mere deviations,

15      Death treats us all the same,
        Power can't much reclaim.
    Nothing is more piteous
        Than a man covetous,
        He reaps for another,
20      While suffering hunger.
    And so if all youngsters
        Were just like their fathers,
        For years because of that
        The world would turn to beg.
25  But God found the answer,
        What some put together,
        Others quickly squandered;
        The world should not be starved.
    Hard to rule after death;
30      You, father, did not err,
        The son just counts his gains,
        Did not inherit brains.[1]
    So these groundless worries
        Are the devil's curses;
35      When they leave our heads,
        Let them find Fokar's chests.[2]
    Bring us wine, let it flow,
        And soon good cheer will grow,
        Sorrow washed down with wine
40      Melts like snow in sunshine.

### Notes

1. In lines 17-33, Kochanowski elaborates upon a popular contrast between thrifty fathers and wasteful sons.
2. The most likely meaning of this phrase is that rich bankers of the Fugger family should worry about such matters as inheritance and disposition of money. Jakob Fugger (1459-1525) of the imperial free city of Augsburg was one of the wealthiest merchant bankers in the world. Fugger acquired his fortune from trade, finance, mining, and investments in new industries. He was also the founder of the Fuggerei, the oldest social welfare settlement, built in 1519, which to this day houses the poor elderly in a building with inner courtyards, resembling an Italian palace. Some mem-

bers of the Fugger family settled in Poland, where they were called Fokars, Fukars, or Fukiers.

Another reading suggests that all worries should hide in Fugger's coffers, from where they would not be able to escape.

## Book II

### Song VII

The sun is burning, earth turns truly to ashes,
  The world's veiled in dusty lashes,
  Rivers are running nearly dry
  And parched plants are crying out for rain from the sky.
5 Children take jug to well, table in linden's shade,
  Where the family master's pate
  Is protected from hot summer
  By the leaves, a pleasant reward for the planter.
My lute, stay with me; for your chords so kind
10 Bring comfort to my troubled mind,
  And all of my sleepless concerns
  Fly beyond the Red Sea on the wind's swift currents.

### Song VIII

Do not turn gray, Nicholas, with worry,
  Who will be king: a decree is ready
  Before the Lord, not written with a quill,
  But carved with a chisel in hardened steel.
5 Let's not await a master from the north,
  Nor from the east, the west, or from the south:[1]
  He will be the king whom God designates;
  All human hearts with ease He persuades.
He turned into laughter our vain counsels,
10 Passing over our better-known neighbors,
  He brought us a king from a distant land,
  But soon after someone else took command.
Where are now those boundless mountains of gold?
  Where are the Gascons and armed troops enrolled?[2]
15 What for were cannons and our tournaments?

Hopes filled with air burst in disappointments.
Fortune gives orders to the ships at sea,
In battles, Fortune bestows victory;
Councils and diets take advice from her,
20 While human designs turn into blunder.
Out wordy speakers, stop this grave discourse!
Let us attach on a pole at a course
A gold crown: may chance place it in the hand
Of a faster, if not a wiser man.[3]

### Notes

1. John III Vasa of Sweden, Ivan the Terrible of Russia or his son Fiodor, Stefan Batory of Transylvania, and Habsburg candidates competed with a French prince, Henri Valois, for the crown.
2. King Henri Valois vouched to support four thousand hired Gascons as well as to arm and array the troops. He abandoned the Polish throne in 1574, after a reign of 118 days.
3. According to Kadłubek's *Polish Chronicle*, written in the twelfth century, candidates raced for the crown as if they were knights in a tournament.

### Song XXIV[1]

Endowed with a pinion[2] that is mighty and rare,
    A poet of two forms,[3] I will take to the air:
    I will not remain on this earth any longer,
    But, above envy, I will look with disfavor
5 At crowded cities. Not I, the one lowly-born,
    Not I, whom you call your friend, by Death shall be borne,
    Dear Myszkowski,[4] nor will I be held prisoner
    By the black arms of the mournful Stygian water.[5]
    At once with rough skin my shins are being covered,
10 At once my crown is turning into a white bird,
    Small feathers are sprouting all over my fingers
    And enormous wings are growing from my shoulders.
Even now more swiftly than the brave Icarus

>     I'll visit the bare shores of the loud Bosporus[6]
> 15  And Syrtes,[7] the bird consecrated by Muses.[8]
>     And the plains far beyond northern territories.
>        Moscow and the Tartars will find out about me
>        And the English who live in a far-off country,
>        Germans, brave Spaniards will hold me in high esteem,
> 20     And those who drink water from the Tiber's deep stream.[9]
>     Let there be no sobs at my empty funeral,[10]
>        Nor any laments or any complaints at all:
>        Forego candles, bells and richly adorned gravestone
>        And the psalms that are chanted in a wailing tone.[11]

### Notes

1. This song is a free translation of Horace's *Ode* II, 20.

2. The original singular 'penna' in Latin, meaning 'feather', was poetic usage. It is possible that Kochanowski, by translating this word into Polish as 'pióro' ('feather' or 'quill'), intended to draw the reader's attention to the dual role of the 'quill' as an attribute of the bird and the poet. The Romans, however, did not write with quills.

3. Two forms refer to two natures, i.e., a man changing to a swan. The transformation of poet to a swan is familiar in Greek. In Christianity, the expression was used to describe human and divine natures of Jesus.

4. The poem is addressed to Piotr Myszkowski (1505-1591), Bishop of Płock, since 1577 of Cracow, Deputy Chancellor of the Crown, who was a friend and patron of Kochanowski.

5. Styx was the principal river of the underworld.

6. Bosporus is the strait between Turkey in Europe and Turkey in Asia.

7. Syrtes were two wide gulfs on the north coast of Africa, where navigation was considered perilous in antiquity.

8. The swan was consecrated to Apollo and the Muses.

9. The Italians.

10. The poet has been changed into the swan and his body disappeared, leaving the tomb empty, the ceremony useless.

11. The elaborate funeral ceremonies in Poland, with richly decorated biers and coffins, were often accompanied by loud displays of sorrow.

*Saint John's Eve Song About Saturday Festive Night*[1]

When the sun's rays from Cancer[2] pour
    And the nightingale sings no more,
    Saturday fires, at Time's behest,
    Were lighted in the Black Forest.[3]
5  Both visitors and the household
    Rushed promptly towards the bright glow;
    Three bagpipes played in unison
    And the orchards echoed their song.
They all were seated on the grass,
10    Then six pairs stood up as is just
    Of maidens who alike were dressed
    And girt with artemisia[4] sash.
All the maidens were taught to sing
    And had no equal in dancing;
15    And so in sequence they began,
    The first of them took lead and sang:

### First Maiden

Sisters, the fire is now ablaze
    And for the dancers they've made space;
    So why not join together hands
    And in one voice begin our chants?
5  O fair night, grant us good weather,
    Guard us from winds and flood water.
    The time has come for us tonight
    To wait outdoors for morning light.
This was passed on by our mothers,
10    They learned it in turn from others,
    That on the feast day of Saint John,
    Saturday fires were burning on.
Children, heed my admonitions,
    Firmly keep the old traditions,
15    Let holy days be holy days,

Since it has been like that always.
In the past they kept holy days
          And yet their work was done apace;
          The earth produced abundantly,
20        For God rejoiced in piety.
We work this day without delays,
          We disregard the holy days;
          Although we work hard in the field,
          We do not have much of a yield.
25 Sometimes we are smitten with hail,
          Sometimes ruined by a hot gale;
          Each year our harvests get poorer,
          Bigger expenses then occur.
You work by day, you work by night--
30        All this in vain if God doesn't guide:
          You need God, children, and Godhead,
          If you want to have enough bread.
Let us entrust all to His grace,
          And not alone the worry face:
35        The good years may even recur,
          It's not yet the end of the world.
And at present this glorious night
          Let's celebrate as an old rite:
          Tending fires until early dawn,
40        With joyous music and with song.


## Second Maiden

This is inded my greatest fault,
          I truly like to dance a lot.
          But, neighbors, tell me once again,
          Does not each girl enjoy the same?
5 Each of you girls smiles back at me,
          And seems to show that you agree;
          So let's move forward walking straight,
          Though better still is skipping gait.
The skipping dance is most easy,
10        And also it is most lively,
          When the musicians beat the drums:
          The feet themselves begin to dance.
So it's your chance now, if you can,

             And play, my drummer, most handsome:
15         Around here sits the whole village,
             Amid them, men of privilege.
You seem to claim she is not here,
             The maiden to your heart so dear,
             If you say so--we'll take it in,
20         But it is not what we will think.
So lend your hand to this good goal
             And shepherd with care our gambol.
             Maybe you'll find in this array
             One who for us all will repay.
25  I do not know how to worry,
             The same I advise to many:
             Because we grow old when we fret,
             Much sooner than we would expect.
But where good cheer holds its spell,
30         In better health we will all dwell;
             And though in age you may advance,
             As a best man you'll have a chance.[5]
Fair circle, follow, follow me,
             Singing back my songs happily!
35         And you look out, the next in line,
             So that you are not left behind.

### Twelfth Maiden

Peaceful village, joyful village,
             Who can speak of your advantage?
             Who can recall your comforts, gain,
             Who can recall them all again?
5   Man dwells in your care honestly,
             Not engaging in usury;
             His whole endeavour is righteous,
             He's growing rich without distress.
Some people labor at the court,
10         Others sail to many a port,
             Where man is driven by the winds
             And death is waiting in the wings.
You find a man who rents his tongue
             And sells his counsel by the pound;
15         Others pay for profit with blood,

Venturing their lives to hazard.
The ploughman thrusts his plough in soil;
    From this he provides food for all,
    For himself and for his whole flock,
    For his hands and for his livestock.
For him the orchards their fruit yield,
    For him the bees honeycombs build,
    For him the wool from sheep is shorn
    And flocks of lambs his fold adorn.
He mows the meadow and the field
    And to the barn brings in his yield.
    When sowing chores are all complete,
    Around the hearth we'll take a seat.
There we will sing many a song,
    There we will tell some riddles long,
    With gracious bows we'll walk and prance
    And do the blind and running dance.[6]
At night the master takes his nets,
    Out to the hunting site he sets
    Or in the forest puts his springs
    And always something home he brings.
He lays many traps in the brook,
    Sometimes will use a pole and hook;
    And the flocks of birds all around
    Utter many a joyful sound.
The herds frolic by the water,
    While the shepherd, in cool shelter,
    Upon his pipe plays simple songs,
    While close at hand dance forest Fauns.
Then the housewife, working with zeal,
    Busies herself with evening meal,
    She has at home such big supplies;
    At market stalls she never buys.
She will also count the cattle,
    When lowing homeward they amble;
    And to milk she will lend a hand;
    Does her best to help her husband.
All the grandchildren, not yet grown,
    To their elders are bowing low,
    They learn that a little will do,
    Preserve modesty and virtue.
It is daytime, but the bright glow

                Into the sea once more would flow,
                Before my voice could tell again
60              Of village comforts and its gain.

                            Notes

     1. The night of festivities, an old pagan custom, took place before the day of Saint John the Baptist, celebrated on June 23.
     2. The sun enters the sign of Cancer on 22 of June.
     3. *Czarnolas*, the Black Forest, was the name of Kochanowski's estate.
     4. Artemisia--a shrub or herb with strongly scented foliage of the aster family. Artemis was a Greek goddess represented as the virgin huntress.
     5. Another reading: 'To court the girls you'll have a chance'.
     6. The dance with bows is probably the polonaise, while the blind dance ('cenar') may be translated *Blind Harry* and the running dance ('goniony') *Hide and seek*. The last two were popular, frivolous and fast dances.


                            Song

     What do You want from us, Lord, for Your lavish gifts?
       What for the benefactions, which have no limits?
     The Church will not contain You, You are everywhere:
       On the earth, in the depths, the sea, the open air.
5    You do not want gold, I know, as it is all Yours,
       Whatever in this world man names as his resource.
     With our grateful hearts we sing your glory, O Lord,
       For no offering more proper can we afford.
     You are the Lord of the whole world, You built the sky,
10     And embroidered it splendidly with gold stars high.
     Of the earth untraversed, You lay the foundation,
       And covered its bareness with rich vegetation.
     By Your own command the sea stands within its shores
       And is fearful to leap over its assigned course.
15   Inexhaustible waters enrich the rivers,
       Bright day and shadowy night keep their hours diverse.
     By Your will Spring brings flowers, in abundance born,

By Your will Summer wears wreaths made from ears
    of corn.
Autumn gives out wine and apples of various kinds,
20   Idle Winter rises, when ready meal she finds.
By Your grace the dew descends on frail plants at night,
    And the rain brings new life to withered grains aright.
From Your hands all animals look for sustenance,
    And You nourish them all in Your munificence.
25 Be praised forever, everlasting Creator!
    Your grace and Your goodness will not cease evermore.
Shield us, as long as You deign, on this earth so low,
    But in the shade of Your wings let us always go!


*Text*: Kochanowski, Jan. *Dzieła wszystkie*. Vol. IV. *Pieśni*. Ed. by Maria Renata Mayenowa and Krystyna Wilczewska with Barbara Otwinowska and Maria Cytowska. Wrocław: Ossolineum, 1991, 110-113, 121-122, 129-130, 158-161, 183-185, 185-186, 213-214,214-221, 242-246, 246-249.


## DAVID'S PSALTER

### Psalm 91

Qui habitat in adiutorio altissimi.

He that seeks refuge in His Lord's safeguard
    And trusts in Him fully with his whole heart,
    Can boldly say: "God is my defender,
    No mortal terror will fright me ever."

5    He will release you from the hunter's snare
    And save you in times of pestilent air;
    Under His wings will keep you forever,
    'Neath His feathers you'll rest in safe shelter.

His truth shall be your shield and strong buckler,
10    Behind them, don't fear any night terror,
    Neither any arrows, nor the dismay
    That mishap scatters by the light of day.

A thousand mortals shall fall on your side,
    Then a thousand more; the sword looming nigh
15    Will not come near you; with your eyes only
    You'll see the vengeance wreaked on the guilty.

Since you told the Lord: "You are my support,"
    And God the most high is your last resort,
    No evil shall come to your existence,
20    Nor any harm enter your residence.

He shall give His angels charge over you,
    Wherever you go, they will be there too
    To bear you up in their hands; left alone
    You would dash your foot against a sharp stone.

25    You shall tread safely upon fierce adders
    And also upon ill-tempered vipers;
    You will sit harmless on the wild lion
    And you will ride on the giant dragon.

Hear what the Lord says: "Because he loves me
30    And is acting towards me honestly,
    I won't forget him, whatever his grief,
    I will be ready to bring him relief.

His voice shall not be left without response,
    I will come in mishap; of my defense
35    He can be certain, also of honor,
    Of very long years and of my favor."

*Text*: Kochanowski, Jan. *Dzieła wszystkie*. Vol. I. *Psałterz Dawidów*. Part 1. Ed. by Jerzy Worończak et al. Wrocław: Ossolineum, 1983, 283-284.

## LAMENTS

### TO URSULA KOCHANOWSKA,

A GRACIOUS, DELIGHTFUL, UNCOMMONLY TALENTED CHILD, WHO HAVING SHOWN GREAT TOKENS OF ALL MAIDENLY VIRTUES, SUDDENLY, WITHOUT WARNING PASSED AWAY IN HER UNRIPE YEARS, TO THE GREAT AND UNBEARABLE SORROW OF HER PARENTS, WRITTEN WITH TEARS BY JAN KOCHANOWSKI, HER UNHAPPY FATHER, FOR HIS DEAREST DAUGHTER.

MY URSULA, YOU ARE NO MORE.

> *Tales sunt hominum mentes, quali pater ipse*
> *Jupiter auctiferas lustravit lumine terras.*
> "Such are the minds of men, as is the light
> Which Father Jove himself doth pour
> Illustrious o'er the fruitful earth."[1]

### Lament I

All the cries, all tears of Heraclitus,[2]
    All wails, and complaints of Simonides,[3]
All worries in the world, and all laments,
    And sorrows, and griefs, and wringing of hands,
5    All you do soar to my house together
    And help me mourn for my precious daughter,
From whom vile death[4] has separated me
    And of all my joy deprived suddenly.
Thus a snake,[5] singling out a hidden nest
10    Plucks frail nightingales, feeds its covetous
Throat, while the wretched mother will twitter
    And time after time fall on the killer.
In vain! The fierce beast turns on her to spring,
    And she barely saves her feathers, poor thing.
15    "You cry in vain"--some of you may assert.
    But what, by God, is not vain in this world?
All is in vain.[6] We grope where milder it may be,
    But are pressed from all sides: life is just vanity.[7]

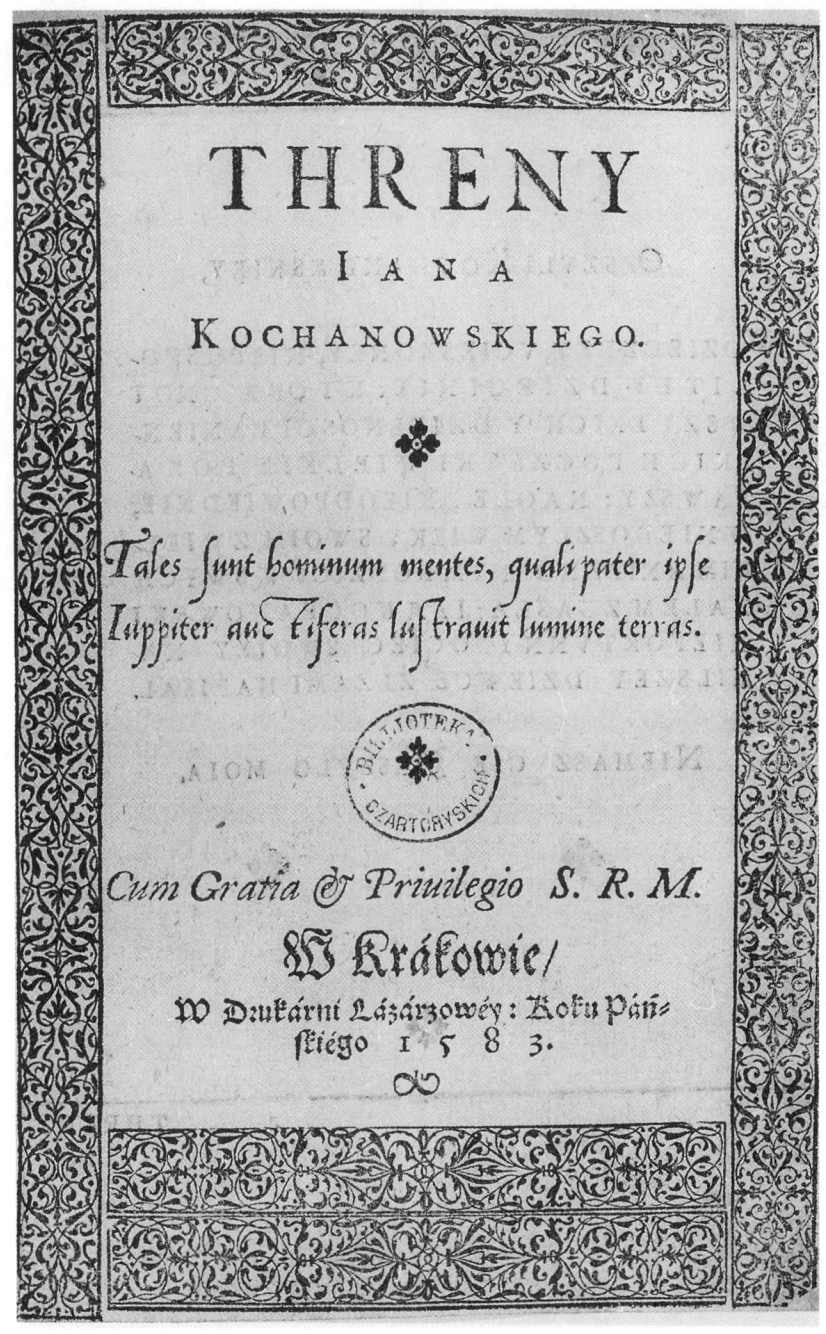

XII. Title page of Jan Kochanowski's *Laments,* Cracow, 1583

I don't know what's easier: on view in grief to wail,
20      Or upon human nature by force to prevail?[8]

## Notes

1. Cicero's Latin version of Homer's *Odyssey*, 18, 136, 137, cited by Saint Augustine in *The City of God* (5, 8, 152, New York: The Modern Library, 1950). A similar thought that people's fates are affected by the light flowing from a supreme being can also be found in *Lament II*, 19-20, and *Lament XVI*, 37-38.

2. Heraclitus of Ephesus (556-486 B.C.), a Greek philosopher. His haughty views and melancholy disposition caused him to be considered a pessimist, crying over the insignificance of human fate.

3. Simonides of Ceos (556-c.468 B.C.), a Greek lyric poet, wrote elegiac poems, and numerous threnodies and epitaphs.

4. Impious death, 'impia mors', acts wickedly and cruelly, in devilish and sinful fashion, breaking divine and human laws. See also *Lament IV*, 1.

5. In the Christian tradition, the serpent stands for the Evil one and is iconographically identified as both the Satan and Death. An apocryphal story, in Polish literature referred to in *Conversation Between Master Polycarpus and Death*, had Death being born from the apple in Paradise. Kochanowski probably adapted this passage from *Iliad* (2, 308-317), substituting 'nightingales' for 'sparrows'.

6. Cf. "Vanitas vanitatum et omnia vanitas" (Ecclesiastes 12:8).

7. 'Life is just vanity' is an echo of "Surely every man is a mere breath!" (Psalm 39:11). King James Version: "Surely every man is vanity." In his translation, Kochanowski says: "Man is error, wretched error" (39:48).

8. This dilemma whether in distress we should openly show our grief or stoically control emotions is treated more fully in *Lament XVII*.

## Lament II

    If I'd ever used my quill for children,
        And put together light verses for them,
    I should have just as soon rocked the cradles,
        Writing, like others, plain rhymes for nursemaids,
5  With which they could put to sleep newborn babes
        And calm down the crying of their charges.
    Much better to gather such trifles for play
        Than, as misfortune has caused me today,
    Cry by the mute grave of this loved child of mine
10   And grieve the harshness of cruel Proserpine.[1]
    But I couldn't choose in these matters[2] freely:
        The first I shunned as something untimely
    For the ripe mind; fate, irreparable loss
        Have forced me to follow the other course.
15 Nor can I now easily determine,
        What fame in the future my tears[3] will bring.
    I wouldn't sing for the living, I must for the dead,
        And mourning another's death, my bones are withered.[4]
    It is in vain[5]; such fate as follows men,
20   Brings either peace of mind or discontent.[6]
    Law full of injustice![7] Cruel, relentless,
        Unbending princess[8] of vanishing shades!
    Is that why my daughter, still ignorant
        How to live in this world, had to die young?
25 And having not seen enough of sun's light,
        She went to the regions of endless night.
    I would she had not seen, poor girl, this earth,
        For what more did she know than birth and death.
    And instead of joys, owed parents in time,
30   In profound sorrow she left them behind.

### Notes

1. Persephone (in Roman religion Proserpine), was in Greek mythology the daughter of Zeus. She was carried off by Hades (Pluto) and made his queen in the lower world. For Kochanowski, she personifies death.
2. The first alternative for Kochanowski was to write lullabies for children; the other, to write laments.

3. 'Tears', or the act of crying, refers here to his writing of the *Laments*.

4. A biblical phrase to express suffering, e.g., "Our bones are dried up" (Ezekiel 37:11) or "a downcast spirit dries up the bones" (Proverbs 17:22).

5. The phrase 'It is in vain' refers to the uselessness of admonitions to maintain moderation in grieving (as in I, 15).

6. Kochanowski paraphrased in lines 19-20 the motto, taken from Homer's *Odyssey*.

7. The law which is lawless (cf. the Latin proverb "Summum ius, summa iniuria", which can be translated to mean that the highest law is the greatest violation of the law). Kochanowski refers here to the law of death which applied prematurely to his daughter.

8. The harsh princess of death is Proserpine.

## Lament III

You have scorned me, my delightful heiress!
    Your patrimonial land inheritance
Seemed much too meager to satisfy you.
    It would never have equalled, it is true,
5   Your budding mind, your lovely qualities,
    From which we could see your future virtues.
Your words, your play, o your delightful way!
    How woeful am I without you today.
And you, my joy, will never come to stay,
10    Nor will you ever restrain my dismay.
What's left, what's left, but only to prepare,
    And follow in your little footsteps there.[1]
I'll see you, God willing, and you'll put back
    Your tiny arms around your father's neck.

### Notes

1. 'There' refers to Kochanowski's destination in search of his daughter, most likely in heaven.

## Lament IV

O cruel death, you violated mine eye,[1]
   When I beheld my own beloved child die.
I saw you shake the fruit that was unripe,
   While wretched parents' hearts were bleeding white.
5 Never could she, without my profound woe,
   Have passed away, never without sorrow
And my heartfelt pain, on whatever day
   She would have left me on earth in dismay.
As I, at her death, could have never been
10  More sorrowful, more sad or more aching.
For had God granted her more of life's light,
   She could have brought my eyes much more delight.
While I, at least, could have finished my time
   And come before all-ending Proserpine,
15 Not feeling such a deep grief in my heart,
   Which in this mortal world has no twin part.
I am not surprised that Niobe[2] turned to rock
   Amid the lifeless bodies of her dearest flock.

### Notes

1. A metaphor 'to violate our eyes' is found in Latin lyrical poetry: 'violarit ... oculos nostros' (Ovid, *Heroides*, 17, 1). The full meaning of this phrase in the sixteenth century Polish is 'against the law of nature to force someone to look at the death of his own child'.

2. According to Ovid's *Metamorphoses*, Niobe, the queen of Thebes, boasted to Latona, mother of only Apollo and Diana, that she herself had seven sons and seven daughters. To punish her, Apollo and Diana killed her sons and daughters with their arrows. In despair, Niobe wept for them until she turned into a column of stone (on Mt. Sipylus in Lydia), from which her tears continued to flow. (Ovid, *Metamorphoses*. Translated and With Introduction by Mary M. Innes. Hammondsworth: Penguin Books, 1977, 6, 165-312). Cf. *Lament XV*, footnotes 4 and 5.

## Lament V

Just as an olive shoot 'neath a tall tree
   Grows up from the ground in its mother's lead,
Though not yet bearing any leaf or limb,
   Still rising up as a slender sapling:
5 If a hasty gardener, weeding out
   Sharp thorns and rank nettles, cut that small sprout,
It wanes now and stripped of native power,
   Drops at the feet of its beloved mother.
That's what befell my dearest Ursula;
10   Growing 'neath her parents' eyes, she barely
Rose above ground, when she breathed her last breath
   Swept by the striking foul force[1] of cruel death,
At the grieved parents' feet. O harsh Persephone,
   How could you let so many tears flow fruitlessly?

### Notes

1. Another reading of this line: 'embraced by the pestilent breath of cruel death'. The striking evil force, however, is connected with the evil serpent and impious death of *Lament I*, and with the contents of *Lament XI*.

## Lament VI

My delightful singer, Slavic Sappho,[1]
   Who were to get by hereditary law,
Both a share of my estate and the lute![2]
   You've already displayed this attribute,
5 As you created many a new song,
   Which your small lips would sing the whole day long,
Like a frail nightingale in the green plant,
   That sings the whole night its delightful chant.
You fell silent too soon, and instanter
10   Cruel death scared you off, dear sweet chatterer.
You haven't fully filled my ears with your songs,
   And for this little, I pay much with sobs.
You didn't cease to sing, even before death,
   But kissed your mother, bidding with last breath:
15 "No more, mother, to serve I'll be able

Nor take a place at your gracious table;
   Time to lay down my keys, to go further,
   And leave my dear parents' home for ever."[3]
   This song and what a father's heartfelt hurts
20 Won't allow recalling, were her last words.
   And her mother, listening to this woeful goodbye,
     Must have had a sound heart that from grief it didn't die.

### Notes

1. Sappho, a Greek lyrical poet from the island of Lesbos was born about the middle of the seventh century B.C. She wrote nine books of odes, epithalamia, elegies, and hymns. Her poetry was much admired in antiquity. The adjective 'Slavic' in the sixteenth century could refer also to Polish.
2. The lute stands for the poetic talent.
3. It is not clear whether Kochanowski quoted here a bridal folk song or wrote it himself on the basis of such a song.

### *Lament VII*

   Sorrowful clothing, pitiful apparel,
       Of my most dear daughter.
   Why do you draw my disconsolate eyes?
       You just add to my trials.
5  She will not clothe her small limbs any more--
       Of hope no more, no more!
   An iron sleep has gripped her, hard, wakeless.
       Her patterned summer dress
   And ribbons, and golden belts are useless,
10     Mother's gifts now fruitless.
   Not to such a bed, my dearest daughter,
       Was your hapless mother
   To lead you; not such dowry she promised
       To give, as she bestowed.
15 She gave but a small shirt, a tunic worthless[1];
       Father put a clod of earth
   'Neath your head. Alas, dowry and its mistress
       Are closed in a single chest.

Notes

1. Another reading: "a worthless hairband."

## Lament VIII

You've turned my household into empty space,
    My dear Ursula, leaving with no trace.
It's full, yet feels as if no one is here:
    With one tiny life, so much disappeared.[1]
5    You talked for us all, sang for all of us,
    And always ran to all nooks of the house.
You never let your mother feel upset
    Nor let your father think too much and fret.
Hugging gracefully one, then another,
10    And bringing joy with your merry laughter.
Now all is hushed, emptiness is reigning,
    No merriment, no one bursts out laughing,
From every side we are gripped by desolation,
    And the heart looks in vain for its consolation.

Notes

1. Servius Sulpicius, in his consolation letter to Cicero after his daughter's death, stated that "all that man should hold no less dear than children--country, dignity, standing, distinctions--has been snatched away from us" and asked: "can you be so greatly moved by the loss of one poor little woman's frail spirit?" Kochanowski's reply is affirmative. (*Cicero's Letters to His Friends 2.* [*Fam.*] Translated with Introductions by D.R. Shackleton Bailey. Harmondsworth: Penguin Classics, 1978, 4, 5, 5).

## Lament IX

If we could buy you, Wisdom, for pure gold,
    Since you can root out, if it's truly told,[1]
All desires and all human trouble,
    And nearly change a man to an angel,

5    Who knows no pain, nor feels any dolor,
        Yields not to ill chance, nor bows to terror.
You regard lightly all human matters,
        And show a constant poise in happiness
And sadness[2]; fear of death incapable,
10       You stand fearless, unchanged, unconquerable.
You judge riches not with gold, great treasure,
        But with one's needs and natural measure[3];
And with your eagle eye you will behold
        A wretched man beneath the roof of gold[4];
15   You don't grudge poorer men their just possessions,
        If they'd only heed your admonitions.
I'm a hapless man who for years untold
        Was striving just to look at your threshold.[5]
And now, from the highest steps[6] cast down suddenly,
20       I'm counted with others, as one among many.

## Notes

1. Kochanowski refers here above all to the adherents of the stoic philosophy, especially Seneca, Cicero, and Horace. There are numerous references to wisdom in the Bible, e.g.:

"Get wisdom; get insight.
Do not forsake her, and she will
    keep you;
love her, and she will guard you." (Proverbs 4:5-6).

"But where shall wisdom be found?
And where is the place of
understanding?" (Job 28:12).

"Therefore I prayed, and
    understanding was given me;
I called upon God, and the spirit
    of wisdom came to me." (Wisdom of Solomon 7:7).

2. "When life is hard, your soul possess
    In calm serene; when times are fair,
    Refrain from triumph's haughty air,
    For, Dellius, death will come no less" (Horace, *Odes*, 2, 3, 1-4).

3. "He, who but asks 'Enough,' defies

Wild waves to rob him of his ease;" (Horace, *Odes*, 3, 1, 25-6).
  4. The man is miserable even though he lives in a palace. "Sitting 'mid worthless wealth, a beggar still." (Horace, *Odes*, 3, 16, 24).
  5. "Happy is the one who listens to me,
    watching daily at my gates,
    waiting beside my doors." (Proverbs 8:34)

"give me the wisdom that sits by
    your throne,
and do not reject me from among
    your servants." (Wisdom of Solomon 9:4)
  6. According to Seneca, there were three classes of people making progress towards the highest rank of Wisdom (see Seneca, *Ad Lucilium Epistulae Morales With an English Translation by Richard M. Gummere*, 3 vols., Cambridge: Harvard University Press, 1962, The Loeb Classical Library, Vol. II, letter 75, 8-18, and also letter 90, 25-29).

## Lament X

My gracious Ursula, where are you gone?
    Along which way, to which land are you borne?
Are you raised high above all the heavens
    And numbered there among little angels?
5   Are you in Paradise? Or carried to
    The Blessed Isles?[1] Does Charon[2] ferry you
Across lakes of sorrow and make you drink
    Waters of oblivion so you know nothing
Of my tears? Have you shed maid's form and dreams
10    And taken the nightingale's shape and wings?[3]
Or purged in Purgatory, if a minute
    Bodily stain has yet remained on you?[4]
Did you go after death to where you were,
    'Ere you were born to bring me deep despair?
15  Wherever you are, if you are,[5] pity my dole,
    And if you are not able as your former whole,[6]
Console me, as you can, and make an appearance
    As a dream, a shade, or an illusory substance.

## Notes

1. Islands of the Blest, in Greek mythology, in the stream Oceanus, far away in the west, were extremely fertile islands, where the blessed among the dead lived again in bliss.
2. Charon, in Greek mythology, was the boatman who conveyed the dead across the Styx to Hades. Lethe ('oblivion'), was in Latin poets a river or a spring in Hades. Its water was drunk by souls about to be reincarnated, so that they forgot their previous existence. Kochanowski's source was Virgil's *Aeneid*, 6, 297-305 and 714-716 (*Virgil's Works*. Translated by J. W. Mackail, New York: The Modern Library, 1950).
3. This is a reference to the doctrine of transmigration of souls, described in mythology and poetry, e.g., by Ovid in *Metamorphoses*.
4. These words refer most likely to the Christian Purgatory.
5. This expression of doubt in the eternal life is an echo of a formula used in Roman funeral poetry, e.g., in Ovid's *Amores*, III, 9, 59: "And yet, if aught survives but shade and name" (Tr. by A.D.Melville, Oxford: Oxford University Press, 1990).
6. 'A former whole'--with body and soul. Kochanowski is hoping that his daughter might come as a dream apparition, a shade or a bodyless vision. Ursula indeed appears to him in a dream in *Lament XIX*.

## Lament XI

"Virtue--a trifle!"--said vanquished Brutus.[1]
    Trifle, all know, trifle in all cases.
Who was ever saved by his piousness?[2]
    Who was preserved from ill chance by goodness?
5  Some unknown foul force[3] disturbs men's affairs,
    For good and bad alike it little cares;
Where its spirit breathes, none will find haven,
    Just or not, at random will be stricken.
And yet we still pretend to be wise men.
10    Proud 'mid simpletons, though little we ken,
We climb to heaven, thus striving to spy

The Lord's mysteries,[4] but the mortal eye
Is too dull; light dreams, idle dreams delude
   Though perhaps never will be proven true.
15 O, sorrow, what are you doing to me?
   Will I lose both: solace and sanity?[5]

### Notes

1. Marcus Junius Brutus (85 - 42 B.C.), Caesar's assassin and a symbol of republican virtues, was defeated at Philippi by Octavius Augustus. According to tradition, in his last words before he committed suicide, he stated that virtue "was but a name."

2. "Think now, who that was innocent
      ever perished?
   Or where were the upright cut
      off?" (Job 4:7). Also Ovid, *Amores*, 3, 9, 27 ff.

3. Also 'devil', the evil, black force with magic powers. In Lucretius we have: "So true it is that some hidden power grinds down humanity ..." (*De rerum natura with an English Translation by W.H.D. House.* Cambridge: Harvard University Press, The Loeb Classical Library, 1937, 5, 1232-3).

4. "Nought is there for man too high;
   Our impious folly, e'en would climb the sky,
   Braving the dweller on the steep,
   Nor let the bolts of heavenly vengeance sleep."
   (Horace, *Odes*, 1, 3, 37-40).

This motif has also a biblical tradition:
   "Though his height mount up to the heavens,
   and his head reach to the clouds,
   he will perish for ever like his own
   dung;" (Job 20:6-7)

"Who has gone up into heaven,
   and taken her,
and brought her down from the
   clouds?
Who has gone over the sea, and
   found her,
and will buy her for pure gold?" (Baruch 3:29-30).

5. Expressing his despair, the poet is asking if he is to lose both consolation and his mind. The word 'consolation' may refer to his daughter or to religious solace.

## Lament XII

No father, it appears, loved more his child,
    No father cried over it more than I.
As scarcely ever there was born a child,
    That to parents' love had such a great right:
5  Neat, polite, kind, not hard to satisfy,
    As someone taught to speak, sing, versify;
Everyone's behavior to show and mime,
    She knew maidenly custom and pastime.
Prudent, courteous, friendly, not capricious,
10    Eager, graceful, modest, unpretentious.
She never asked for food at break of day,
    Until to the Lord she finished to pray.
Nor lay down till she paid respects to mother
    And conveyed parents' health to the Savior.
15  To greet her father she'd cross all doorsills,[1]
    Always showed joy and met him from travels.
She helped with chores, and in every instance
    She was ahead of her parents' servants.
And she would do it at such early stage,
20    As she was not yet thirty months of age.
So many virtues of great excellence
    Her youth couldn't bear; she fell of abundance
'Ere she saw harvest. O my shoot most dear,
    You haven't ripened, and I, loath to wait here
25  Till the right time, sow you in sad earth anew;
    But I bury hope together with you,
As you will never grow up, nor will you ever
    Before my sorrowful eyes come out in flower.

### Notes

1. It was quite difficult for a child of two years and a half to get over high thresholds.

## Lament XIII

My fair Ursula, I wish you didn't die
　　Or that the light of day you did not spy.
I pay for little joys with deep mourning,
　　Because of your unexpected parting.
5　You duped me, like a fading night fancy,
　　Which pleases with piled gold greedy senses.
Then quickly flees and in reality
　　Leaves of this hoard just wish and cupidity.
That's what you, dear Ursula, did to me:
10　　Kindled in my heart great expectancy,
Then you suddenly left me in distress
　　And carried away all my happiness.
You've taken from me, briefly, half my soul,[1]
　　The rest I'm left with for eternal dole.
15　Stonemasons, put down here a carven stone,
　　With this sorrowfu epitaph etched on:
HERE LIES URSULA KOCHANOWSKA, HER FATHER'S AFFECTION,
　　OR MORE APTLY HIS TEARS AND HIS LAMENTATION.
DISORDERLY DEATH, YOU HAVE DONE IT ALL AWRY:
20　　NOT I FOR HER, BUT RATHER SHE FOR ME SHOULD CRY.

### Notes

1. "Of thee, my soul's best part, bereft,
　　Shall I, the other half, delay,
　　With all ties gone and nothing left
　　Save cheerless life? That fatal day

　　Shall wreck us both." (Horace, *Odes*, 2, 17, 5-10).

## Lament XIV

Where's that ill-starred[1] gate through which years ago,
　　In search of his loss, Orpheus[2] downward strode?
O, could I the same path also travel,
　　Seek my dear daughter and cross the river,
5　Where a horrid boatman[3] ferries pale ghosts
　　And drives them to the mournful[4] cypress groves.
Yet you, my gracious lute, don't forsake me,

|      | But come along to the chamber entry |
|------|--------------------------------------|
|      | Of harsh Pluto:⁵ maybe we'll soften him |
| 10   | With tears and this disconsolate singing, |
|      | So that he'll give back my dearest daughter, |
|      | And curb my unmitigated dolor. |
|      | He will not lose her; all must here endure, |
|      | He'll just let this unripe berry mature. |
| 15   | How could that god have such a stone-like heart, |
|      | That a sad man wouldn't win by pleading hard? |
|      | What to say?⁶ Maybe to stay, since I am now there, |
|      | And together with my life cast off deep despair. |

### Notes

1. The gate is called 'ill-starred' because those who walked through it were considered unfortunate, as they were deprived of life.

2. Orpheus, a legendary pre-Homeric poet, was so marvelous a player on the lyre that even the wild beasts were spellbound by his music. When his beloved wife Eurydice died, Orpheus went down to Hades to recover her and by his music conduced the rulers of the lower world to let her go, but on condition that he should not look back at her as she followed him. When they approached the world of the living, Orpheus forgot the condition and looked back, and Eurydice immediately vanished forever.

3. Charon, see footnote 2, *Lament X*.

4. The cypress forest, filled with vile specters, was dedicated to the god of the lower world, so it was 'mournful'.

5. Pluto was the ruler of the lower world. While pleading for the return of Eurydice, Orpheus argued that Pluto and Persephone could not suffer any loss by releasing Eurydice, since everyone must eventually come back to the lower world. Kochanowski, identifying himself with Orpheus, repeats this argument.

6. The rhetorical question "What to say?" implies that the author's initial plea was answered negatively. He feels helpless and considers remaining with his daughter in Hades.

## Lament XV

Golden-haired Erato[1] and you, sweet lute,
    That comfort people in their anguished mood,
Calm my distressed thought just for a moment,
    'Ere I turn into a stone monument,
5  That's shedding bloody tears through live marble,
    A mark of deep grief, a sign of great trouble.
Am I wrong or viewing human mishaps,
    We deem more modestly our own collapse?[2]
Poor mother (if we ascribe to ill chance,
10    What we bear due to reason's ignorance),[3]
Where are your seven sons and seven daughters?
    Where is comfort? Where joy and your pleasures?
I see fourteen graves and you, pitiable
    And it seems still alive against your will,
15  Embrace cold graves, in which (o, poor woman!)
    You laid your dearest children, cruelly slain.
They lie like flowers by a scythe cut down
    Or beaten by a fierce rain to the ground.
What's your hope? What else are you awaiting?
20    Why not rush to death to discharge grieving?
What do you, Phoebus and vengeful goddess,[4]
    Do with unerring bow and swift arrows?
Either in wrath (for her guilt) or in pity
    End, by God, her feeble longevity.
25  A new revenge, new trial matched her proud tone:
    Weeping for her young, Niobe turned to stone.
And as timeless marble stands at Mount Sipylus,
    Yet even 'neath the stone live hidden wounds.
As her heartfelt teardrops seep through the rock[5]
30    And fall in a clear stream from the hilltop,
Whence beast and fowl drink; and in endless bonds
    She stands at cliff edge, in path of strong storms.
This tomb has no corpse, this corpse has no tomb,
    But it is at once its own corpse and tomb.[6]

### Notes

1. Erato, muse of lyric and love poetry.
2. "Similarly, too, attention is called to those who have lost their children, by giving instances, and so the sorrow of

those whose grief is excessive is softened by the examples of others who have suffered: in this way the endurance of the others makes mishaps seem of far less magnitude that the estimate first formed of them." (Cicero, *Tusculan Disputations*, Cambridge: Harvard University Press, 1950, 3, 24, 58).
    3. "For the wisdom of this world is folly with God" (1 Corinthians 3:19).
    4. Phoebus (Apollo) and Diana (Artemis) slew Niobe's children. Cf. footnote 2, *Lament IV*.
    5. "... her internal organs too were turned to stone: yet still she wept. A violent whirlwind caught her up, and carried her away to her own country, where she was set down on a mountain top. There she wastes away, and even now, tears trickle from her marble face." (Ovid, *Met.*, 6, 309-312).
    6. Line 33-34 are taken from *The Greek Anthology*. It is an epitaph by Agathias (536-82), entitled *On Lot's Wife* (7, 311): "This tomb has no corpse inside it; this corpse has no tomb outside it, but it is its own corpse and tomb." (*The Greek Anthology with an English Translation by W.R.Paton.* 5 vols. London: William Heinemann Ltd., The Loeb Classical Library, 1939, Vol. II, 169).

## Lament XVI

    Because of adversity and the woe,
    Which truly runs to my very marrow,
    The lute and gracious verse I must put by
        And almost die.[1]
5    Am I awake or vexed by a false dream?
    Which flies from the ivory opening[2]
    And occupies man's thoughts with an issue,
        In life not true.
    O, human error, o, fancies so vain,
10   How easy it is for reason to feign,
    When the world favors us and we profess,
        Peace from distress.
    Well situated, we praise poverty,
    In pleasures--we make light of misery,
15   While a stingy spinner[3] has enough wool,

                    Death counts for null.
            But when penury or grief will stalk,
            Then to live isn't as easy as to talk,
            People take account of death only when
20                  It runs towards them.
            Wordy Arpinian,4 why in tears do you roam
            From your beloved homeland? Not glorious Rome,
            But the world is the City of the wise man
                    In your judgment.
25          Why do you grieve so much for your daughter?5
            After all, you shun only dishonor;
            You treat all the other adversities
                    Almost like bliss.
            "Death," you say, "frightens only the godless"6;
30          Why did you not want to die, virtuous,
            When because of the insults which you said,
                    You risked your head?
            You convinced all but yourself, Arpinian;
            I see, for you too, easier said than done;
35          O, angelic quill,7 in mishap your heart
                    Was, like mine, scarred.
            Man is not stone: whatever fortune comes,
            Such thoughts it will deliver unto us.8
            O, you cursed fate! Do we suffer more,
40                  Touching the sore?9
            O, Time,10 father of longed-for oblivion,
            Do what can't be done by saints or reason,
            Heal my sad soul and put out of my head
                    This grim regret.

                            Notes

    1. This thought, that suffering cannot be soothed by a poetic complaint, is opposite to the opening lines in *Lament XV*.
    2. The ancient Greeks (Homer, *Odyssey*, 19, 562 ff) and Romans (Virgil's *Aeneid*, 6, 893 ff) believed that dreams leave the lower world through two gates, the windows of Hades: delusive dreams through the ivory gate and the dreams that tell the truth through the horn gate. Kochanowski paraphrased Horace, *Ode* 3, 27, 39-42:
    "Am I awake and sinning sore,

Or all in innocence,
By phantoms from the ivory gate
Bemocked?"
3. Parca, or a miserly goddess wove the thread of human life.
4. The question, one of three, is addressed to Cicero (106-43 B.C.), Roman writer and philosopher, born in Arpinum. He claimed in *Tusculan Disputations* ( 5, 37, 108) that being banished is not a great misfortune, quoting Socrates, who held that the wise man is "a native and citizen of the whole world." When banished himself, however, Cicero despaired.
5. This is another ironical question to Cicero who maintained, like the stoics, that the wise man should accept all misfortunes with calm and use them to practice his virtues. In spite of this opinion, Cicero gave himself up to despair after the death of his daughter Tulia.
6. This sentence is a paraphrase of Cicero's conclusion in Book I of *Tusculan Disputations* (49, 118). In his speeches, Cicero attacked Mark Antony, and this was punishable by death. When he faced the emperor's agents, he tried all he could to save his life, but to no avail.
7. Kochanowski considers Cicero the author who could write and speak like an angel.
8. Compare the motto of the *Laments*.
9. This text may refer to Cicero's doubts, expressed in his translation of Aeschylus's *Prometheus*:
"Yes, if a man applies a timely cure
And crushes not the wound with heavy hand."
(*Tusc.*, 3, 31, 76, 317).
10. Time, personified as Chronos, allows distressed people to forget.

### Lament XVII

The hand of the Lord has touched me,[1]
    All my joy has taken from me,
    Now I am just barely alive
    And probably will have to die.
5    When the sun shines brightly rising,
    When it is extinguished setting,

My heart still suffers the same pain,
And its crying will never wane.
I will never dry up mine eye
10     And will forever have to cry.[2]
I have to cry; o, my Savior,
Who can hide from You ever?[3]
In vain we shun the stormy sea,
In vain evade the battlefield:[4]
15     Anywhere misfortune will strike,
Although it may seem most unlike.[5]
I lived my life so modestly,
Almost no one knew about me,
Man's envy and adversity,
20     Did not know where to injure me.
Yet God who knows where to touch us,[6]
And derides human cautiousness,[7]
Dealt me a blow more palpable,
The more I felt invulnerable.
25 And reason, that free from danger
Knew how to talk of disaster,
Today barely knows where it is:[8]
That's how it helped in my sickness.
At times it would like to amend,
30     And free me from deep discontent,
But when reason will sit on scales,[9]
It cannot outweigh my travails.
Quite useless are all human claims,
Not to call losses by their names[10];
35     If one laughs in calamity,
I'd say he's lost his sanity.[11]
And if one treats crying lightly,
I hear what he's saying clearly,[12]
But this won't diminish sorrow,
40     Certainly it will only grow.
For when my soul is mortified,
Willingly or not I must cry;
What's contemptible must be marred
And derision pierces the heart.[13]
45 This medicine, by the living God,
Too heavy for my distressed thought.
If you are of my health a friend,
A milder cure do recommend.

>       So I will keep on shedding tears,
> 50      As all my hope now disappears
>       That reason could bring deliverance;
>       Only God can soothe my sufferance.

## Notes

1. Job 19:21. Many verses in this *Lament* are reminiscent of biblical verses, especially in the Psalms and Job, and of the texts of Cicero and Horace.
2. "But you are ever drowned in tears,
    For Mystes dead you ever mourn;" (Horace, *Odes*, 2, 9, 9-10).
3. "Where can I go from your spirit?
    Or where can I flee from your
    presence?" (Psalms 139:7)
4. "In vain we shun the battle's roar,
    And breakers dashed on Adria's shore;
    Vainly we flee in terror blind
    The plague that walketh on the wind,
    The sluggish river of the dead,
    Cocytus must be visited;" (Horace, *Odes*, 2, 14, 13-18).
5. "And still in unimagined guise
    Comes Death on man" (Horace, *Odes*, 2, 13, 19-20).
6. Satan accused Job of serving God because it was profitable. He urged God to try Job: "But stretch out your hand now and touch all that he has, and he will curse you to your face." (Job 1:11)
7. "He who sits in the heavens laughs;
    the LORD has them in derision." (Psalms 2:4).
8. "Now it's your turn to be in
    trouble,
    and you are too stunned to
    face it" (Job 4:5).
9. "Let God weigh me on honest
    scales" (Job 31:6).
10. "The first remedial step therefore in giving comfort will be to show that either there is no evil or very little" (Cicero, *Tusc.*, 3, 32, 77).

11. " ... if the wise man finds himself inside Phalaris' bull [Phalaris burnt his victims in a brazen bull], he will say: 'How sweet; how indifferent I am to this!'" (Cicero, *Tusc.*, 2, 7, 17).

12. "But the principal precaution to be observed in the matter of pain is to do nothing in a despondent, cowardly, slothful, servile or womanish spirit, and before all to resist and spurn those Philoctetean outcries." (Cicero, *Tusc.*, 2, 22, 55).

"Therefore, where others are accustomed to surrender themselves to distress in the belief that it is right, these men spurned distress in the thought that it was degrading." (Cicero, *Tusc.*, 2, 28, 71). "Leave off at length these woman's sighs" (Horace, *Odes*, 2, 9, 17).

13. "Therefore, as you admitted at the outset, disgrace is worse than pain, pain is clearly of no account; for whilst you shall hold it base and unworthy of a man to groan, shriek aloud, wail, break down and be unnerved; so long as honour, so long as nobility, so long as worth remain, and so long as you control yourself by keeping your eyes upon them, assuredly pain will lead to virtue and grow fainter by a deliberate effort of will; for either no virtue exists or all pain is to be despised." (Cicero, *Tusc.*, 2, 13, 31).

## *Lament XVIII*

    We, O Lord, Your disobedient children,
        In times of merriment
        Remember You rarely,
    And indulge in usual pleasures only.
5    We pay no heed that it[1] flows from Your grace,
        So it will pass apace,
        When You, Lord, will not sense
    Our gratitude for Your benevolence.
    Keep a reign on us, let's not become swelled
10        With vain joys of this world.
        Let us at least know You
    When we're punished, since loved we don't want to.[2]
    But chasten us only like a father[3];
        We melt in Your anger
15        As snow becomes undone,

When warmed by the rays of heavenly sun.[4]
You'll quickly destroy us, Lord most constant,
    If Your divine stern hand
    Above our heads will hang[5];
20 Your disfavor is for us a cruel pang.
Yet Your mercy has been famed since times' dawn;
    First the world will be gone,
    'Ere You'll spurn a meek man,
Though against You he was long adamant.
25 My offenses toward You are legion,[6]
    And yet Your compassion
    Exceeds all iniquity:
Be today, o Lord, merciful to me.[7]

## Notes

1. 'It' refers to happiness described in preceding lines.
2. Kochanowski juxtaposes the state of grief caused by God's punishment for our sins with the state of joy brought about by God's grace.
3. "For the Lord disciplines him whom he loves, and chastises every son whom he receives." (Hebrews 12:6)

"for the Lord reproves him whom he loves, as a father the son in whom he delights." (Proverbs 3:12)

4. "You will make them as a blazing oven when you appear. The LORD will swallow them up in his wrath; and fire will consume them." (Psalms 21:9)

"By the breath of God they perish, and by the blast of his anger they are consumed." (Job 4:9)

5. "And the hand of the LORD was on El'ijah;" (Kings 18:46)
6. "For evils have encompassed me without number" (Psalms 40:12)
7. "Do not thou, O Lord, withhold thy mercy from me." (Psalms 40:11)

*Lament XIX*
or
*The Dream*

    Long into the night sorrow didn't let me
        Close my eyes and calm my weakened body.
    Just one hour before dawn a lingering dream
        Enfolded me within its darksome wings.
5    Just then mother herself appeared to me,
        Holding in her arms my sweet Ursula,
    Who looked as she did when she'd come to pray,
        At daybreak, when from bed she moved away.
    In a tiny white shirt, with curly hair,
10    A rosy face, her eyes to smile prepared.
    I'm waiting what next and my mother says:
        "Asleep, Jan, or does grief cause you distress?"
    Then I sighed deeply and it seemed to me
        That I woke up. And she, silent briefly,
15    Spoke again: "Your inconsolable wail
        Brought me here, my son, onto this vale
    From the far-off lands, and your bitter tears
        Seeped into the concealed chambers of death.
    I brought you in my arms your sweet daughter,
20    So that you could still see her and lower
    Your heartfelt sorrow, which lessens your strength
        So much and invisibly saps your health,[1]
    As fire burns to ashes a cord that's dry,
        Not letting the shortest moment pass by.
25    Do you consider us, the dead, as gone
        For whom the sun never again has shone?[2]
    Yet we, in truth, live life much more worthy,
        Since soul is nobler than this coarse body.
    Dust goes to dust,[3] but would spirit from heaven
30    Die and not be called back to its haven?[4]
    Don't fret about this and your trust revive,
        That your dearest Ursula is alive.
    And she has appeared to you in this guise,
        So you could see her with your mortal eyes.
35    She shines 'mid angels and timeless elements
        Like the fair dawn and prays for her parents
    As she knew how to when she was with you,

Though how to say the words she barely knew.
And if the sorrow grows because her years,
40   Had been broken 'ere she could experience
The pleasures of this world?[5]  O, poor and vain
   Are your pleasures, which have been so ordained,
That they contain more worries and sadness,
   As you can experience for yourself best.
45 Did your daughter bring you such joyousness
   That ever your cheer and your happiness
Could be compared to your present distress?
   You don't say that, I see. So you assess
What you learned and don't grieve that early death
50   Was sent to the daughter which you love best.
She didn't go from pleasures, but from labors,[6]
   From work, from worries, from tears, from dolors.
Which fill the world so much that even though
   What cheers man's nature on this mortal globe
55 Must lose taste, through size of impurity,
   Or because we fear obvious falsity.
Why these tears, by God? What did not she know?
   That she didn't buy a man with her trousseau?
That she didn't hear threats and someone's scolding?
60   That she didn't suffer pains in childbearing?
And she doesn't know what her worried mother
   Found out: what predicament is greater:
To bear or bury them?[7]  See these delights
   With which you commonly sweeten your lives!
65 In heaven true joys, what's more, endless,
   Protected and free from any menace.
Here worries don't rule, here toil is unknown,
   Here ill chance, here mishaps don't find their home.
Here you won't find sickness, here's no old age,[8]
70   Here death fed by tears does not have free range.
We live forever, enjoy inner peace,
   We know the mysteries of existence.[9]
The sun always shines, the day does not wane
   Nor does it draw the blind night in its train.[10]
75 We see the Maker of all things in His fame,
   Which you, in the flesh, try to see in vain.
Swiftly turn your thoughts here and be preserved
   My son, for this richness of joys unchanged.
You've learned what this world and its joy can do,

80     You'd better strive for a greater value.
      Your daughter drew a good lot (you can trust),
        And in her own matters she acted just
      As one who for the first time went to sea,
        And having spotted a great jeopardy,
85     Preferred to get back to the shore. A few
        Who set sails, ran into rocks hid from view[11];
      One was struck by frost, next by hunger's sword,
        Scarcely any got to shore on a board.
      She could not flee death, even if she still
90     Lived much longer than that ancient Sibyl.[12]
      What was still to come, she preferred to foil;
        That's why on this earth she suffered less toil.
      Some are left alone after parents' death
        And they live, poor orphans, in wretchedness.
95     Some are rudely pushed into married state,
        Only God knows who receives the estate.
      Others are abducted, by our own men,
        And in Tartar hordes many must remain,[13]
      Where in pagan slavery, in shamed service,
100    They drink their tears,[14] in wait for all-soothing death.
      Your gracious daughter has no more these fears,
        As she's borne to heaven in her young years.
      Having not yet suffered an earthly strain,
        Nor smeared her precious soul with a sinful stain.
105 So her matters, my son, (there is no doubt),
      Went well and don't worry on that account.
      You weigh your losses and your delusion
        So you do not forget that your reason
      And poise are dearer. To this then adhere
110    Howsoever you feel stripped of good cheer.
      When a man is born, he's ruled by such law,
        That he's a target in each luckless draw.[15]
      This is hard to dodge; do what we can:
        If we won't go freely, we'll go restrained.[16]
115 What burdens all alike, I don't know why
      Would be just for you, my son, hardest trial.[17]
      Your daughter was mortal, just as you are:[18]
        She lived until her destined course was barred.
      Briefly, it's true, but man has no power.
120    And it's not easy to judge what's better.[19]
      God's judgments are hidden,[20] what He's resolved,

            Would best be also by us approved.[21]
        Tears in this case are worthless, once the soul
            Leaves body, vain our wait to make it whole.
125 But man isn't fair to fate in these matters,
        As a rule he notes only disasters,[22]
        And does not want to heed nor keep in mind
            What at times may come by his own design.
        Fortune's power is such, my dearest son,
130     That we should not grieve when things are undone,
        But rather thank that something did withstand,
            Since misfortune had it all in its hand.
        So you as well, yielding to common law,
            Don't permit despair at your heart to gnaw.
135 And look at what escaped misfortune's reign:
            If man bore no loss, he should call it gain.[23]
        Lastly, what of your expenses and cost
            What of your labor and the years you lost,
        Nearly all of which you spent over books,[24]
140     Enjoying little common life pursuits?
        Now you should gather fruit of your grafting[25]
            And save weak nature when it's faltering.
        You consoled others in the same mischance,
            Will you show less care in your own instance?[26]
145 Now, master, heal thyself![27] Time, makes all hale,
            But the one who disdains the common trail
        Won't deign to wait for such late remedy:
            His mind should cure what time heals for many.
        And what method does time use? It'll supplant
150     Old states with newer, at times more pleasant,
        Sometimes such that a thoughtful man will see
            'Ere they happen and with this subtlety
        He doesn't weigh past things, looks toward future
            And sets his heart for good and bad fortune.[28]
155 You adhere to this, my son, and the human lot
            Bear like a man.[29] There's one Lord of grief and reward."[30]
        She vanished. I woke up. But with no certainty
            If I heard it in a dream or reality.

### Notes

1. "For sorrow results in death,

and sorrow of heart saps one's strength." (Sirach 38:18).

2. In the Bible, the light, especially sunlight, means life, while darkness and extinguishing of light, mean death. See also *Lament II*, 25-26.

3. "In the sweat of your face
you shall eat bread
till you return to the ground,
for out of it you were taken;
you are dust,
and to dust you shall return." (Genesis 3:19)

4. "and the dust returns to the earth as it was, and the spirit returns to God who gave it." (Ecclesiastes 12:7).

5. "The infant had not yet tasted the sweetness of life" (Cicero, *Tusc.*, 1, 39, 93).

6. "What does cause anguish, or rather torture, is the departure from all those things that are good in life. Take care it may not more be truly said, from all its evils." (Cicero, *Tusc.*, 1, 33, 83).

"For we should mourn in sorrowing throngs the house
Where a man child is born to light of day,
When reckoning o'er the ills of human life:
But who by death has ended grievous toils,
Him let his friends bear forth with praise and joy."

(Cicero, *Tusc.*, 1, 48, 115, quoting Euripides's *Cresphontes*).

7. Some of these expressions are similar to the questions posed by Servius Sulpicius in his consolation letter to Cicero after his daughter's death: "What was there after all to make life so sweet a prospect for at this time? What did she have or hope? What comfort for her spirit? The thought perhaps of spending her life wedded to some young man of distinction? (...) Or the thought of bearing children herself (...)?" (Cicero, *Fam. 2*, 4, 5, 3).

8. This description contains some opposite elements of the ones used by Virgil in his depiction of hell: "there dwell wan Sickness and gloomy Eld, (...) and Death and Travail and thereby Sleep, Death's kinsman" (*The Aeneid*, 6, 274-277).

9. According to Cicero, the soul's happiness derived from the ability to understand all things: "assuredly, we shall be happy when we have left our bodies behind and are free

from all desirings and envyings; (..) we feel the wish for an object of our observation and attention, (...) and we shall devote our whole being to study and examination, because nature has planted in our minds an insatiable longing to see truth; (...)" (Cicero, *Tusc.*, 1, 19, 44).

10. "And your life will be brighter than
the noonday;
its darkness will be like the
morning." (Job 11:17).

The phrase 'blind night' is used frequently in the classical literature, e.g., in Virgil's *Aeneid*, 2, 397.

11. A comparison of life to sailing a stormy see and death to arriving in a peaceful haven was popular in the classical literature. "Would that we might be wafted there under full sail! but if contrary winds shall throw us back, all the same we must be brought again to the same point a little later." (Cicero, *Tusc.*, 1, 49, 119). The rocks and shoals hidden from view, signifying life dangers, appear as 'blind rocks' ('caeca saxa' or 'caeca vada') in Virgil's *Aeneid* (1, 536; 3, 706 and 5, 167).

12. Sibyl, a prophetess, who lived at Cumae near Naples, was famed for her longevity (she was reported to live one thousand years) and her wise prophecies.

13. Kochanowski speaks here of the abuse of orphans, some cases of abduction of women in Poland, and of the raids of the Tartars.

14. "For I eat ashes like bread,
and mingle tears with my drink," (Psalms 102:9).

15. "it is the law of our entry into this world that no one can permanently escape evil." (Cicero, *Tusc.*, 3, 29, 59, 295-7.

16. 'Go restrained' may refer to walking like oxen pulling a heavy cart, constrained by an oppressive yoke. See also "For Fate the willing leads, the unwilling drags along", quoted in Seneca, *Letters From a Stoic*. (Selected and Translated With an Introduction by Robin Campbell. Hammondsworth: Penguin Books, 1969, 107, 11).

17. "But can that which is necessary for all be wretched for one alone?" (Cicero, *Tusc.*, 1, 49, 119).

18. "I knew that I had begotten a mortal". (Cicero, *Tusc.*, 3, 14, 30).

19. It is not easy to say whether it is better to live short or long.

20. "O the depth of the riches and wisdom and knowledge of God! How unsearchable are his judgments and how inscrutable his ways!" (Romans 11:33).

21. "O my Father, if it be possible, let this cup pass from me: nevertheless, not as I will, but as thou wilt." (Matthew 26:39, King James Version). These words were recited in the sixteenth century by the bed of a dying person.

22. "Whatever day your fortune grants,
    That day mark up for gain;" (Horace, *Odes*, 1, 9, 14-15).

23. See "Luck that passes expectation should be reckoned all as gain", quoted by Cicero, *Tusc.*, 3, 14, 30.

24. See similar phrases in Cicero, *Tusc.*, 2, 25, 60: "I had given such devoted attention to philosophy" and "I have spent many years in studying philosophy."

25. "Your people shall all be righteous;
    they shall possess the land for
    ever,
    the shoot of my planting, the work
    of my hands
    that I might be glorifed." (Isaiah 60:21).

26. "And there is none of wisdom so possessed,
    Who with mild words has soothed another's woes,
    But does not, when a turn of fortune comes,
    Fall broken by his own calamity;
    So words, for others wise, his own need fail"
    (Cicero, quoting Sophocles in *Tusc.*, 3, 39, 71).

27. Latin "Medice, cura te ipsum." "Physician, heal thyself" (Luke 4:23).

28. "Lighten grief with hopes of brighter morrow;
    Temper joy, in fear of a change of fortune;
    Bear the winters, knowing despite their fury,
    Jove will recall them." (Horace, *Odes*, 2, 10, 13-16).

Servius Sulpicius, in his letter to Cicero, wrote: "There is no grief that is not lessened or softened by the passage of time. For *you* to wait for this time to pass, instead of anticipating the result by your own good sense, does you discredit." (Cicero, *Fam.* 2, 4, 5, 6).

29. "Humana humane ferenda"--"The lot of man must be endured in the spirit of a man" (Cicero, *Tusc.*, 3, 16, 34).

30. "For he who brought these calamities
   upon you
   will bring you everlasting joy
   with your salvation." (Baruch 4:29).

"For God, who rules over all things, has made this day to be a joy to his chosen people instead of a day of destruction for them." (Esther 16:21).

The end of *Laments*.

# EPITAPH

## TO
## HANNA
## KOCHANOWSKA[1]

AND YOU TOO, HANNA, YOUR SISTER QUICKLY FOLLOWED
AND AHEAD OF TIME VISITED THE LOWER WORLD,
SO YOUR HAPLESS FATHER MOURNED YOU BOTH TOGETHER,
AND PREPARED HIMSELF FOR MORE ENDURING PLEASURE.

### Notes

1. A few months after the death of Ursula, Kochanowski lost a younger daughter, Hanna. He published this brief epitaph for her at the end of the *Laments* in 1580.

*Text*: Kochanowski, Jan. *Dzieła wszystkie*. Vol. II. *Treny*. Ed. by Maria Renata Mayenowa and Lucyna Worończakowa with Jerzy Axer and Maria Cytowska. Wrocław: Ossolineum, 1983, 46-97.

## THE DISMISSAL OF THE GREEK ENVOYS

Staged in 1578, *The Dismissal of the Greek Envoys*[1] is a dramatization of an episode from Homer's *Iliad*, a frequently retold tale of the beautiful Helen who was abducted by Alexander and brought to Troy. Two Greek envoys arrive in Troy, demanding her return. King Priam and his council gather to debate how to respond. When Alexander persuades his countrymen to reject the envoys' demand, Cassandra, Priam's daughter, predicts the destruction of Troy. The Greek army makes preparations to launch an attack.

Even though the play is based on Greek and Latin dramatic works, for example, by Sophocles, Euripides, and Seneca, it is not a mere imitation. *The Dismissal* is a drama with political and local overtones. It does not show a tragic hero, indispensable in the Greek theatre, but foretells the fall of the state, brought about by the irresponsible decision of its rulers and immoral behavior of some citizens. This warning, which could apply to the Polish republic, carried a sense of urgency as the play was staged before King Stefan Batory and Jan Zamoyski, Vice-Chancellor of the Crown.

In the play, Kochanowski used for the first time in Polish poetry blank verse of eleven, twelve, and thirteen syllables, rendered in this translation by lines of four, five, and six feet.

1. The title *Dismissal of the Greek Envoys* is not accurate. The original word 'odprawa' or its synonym 'załatwienie' referred in the sixteenth century to the whole proces of dealing officially with petitioners, as in modern Polish 'odprawa pasażerów'--'processing of passengers' or 'dealing with passengers', for example, at customs. In the language of diplomacy it referred to receiving and responding to the envoys at a special audience. It happens that in this play the response is negative and the envoys leave, hence the "dismissal." The main issue facing the protagonists, however, is to weigh conflicting arguments presented to the Trojan council and to give response to the envoys. Thus the title *The Response to the Greek Envoys* would be more accurate. However, *The Dismissal of the Greek Envoys* is well established and has been retained here.

XIII. Title page of Jan Kochanowski's *The Dismissal of the Greek Envoys*, Cracow, 1578

## THE DISMISSAL OF THE GREEK ENVOYS

Presented in the theatre before His Majesty the King and Her Majesty the Queen in Jazdów near Warsaw, on the twelfth day of January, in the year of the Lord 1578, at the festivities given by His Grace Vice Chancellor of the Crown.

To my Gracious Lord, His Grace Jan Zamoyski of Zamość, Vice Chancellor of the Crown, etc., etc. I commend my services to the favor of Your Grace, my Gracious Lord.

Only yesterday were there delivered to me at the same time both letters that Your Grace wrote to me concerning this tragedy. But as I had not known earlier about those letters, I had supposed that because of those delays, my tragedy was also to be delayed or rather it was to remain with me--to feed moths or for funnels for an apothecary. When I read Your Grace's letters, there was no time to correct it, for I had to *insumere*[1] the whole for copying. *Quicquid id est*,[2] and I think it is foolishness, and Your Grace will probably say the same, I am sending it to Your Grace so much the more boldly, though it is not much, since I had told Your Grace earlier that it was not *ad amussim*,[3] for the master is not equal to the task. Our ears also are not used to the rest.[4] *Inter caetera*[5] there are three choruses, the third seemingly imitates the Greek choruses, for they have a special form for them; I do not know how it will sound in Polish. But on this let Your Grace pass *arbitrium*[6] or rather on the whole. I would be very glad if I could myself *praesens*[7] now offer my services but my poor health will not permit it. I would not like, however, to miss the reception[8] at Your Grace's if *salus*[9] will allow me. Therefore I commend myself to the favor of Your Grace my Gracious Lord.

*Dat.*[10] at Czarnolas on the twenty second day of December, in the name of the Lord MDLXXVII.
The devoted servant of Your Grace my Gracious Lord,

Jan Kochanowski

1. *insumere* - 'to use.'
2. *Quicquid id est* - 'whatever it is', 'be it as it may'.

3. *ad amussim* - here 'according to the rules'.
4. The Poles are not accustomed to other things.
5. *Inter caetera* - 'among other things'.
6. *arbitrium* - 'judgment'.
7. *praesens* - 'in person, personally'.
8. Following the wedding festivities, a banquet was given in the house of the bridegroom.
9. *salus* - 'health'.
10. *datum* - 'given, dated'.


Dramatis personae

Antenor
Alexander, also called Paris
Helen
An Old Lady
Messenger from Paris
Ulysses and Menelaus, the Greek envoys
Priam, King of Troy
Cassandra
A Captain
A Captive
Chorus of Trojan maidens

In Troy

[A square in front of the palace. The Chorus of Trojan maidens is seated on the steps of the palace. Antenor is standing in the center of the square.]¹

Antenor

    I have long expected and said loudly
    That such a great insult and injury
    Would not be suffered by the valiant Greeks:
    We already have with us their envoys
5    Who present here the following demand:
    That Helen must be surrendered to them,
    She, whom Alexander, in years gone by,
    While he was in Greece, a guest not quite true,
    Abducted from her husband and then brought

10   Across the rough sea to the town of Troy.
     If we send her back into her husband's
     Hands, we will be able to live in peace,
     But if the envoys go back with nothing,
     Same day we'll hear the tiding that the Greeks
15   Come from the sea and attack the country.[2]
     I see Alexander takes care of this:
     He contrives secret plans, wins supporters,
     Sends gifts, has not even overlooked me;
     But I, my home, and my inheritance
20   Are not for sale. Let my God forbid me[3]
     From taking my honor to the market.
     He who calls upon gold to speak for him,
     Does not trust in the justice of his cause.
     But he is also an imprudent man
25   Who, putting the republic in danger,
     Receives gifts as if only he alone
     Were to remain safe when all will perish.
     Time to go to council, as today the king wants
     To receive the envoys. Is this Alexander?[4] Yes.

Alexander, Antenor

Alexander

30   As almost everyone has promised me,
     Respected Antenor, be well disposed
     Towards my case against the Greek envoys.

Antenor

     I will do willingly, most esteemed prince,
     Whatever is required by justice
35   And the interest of our republic.

Alexander

     There's no excuse, when a friend asks for help.

Antenor

     I agree when he asks for the right thing.

Alexander

> To wish better the stranger than the friend
> Methinks it is not too far from envy.

Antenor

40 > To serve the friend more than to serve the truth
> Seems an offense against all honesty.

Alexander

> A hand washes a hand, a foot supports
> A foot, a friend is the port for a friend.

Antenor

> Honesty is a great friend: to make it
45 > A servant is not a friendly action.

Alexander

> They say a friend in need is a friend indeed.

Antenor

> It's also a need, when conscience suffers.

Alexander

> Clear the conscience if one stands by a friend.

Antenor

> Even more clear when one remains with truth.

Alexander

50 > It is your truth to give help to the Greeks.

Antenor

> Each one who is right is a Greek to me.

Alexander

> I can see that you have judged me quickly.

Antenor

> Man's conscience is to judge everybody.

Alexander

> It's known that the envoys stay in your house.

Antenor

55 > My house is open to each honest man.

Alexander

> Specially if his hands are not empty.

Antenor

> Because I must make gifts to the judges,
> As I seized someone's wife, who they came for.[5]

Alexander

> I don't know of the wife, but you take gifts,
60 > Mainly from Greeks; mine are too small for you.

Antenor

> Both wives and gifts I'm unwilling to take.
> I see you speak just as intemperately
> As you live; I have naught to do with you.

Alexander

    I regret I asked you for anything,
65  I trust my gods that without your goodwill
    I'll find someone to back up my affairs.

Antenor

    Such as you are.

Alexander

              God grant, an honest man.

[Chorus rises from the steps, stands in the center of the stage and sings]

    If youth could consort with good sense!
    There ne'er will be such affluence
70  Of gold in the earth and of sea-born pearls
    With which the young could get hold of prudence.
      Less grief in the world would occur,
    If these two things[6] joined together,
    The young would know more lasting merriment,
75  Not bringing woe to themselves and kinsmen.
      But now, they disregard reason,
    Satisfy only their passion,
    They lose health and fame, they lose possessions
    And bring the homeland dire tribulations.
80     O God, who are high in heaven!
    It is hard for you, I discern,
    To grant youth and sense; youth pays for reason,
    Which we would like to possess, while still young.
      Lo, I see Helen: what does she at present think,
85  Poor woman, knowing that today at the council
    They have final debates, if in Troy she should stay
    Or in Greece and Sparta[7] she should venture to live?

[Helen comes out from the palace]

Helen

    I have seen it all as if in the looking-glass
    That shameless Alexander would not enjoy long
90  His advantage, but that the overpowering Greeks
    Would unsettle his repose and his merriment.
    So like a voracious wolf that dispersed the flock
    He ran as far as he could, while they, like shepherds
    With dogs, followed him. And it might yet come to that;
95  The wolf will have to give up the sheep at the end
    And will escape in shame somewhere to the forest.
    Alas, what will my return voyage home be like?
    Probably I will be chained by the neck astern,
    Flanked from all sides by the fleet of Grecian vessels.
100 With what countenance will I greet my dear brothers?[8]
    How will I, now shameless, appear before your eyes,
    My dear husband, and then how will I give account
    Of my actions? Will I dare to look at your face?
    I wish that you never had visited Sparta,
105 Miserable son of Priam! Because what else
    Did I lack? A daughter of illustrious princes
    I married into an illustrious princely house;
    God gave me beauty, and progeny,[9] and good fame
    Valued most. I lost all because of a bad man.
110 My homeland is far away, I do not see friends,
    I do not know if my children are still alive;
    As for myself, I am not different from a slave,
    Subject to painful taunts and evil fame; what else
    Fortune plans for me, only you can know, my Lord.

Old Lady,[10] Helen

    Old Lady

115 Do not worry, dear child, for so
    It must be in this world: once joy,
    Then sorrow comes; from these two threads
    Our life is woven. Our joys are
    Insecure, but worries must yield,
120 When God wishes and the time comes.

Helen

>My mother, this wreath is woven
>Unevenly! The mortal man
>Feels much more worries than pleasures.

Old Lady

>Man takes more to heart what ails him
>Than what satisfies his purpose.
>That is why it seems there is more
>Of what grieves than what pleases him.

Helen

>By God, more evil in this world
>Than of good. First, behold there is
>Only one way man can be born,
>But so many ways to perish
>That we can not guess them at all.
>The mortal man possesses too
>Only one health, and against it
>Are countless hosts of sundry ills.
>Also she who rules all of us
>Whose hand controls and governs all,
>Fortune herself confirms my words,
>There's far less happiness on earth
>Than what men call evil. For she
>Makes a few rich, but look at all
>That she plagues with grave misery.
>It is not her envy or greed,
>She does it pressed by want. It means
>That even now, when she wishes
>To favor one, she often takes
>From another, ere granting it;
>From this it can be understood
>What I said many times: by far
>Less happiness than mishaps here.

Old Lady

> If more or less, or same amount
> Of both--no gain for us to know.
> Let's pray to God that each of us
> Suffers the least of misfortune,
> 155 Since suffering none is not man's lot.
> But why no news from the council
> For so long! I know that Alexander
> Without delay will let us know
> What was resolved; for us, women,
> 160 More fit to be at home than here.

[They enter the palace]

Chorus

> O you that rule over Republic lands[11]
> And justice for people hold in your hands,
> You, I say, that were given charge to feed
> All the people and the Lord's flock to lead:
> 165 Remember it forever as your faith
> That you sit in the Lord's seat on this earth,
> From where you should not your own affairs mind,
> But take under your care all of mankind.
> Although you hold sway over lesser men,
> 170 High above you sits a mighty Sovereign,
> To whom one day you will tell every deed;
> Those who are guilty, will never be freed.
> This Lord does not take gifts nor does he ask
> Who is a peasant, who wears the count's mask:
> 175 Whether in homespun coat or in gold lace,
> If he transgressed, in chains would be his place.
> So methinks I cause less harm with my sins;
> As only I risk fall for my licence.
> Misdeeds of the mighty ravished cities
> 180 And brought destruction to large monarchies.[12]

[A Messenger enters running, Helen comes out of the palace]

## Messenger

    I bring good news to my mistress.
    I know she has awaited long
    This message, worrying her heart
    With distress and tears. Lo, just now
185 She comes out of the house. O Queen,
    I'm a messenger of good news.

## Helen

    God grant you bring consolation.

## Messenger

    Just as your envoys came, so are
    They going, yet you are with us.

## Helen

190 Were you in council or just told?

## Messenger

    I was present through all and Alexander
    Ordered me to go straight to you.

## Helen

    I do not see yet why I should
    Be truly happy. But tell me
195 What happened.

## Messenger

                  I will, just listen!
    When all the lords were seated in council,
    First the King spoke: "I never take measures
    Without your advice; if I ever did
    (Though I do not recall it), I should not,
200 When the case pertains to my son, so that
    A father's love would not lead me astray.

          Although methinks it was not said in vain:
          'Blood is thicker than water', yet for me
          The bond with the republic counts for more.
205       So what you will decide, I will approve.
          My son took a wife in Greece, I know not
          How; the Greek envoys want to take her back.
          To give her up or not; we must resolve."
             Then Alexander rose and began thus:
210       "Upon the first complaint of the envoys,
          I gave adequate account; I will not
          Idly assail your ears at present, but
          Having said little, I will leave the rest
          To God, my father's grace, and your judgment.
215       You are all aware of the life I led;
          I never cared at all for city feasts;
          I much preferred to chase through the thick groves
          The swift deer or wild boar. Nor did I think
          It was a hardship when sometimes I slept
220       In a forest shed, or shepherded flocks.[13]
          I did not think of Helen at all then,
          Nor had my ear heard her name before that.
          It was Venus, when the three goddesses
          Chose me as judge,[14] Venus herself who first
225       Favored her, and gave her to me as wife.
          I see people ask God for happiness,
          Should I scorn it, when they gave it to me
          Of their own wish? I took it and took it
          With grace. I hope strongly that the deity
230       Who honored me first, will keep favoring me,
          And what she gave, she won't allow to take
          Lightly from me. Even if I had won
          My wife by mortal means, I know not why
          They could just steal Medea from our friends,[15]
235       Yet it would be improper to repay
          Their ruse with the same ruse.
          If I am guilty, so are they no less.
          If they want redress, let them make it first,
          As those who first did wrong. If they do it,
240       Father, hand over not only my wife
          But also myself, let me do penance.
          And if they too want to think that all men
          Owe them justice for wrong, while they owe none,

           God permit, they will not force this on us,
245    Nor will they ever accomplish it here.
           I do not think you, my gracious father,
       Have yet forgotten old wrongs and losses,
       You and this famed state suffered from these lords.[16]
       The ruined walls still lie upon the ground
250    And to this time the fields stand desolate,
       The signs of the Greek sword and cruel hand.
       And if you would not remember it well,
       Hesione must remember, your sister,
       O Father, and my aunt, who to this day
255    Lives with them in slavery, if she still lives.
       This wrong, O King, will not be recompensed
       By one Helen, avenged by one Paris."
           He ceased. A whisper spread among the lords
       In the hall. Just as towards the summer
260    The industrious bees will hum in the hive,[17]
       When they see a new ruler, and they wish
       To leave their queen and start a new household,
       With buzzing in the hive and furtive stir:
       Such a sound arose then among the men,
265    And when it died, Antenor rose to speak:
           "Truth, my King, does not need long arguments:
       Alexander, as a house guest in Greece
       Of a renowned man, not heeding the laws
       That bind guests, took his host's wife for himself.
270    If he had enticed the lowest slave girl,
       He'd be guilty. What if he seized his wife?
       A good, honest man couldn't disregard her
       Or insist on her return without shame.
       He owes him a lot. The man though ashamed
275    Wants her back, and I counsel her return,
       Lest we should add injustice to insult:
       Each of these alone is unbearable,
       Far more when combined! So undoubtedly
       The Greeks will demand Helen not only
280    By their envoys but also by the sword.
           Let Alexander not wed at such cost,
       That he would pay for marriage with the fall
       Of his homeland and our blood! If he trusts
       His goddess's grace, let him fear those two
285    He angered and rebuked with his judgment.

Medea was not captured in our times,
And I know not if that concerns us. This
I see: for this wrong, none has called the Greeks
To account until now: silent were those
290 Who had more right to speak up. I know not
How just is our desire to mask our sin
With someone's crime. It is more our concern,
As in fathers' time, the Greeks raised the sword
In this realm. But even then, King, (we must
295 Admit the truth), our misdeed brought that fall,
So I must fear now a secret judgment
Of the gods, for this offense to suffer
Punishment from the Greeks. This you should heed,
O King, the more since in the first defeat
300 You almost died as a boy, in penance
For your father's sin and an unjust deed."
    So spoke Antenor. Aeneas concurred.
So did Panthous, Thymoetes, Lampus,
And also Ucalegon, but Hiketaon[18]
305 Was of different mind and spoke in these words:
"Do we have to dance just as the Greeks play?
They bid us to fear them and I indeed
Feel afraid. Now they are ordering us
To give Helen back, soon they will demand
310 Our wives and children. The greed for power
Never stays within its bounds; it always
Like a flood pushes over its borders,
Until it swamps all fields. So we, my lords,
Must turn away our horns ahead of time[19];
315 Too late to struggle when the yoke is on.
They ask for justice but threaten with war:
Simply, give, if you will, or I'll seize it.
Justice I owe but not with my disgrace:
He who extorts it, wants to gain from me
320 A lavish redress and to insult me.
    The Greeks have called themselves of old the lords,
And us, *barbaroi*, serfs.[20] But it isn't he
Who is from Pelops' land or Troy who is
A lord. The sharp sword in hand is the lord,
325 It will settle who shall bow the head down.
Till then we must be equal; let no Greek
Hold as true he is so terrifying

As he thinks. If they deem they suffered wrong,
For Alexander carried off Helen,
330 Let them first display to Alexander
How he should recompense them for that crime
Since they themselves have shown how to commit
Such a crime. And yet Alexander took
No brother with the sister, as they[21] took
335 Medea and Absyrtus.
Yet Antenor says it concerns us not:
It does indeed! For the wrong done to one,
All stood up[22]; will they seize us one by one?
I think not; a neighbor in Asia owes
340 His neighbor the same help as in Europe.[23]
It's always required, till the goal is reached.
   As for the King's sister and past losses,
I judge them more important than this case
And not comparable: I hold for those deeds,
345 The noble Trojan blood will be avenged.
I do not advise to let Helen go,
Till they come to terms about Medea."
   These were his words. After that nobody
Made a long speech; they spoke with the same voice:
350 "Just like Hiketaon"; both those who sat,
And who stood behind their benches,[24] same words:
"Just like Hiketaon." Ucalegon
Rose several times to speak, but could not
In the din. Marshals tapped their staves again:
355 "Hark, my lords, Ucalegon is speaking."
The staves did not help; our Ucalegon
Spoke to the Ucalegons, they cared not.[25]
   Then someone called in a very loud voice:
"What use these orations? Let's stand aside:
360 And see who has more."[26] He had just spoken,
When they all stood up, and chose their places.
When they stood aside, they were not equal:
Most with Alexander, a handful there.
Then they asked the King to follow the law,
365 And give his verdict for the bigger group.
   Without much pause the King said: "I gladly
Would see concord, yet since that cannot be,
I may not but go with the bigger group.
So let it be said for the public good:

370 'Let Helen stay in Troy, and let the Greeks
Make a redress to us for Medea'."
With this verdict, the envoys were summoned,
And then Alexander sent me to you
To tell all you have heard; I think by now
375 The envoys are informed, and your husband
Has long waited at home. Let's not tarry.

Helen

Well said: go ahead, I will follow you.

[Exeunt Helen, Old Lady, Messenger]

Chorus

She likes this account; I do not at all.
I know not what will come out of this joy.
380 I see the envoys come, their heads are down;
One can see the response does not please them.

[Enter Ulysses, Menelaus]

Ulysses

O disorderly kingdom, close to fall,
Where neither laws have weight much nor justice
Has a place, but all must be bought with gold!
385 Just one spendthrift man could arrange it so
That all, great and small, defend openly
His lewdness and his disgraceful affair,
Counting the truth as naught, ignore the end,
To which things must come after their counsel.
390 People don't understand or consider,
What a harmful sore for the republic
Is wanton youth: for they have put a price
On virtue and modesty; it's hard to
Be good to them; they wreck homes, make states poor,[27]
395 And, I say, destroy them (Troy, you'll learn it!).
They corrupt many with their influence.
Look, what trains of parasites follow them,

　　　　Who by constant idleness and excess,
　　　　Become as fat as hogs. Do you believe
400　　Anyone of that herd will be of use
　　　　To serve his state? How will he bear armor
　　　　If he sometimes finds his silks are heavy?
　　　　How will he stand guard, if he has now learned
　　　　To sleep past noon? How will he endure blows
405　　Of the foe, if he, by constant drinking,
　　　　Lost his health? So because they are such men,
　　　　And maybe don't see it, they call for war:
　　　　God, let me always fight against such men!

　Menelaus

　　　　O eternal light of heaven and you,
410　　Fruitful earth, and you, wide sea, you, all gods,
　　　　High and low, be today my witnesses,
　　　　That I sought a just thing from the Trojans
　　　　So that for the great wrong and the insult
　　　　I could get some redress; I got nothing,
415　　Only scorn, and my heart is much heavier.
　　　　I lay, mighty gods, my shame and deep grief
　　　　Before you; if I make this plea to you,
　　　　While my heart is pure, avenge this insult
　　　　And that plain wrong; let me sit on the throat
420　　Of Alexander and let my sword drink
　　　　The blood of that vicious man, since he has
　　　　Long fed on this insult and does it now.

　　　　　　　　[Exeunt]

　Chorus[28]

　　　　O white-winged sailer of the sea,
　　　　Raised upon the heights of Ida,[29]
425　　Vessel of beech that brought over
　　　　The fair-faced shepherd, Priam's son,
　　　　Along the wet paths of waters
　　　　Full of brine, to the transparent
　　　　Waves of the Eurotas river!
430　　Who did you bring for a sister,[30]
　　　　To Priam's two noble daughters,

The virtuous Polyxena
And Cassandra, the prophetess?
Following in Helen's footsteps,
435 As if she were a fleeing slave,
Her pursuers soon arrived here.
   Is she the celebrated gift
Or payment, given by Venus,
Most beautiful of goddesses,
440 For the verdict pleasing the judge,
When on Ida, that brings forth springs,
The mortal judge sat in judgment,
Of the immortal visages?
In quarrel and discord was born
445 Your marriage, O son of Priam,
I dare not foretell mishap, nay,
But no other end can occur.
   O mighty Cypris,[31] let my eyes,
Never look at a stranger's face!
450 Let me have a dear companion,
Just one friend for my chamber bed,
If you please; if others want more,
Let them entreat!
The greedy eyes have duped many,
455 But the one who knows how to curb
His desire, will enjoy his days
In long tranquility. The times
Will come, and soon, when a robber,
Will find a robber; he will chase
460 The sweet sleep from his eyes and put
The fear into his peaceful heart,
When the big trumpets will resound,
And foe's earthworks[32] surround the walls.

[Enter Antenor, Priam]

Antenor

Since my trusty counsel went unheeded,
465 O great King, that you order to return
Helen to the Greeks and put out at once
This unquestionable torch of great war,
I warn you now, in good time, what will come,

So you think of the attack and sure war,
470 As sure as you see me now before you.
You have heard the envoys bid you farewell
And all of us too. The border captains
Write that the Greek troops gather at Aulis.[33]
Do not doubt that they will march toward us,
475 Otherwise they would neither send out here
Their envoys nor would they speak so sharply
About their wrong. So without much delay,
Before we lose the remnant of the coast,
Supply well harbors and border castles
480 With foodstuffs and men; bid the dependant
Princes to be ready; enlist soldiers;
Send out spies, besides retain guards at sea
And on the land, so the Greeks won't find you
Easily surprised. Such is my advice.

Priam

485 I see you are afraid, good Antenor,
As if you saw the foe before your eyes.

Antenor

O King, better to fear now, as such fear
Increases both caution and readiness.
Later, planning is in vain, as we have
490 To fight or to flee, no third choice is left.

Priam

I indeed want to care for everything,
So it does not come to such sudden flight.

Antenor

God grant it! But look, who is this woman
With hair disheveled and a face so pale?
495 Her limbs are trembling, her bosom heaving,
She rolls her eyes, turns her head: now she tries
To speak, now is still.

Priam

> This is Cassandra,
> My unhappy daughter. I see she's seized
> By Apollo's spirit; we must listen.

[Cassandra rushes in]

Cassandra

500 Why torture me in vain, stern Apollo,
Who gave prophetic spirit but no weight
To my words, so that all my prophecies
Fly to the winds, lending with men no more
Credence than vain trifles and idle dreams?
505 Who will be helped by my fettered heart or
Trance? Who will find use in the strange spirit
Speaking through my lips and in my senses
Possessed by a grave, unbearable guest?[34]
I resist in vain, I suffer violence;
510 I don't control myself, I'm not myself.
Where am I, by God? I can see no light,
A sudden night falls in front of my eyes.
Behold two suns there, behold two Troys there,
A doe swims just there across the deep sea.[35]
515 This doe brings misfortune and ill omen,
Shepherds, protect the shores, do not let close
That hapless guest anywhere near the land!
Unfortunate this land and luckless shore,
Whereto that doe swims, unblest the forest
520 Where she comes in and rests her fair body.
All her footprints, all her lairs will have to
Swim in blood. She brings in destruction, fire,
And desolation. O my fair homeland,
O walls, creation of immortal hands![36]
525 What end does await you? You, my brother,
Guardian of the homeland, honored pillar
Of your house, are threatened to be dragged by
Thessalian steeds, and your distressed father,
In order to bury your cold body,
530 Must buy it back with gold from the killer.[37]
O priceless spirit, together with you

              The homeland died; the same tomb will cover
              Both of you. And yet you, grim corpse trader,
              Before long will perish yourself as well,
535           Pierced by a swift shaft from unmanly hands.38
              What next? The log lies and yet from the trunk
              A new rod springs, beyond expectation
              Grows up fast.39 And what mighty horse is that
              Standing all alone on the battlefield?40
540           Lead it not to the stall, I advise you,
              Lead not, it kicks and bites, rather burn it,
              If you do not wish to burn in its fires.
              Keep guard, a night comes, a perplexing night.
              A big fire will arise, such a big fire,
545           That all will be seen, as in broad daylight.
              But on the next day nothing will be seen.
              Then, my father, neither trust in your gods,
              Nor cling to the consecrated altars:
              The merciless lion's whelp chases you,41
550           That will pierce you through with its pointed claws
              And will fill its hungry throat with your blood.
              They will slay all your sons, into slavery
              Take your daughters; on their graves they will slay
              Others to honor their dead.42 You will not,
555           Mother, cry over your children, but howl!43

      Chorus

              Let us rush and lead this weary maiden
              Somewhere into a solitary place!

      [The Chorus leads out Cassandra and does not return]

      Antenor

              These words, O King, are not too difficult
              To be grasped, and to you and your country
560           They foretell the fall; I ask you by God,
              Don't take them lightly or as mere trifles!

      Priam

              This sullen seer has not yet said all

So that I would tremble with fear; and yet
She scared me somewhat, especially since
565  I recalled my wife's dream when, just before
Alexander, this evil son, was born,
Being pregnant, she dreamt then at sunrise
That instead of a child, she had a torch.

Antenor

I knew it too, Sire, and remember how
570  The soothsayers explained this child would bring
The country's downfall, which I see is near!

Priam

You recall this well but I had ordered
Not to foster this cursed child; long since
The forest wolves were to tear and scatter
575  His ill-starred bones in the barren mountains.

Antenor

Better that, than we should all die for him.
What captive is this? It's a Grecian garb.

[Enter Captain, leading a Captive]

Captain

O lords: you debate here, while in the field
The Greeks give battle. Yesterday at noon
580  Their five galleys attacked the Trojan shores.[44]
Although they did not take captives or burn,
But what cattle were in the fields, they seized.
Few in numbers, we made several attempts
To attack them, but after a time had
585  To give up; yet we have killed some of them,
This single man was captured. When questioned,
He made it known that a thousand galleys
With Grecian troops are ready in Aulis,
Awaiting only the envoys' return.

590 But if they do not come back with Helen
(And I could see they embarked without her),
Then the whole army will move and set sail
Straight for Troy. Is it so?

Captive

                Unfailingly.

Captain

Led by Agamemnon?

Captive

                Menelaus's brother.

Priam

595 Command to jail this man and guard him well!
Now this, Antenor, is quite different from
Prophecies or women's dreams; they all go
In the same direction.[45] Tomorrow then
Let us convene early and do not leave
600 Till we plan defense.

Antenor

                I see we need it.
Though I find this talk dire and ominous;
Every year they bid us to plan defense;
Let's discuss war too, not always defend:
Let's plan how to strike; better than just wait.

## Notes

1. There are no stage directions in the original text. They were supplied by Tadeusz Sinko in his edition of the play and are marked here by the square brackets.

2. Kochanowski implies that the Greek army was waiting on ships off shore for the response to their ambassadors' demands; see lines 649-667.

3. Referring to God by ancient heroes was a typical anachronism in the Renaissance drama.

4. Obviously Antenor knows Alexander. His words: "It seems I see Alexander? Yes, it's him" are modelled on a standard practice in the Greek theatre of introducing to the audience a character entering the stage.

5. Antenor's statement is ironic.

6. The two things are youth and good sense.

7. A figure of speech, allowing for repetition.

8. Helen's brothers were Castor and Pollux.

9. According to Homer, Helen had but one child, Hermione.

10. The Old Lady is Helen's nurse.

11. Compare the chorus of citizens of Mycenae in Seneca's *Thyestes*, 607-622 (Tr. by E.F. Watling. Harmondsworth: Penguin Classics, 1974):

You--to whom the ruler of earth and ocean
Gives the dread power of life and death--be humble;
That overweening face does not become you.
No threat of yours that makes your subjects tremble
Is greater than that your master holds above you.
Kings of the earth must bow to a higher kingdom.
Some, whom the rising sun sees high exalted,
The same sun may see fallen at its departing.
No man should put his trust in the smile of fortune,
No man abandon hope in a time of trouble.
The Spinner of Fate twines good and bad together,
Never lets fortune rest, keeps all things moving.
Never was man so sure of the good gods' favour
That he could promise himself a safe tomorrow.
Under God's hand, life's circle is ever revolving,
The swift wheel turning.

12. "When doating monarchs urge
    Unsound resolves, their subjects feel the scourge." (Horace, *Epistles*, 1, 2, 21-22. *The Complete Works of Horace.*)

13. Paris was a shepherd in his youth. His father, aware of the prophecy connecting the fall of Troy with the birth of his son, ordered him abandoned in the mountains. Found there by shepherds, he was brought up by them. He returned to Troy when he arrived with Helen from Sparta.

14. Eris (Strife), threw down a golden apple, inscribed 'For the fairest'. Hera (Juno), Athene (Minerva), and Aphrodite (Venus) all claimed it, and the judgment was left to Paris, the handsomest of mortal men. Paris awarded the apple to Venus and with her help carried off Helen.

15. Medea, the daughter of the king of Colchis, fell in love with Jason, leader of the Argonauts, the chief heroes of Greece. She helped him to recover the golden fleece. In their flight from Colchis, Medea murdered and cut into pieces her young brother Absyrtus and scattered the fragments so that her father might be delayed in his pursuit.

16. Paris talks here about the destruction of Troy by Hercules. Hercules slew Laomedon, Priam's father, and gave Hesione, Priam's sister, to Telemon. Paris does not mention that before that Laomedon refused to give Hercules the horses he promised him for saving Hesione from a seamonster.

17. This description of the bees in the hive is based on Virgil, *Aeneid*, 1, 430-436 and 6, 706-709.

18. Aeneas, the hero of *Aeneid*, was one of Priam's sons, Panthous and others were Trojan elders in Homer's *Iliad*.

19. The ox does not bend its head to have the yoke put on but turns it away.

20. This reference is to Euripides, *Iphigenia at Aulis* (1397-1398):
"The foreigner must never rule this land,
Our own land! They are slaves and we are free."
(*The Complete Greek Drama*. Tr. by F.M. Stawell. Ed. by Whitney J. Oates and Eugene O'Neill, Jr. 2 vols. New York: Random House, 1938).

21. Jason and the Argonauts.

22. All the Greeks took up arms for the wronged Menelaus.

23. Troy was located in Asia Minor.

24. In Poland, the senators were seated, while the deputies stood in the Diet. In line 355, Kochanowski mentions the marshals, another Polish detail.

25. The play of words: 'ouk alegon' in Greek means 'not caring.'

26. The Romans voted by going to one or the other side of the room.

27. "There is no greater wrong than disobedience.

> This ruins cities; this tears down our homes,
> this breaks the battle-front in panic-rout."

Sophocles, *Antigone*, 672-674 (Tr. by Elizabeth Wyckoff, in *Greek Tragedies*, Vol. 1, ed. by David Grene and Richmond Lattimore. Chicago: University of Chicago Press, 1960).

28. This ode imitates the Greek choruses in form and substance.

29. The ship that carried Paris to Greece was built from the trees growing on the mountain of Ida, near Troy. The Eurotas was a major river of Greece. Alexander's ship came to the shore at the mouth of the Eurotas. It was in Sparta, the kingdom of Menelaus, where Alexander met Helen.

30. Helen became a sister-in-law to Cassandra and her sister Polyxena. Cassandra, loved by Apollo, received from him the gift of prophecy, when she promised to yield to him. She resisted Apollo, who rendered the gift useless, causing her prophecies never to be believed.

31. Cypris, Lady of Cyprus, who sprang from the foam of the sea, was another name for Venus.

32. The reference to 'earthworks' is another anachronism in the play.

33. Aulis, town in Boeotia, where Agamemnon assembled the expedition against Troy.

34. Cassandra is talking about Apollo, who is speaking through her. Cassandra's dream was a conceit of Renaissance drama.

35. In Cassandra's prophecy, the doe stands for Helen.

36. The walls of Troy were erected by the gods Apollo and Poseidon.

37. According to Homer, Hector was defeated by Achilles, who dragged his body around the walls of Troy. To bury the body of his son, Priam had to ransom it.

38. Achilles was killed by an arrow shot by Alexander.

39. Neoptolemus, son of Achilles, revenged his father's death. He murdered Priam, who was seeking sanctuary at his household altar.

40. The story is told by Virgil in *Aeneid*, 2. The Greek warriors concealed themselves in the wooden horse, left on the sea shore. Convinced that if brought within the city, the horse would make it impregnable, the Trojans dragged it inside. The Greeks came out from the horse at night and took the city.

41. Again the reference to Neoptolemus.
42. Polyxena was slain at the grave of Achilles by Neoptolemus.
43. Hecuba, Priam's wife, wailing for the loss of her children, was turned into a dog.
44. It is not clear why the attack would begin 'yesterday', before the envoys' deputation was over.
45. Priam is saying that Cassandra's prophecy, Hecuba's dream, and Captain's report lead to the same conclusion.

*Text*: Kochanowski, Jan. *Dzieła polskie*. Ed. by Julian Krzyżanowski. Warszawa: PIW, 1978, 583-605.

## A Treatise on Virtue[1]

We love virtue in a foe and in strangers. But this word virtue' embraces a great deal.

First, it embraces wisdom which teaches what to seek and what to avoid.

Then, justice, which tells us to give everyone his due.

Third, the loftiness of the mind which rests upon the contempt of temporal things.

Fourth, modesty in speech as well as in deeds.

From these four virtues, as if from four wells, many other virtues which improve man's habits take their origin.

The mind, on the other hand, absorbs the arts, which are numerous. The first place is occupied by the military and legal arts, after them come the humanities.

Therefore two things ennoble man: his habits and his mind; the habits come from virtue and the mind from the arts. To have both of these things is priceless for a man. But if you are to be left with only one, it is better to stay with virtue than with learning, for learning without virtue is like a sword in a madman's hand, harmful to him and others, while virtue, even when left completely alone, is praiseworthy and useful.

Thus people love virtue, and next to it learning; they also love gains. You can easily attract simple people with generosity and gifts. But such a friend is not constant, because he loves the gift more than you and when there is nothing more to be given, the friend will be gone, except those who remember good deeds, and they are very few.

Thus two things are required in this situation. First, you should give generously to others. Second, you should give to those who are worthy, because by doing good to good people, you do good to yourself.

You can also be useful to another person with words, giving him good advice when he needs it or warning him against involvement in some improper matter; for all this people will love you.

The third thing is to maintain respect when pleasures are involved, keeping it well in mind not to sin against virtue and decency, in order to be nice to someone. It is good to praise a person not in his presence, but to other people if you want him for a friend.

But since it is impossible to be liked by all (for what one loves, another abhors), it will be enough for the one who seeks respect to behave in a virtuous and decent fashion. If he is not loved, it will not be his fault (as he did all he could), but the fault of those who do not love virtue.[2]

It is not good to win too many friends after all, for love which is torn into many pieces is not so strong as one that is shared and tied together, and he who loves but little is also loved little.

My advice then is to have few friends, but friends who can be trusted, such as Pylades and Orestes, Pirithous and Theseus, Damon and Pythias, Scipio and Scaevola.[3]

To win such friends one should use the advice given above, but also special art, and most of all kindness. But as it was said, virtue should not be involved, in accord with the Greek saying, up to the altar.[4]

Also, similar habits, similar occupations usually attract one man to another--for example, a soldier to a soldier, a hunter to a hunter.

As gold in a fire, so a friend is proven in need. Remember then, when a friend is in need, it is your opportunity to show if you are truly his friend. For the flatterers will follow you like a shadow on a bright day as long as you are fortunate. But when fortune fails, they will disappear no one knows where, just like a shadow when the sun goes behind a cloud. It is therefore appropriate for a righteous man to stand firmly by his friend, to spite fortune, which is fickle.

And because virtue is the foundation of friendship, man should make an effort to be as good as he can, and then being good himself, seek friendship with the good.

A lazy, spendthrift, greedy, quarrelsome person is not a good friend. Benevolence, hope, love, learning, complaisance, praise--all that wins us love of others.

What did Hercules do to be loved?[5]

There are two causes that awaken love in men: the proper deed and this which has in it the quality of love or is worthy of being loved.

## Notes

1. This is a fragment of an unfinished treatise on virtue, learning, and friendship.

2. This thought is based on Cicero's *De Amicitia* 101-104, where Laelius argues that Virtue alone forms and preserves friendship.

3. Famous pairs of friends in ancient mythology and history. Pylades, son of Strophius, was a a constant friend and companion of Orestes. Theseus descended with Pirithous to Hades to help him carry off Prersephone. Damon pledged his life for his condemned friend Pythias. Scipio and Scaevola were associated as great friends in the philosphical writings of Cicero.

4. A Greek proverb. It was said that Pericles, when asked to give false evidence, answered: "I should support my friends, but I am a friend until I reach the altar." It was customary to put one's hand on the altar, while swearing by gods.

5. In the well-known parable told by Prodicus of Ceos, Hercules was faced in his youth with the choice between two women, representing Pleasure (offering a life of enjoyment) and Virtue (a life of toil). He chose the latter and was exalted as an ideal of human virtue by the Stoics and Cynics.

*Text*: Kochanowski, Jan. *Dzieła polskie*. Vol. 3. Ed. by Antonina Jelicz. Warszawa: PIW, 1953, 225-227.

# MIKOŁAJ SĘP SZARZYŃSKI (c. 1550-1581)

Not much is known about the short life of Mikołaj Sęp Szarzyński. He was born near Lwów. In May of 1565 he entered the university of Wittenberg and in September of the same year the university of Leipzig, both renowned as centers of Protestantism. Many historians of literature assume that Szarzyński was a Protestant and only later converted to Catholicism. It is likely that he studied in Italy. In 1567 he returned to Poland and devoted himself to managing his estate. A collection of his lyrical poems, *Rhythms or Polish Poems*, was published posthumously in 1601 by his brother Jakub.

Szarzyński introduced the sonnet into Polish literature and used it to speak in original language and striking images about his fears and his longing for the union with God.

## Sonnet I

### On the Brevity and Uncertainty of Human Life in the World

Alas, how forcefully the turning spheres
And swift Titan[1] rush the fleeting seasons,[2]
While greedy death can cut off woeful passions--[3]
With lengthy steps just behind us it nears.

5   I see better, with time, the big shadow
Of the sins[4] that gnaw often at my heart,
Brought by constant lust to the state of fright,
In tears I blame my youthful deeds, so low.[5]

Struggles for power, pleasure, and richness,
10  Even if not useless yet still bring rot,
Because they lead away our eagerness
From proper contentment (what we call God).[6]

Worldly goods.[7] Hundredfold happy who knows
In good time the true shape of these shadows![8]

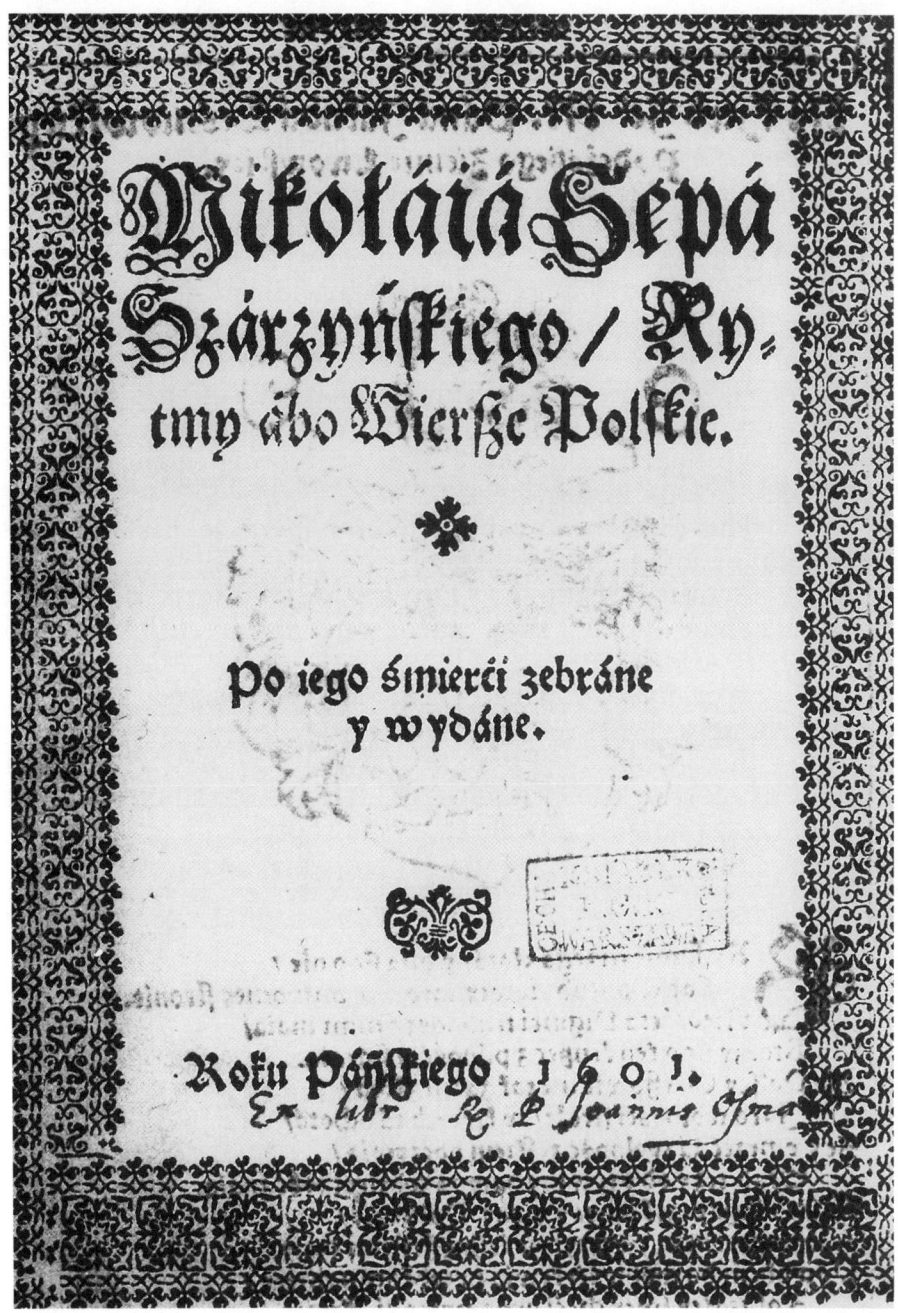

XIV. Title page of Mikołaj Sęp Szarzyński's *Rhythms or Polish Poems*, 1601

## Notes

1. Hyperion, in Greek mythology one of the Titans, was the father of the Sun, or the Sun itself. According to ancient beliefs semicircular spheres were floating above the earth.
2. The first two lines are a paraphrase of the opening lines of Horace *Ode*, 2, 14 ("Eheu fugaces, Postume").
3. Critics have suggested other readings of line 3, e.g., "greedy death may cut off desire with woe" or "death, greedy to cut off pleasure with misery." In the first of these readings, death, greedy to take human life, cuts off life from its delights, by means of despair, eternal damnation.
4. Sęp Szarzynski shows man wandering in the state of sin, which means in darkness.
5. The author may be referring here to his youthful Calvinism or to his erotic poetry.
6. Another reading: "O power, o pleasure, o wealth, even if gained fairly, they harm our devout attempts (to achieve salvation)."
7. Worldly, temporal goods are contrasted with the eternal values.
8. According to Plato, worldy things are reflections (shadows) of true ideas (shapes). It is a paradox that the shadows have shapes, rather than the reverse.

## Sonnet II

*On These Words of Job: Homo natus de muliere brevi vivens tempore etc.*[1]

Conceived in shame, his life in pain begun,[2]
Man lives here in this world only briefly,
Mid changes, miserably, fearfully;
He'll perish--a shadow left by the sun.

5    And from such a man (O infinite Lord,
Living in and for Yourself in glory
And joy), You demand almost avidly
To be shown love and want to be adored.

The works of Your mercy are true wonders.
10   The Cherubim[3] (the abyss of wisdom)
Regards them marveling and from here burns
In happy love the true flame, Seraphim.[4]

O holy Lord, grant us, let us have, too,
What you command, and return it to You![5]

### Notes

1. "A mortal, born of woman,
    few of days and full of
    trouble,
  comes up like a flower and
    withers,
  flees like a shadow and does not
    last." (Job 14:1)
2. "Who can bring a clean thing out
    of an unclean?" (Job 14:4)
3. The cherubim was one of the order of angels, symbolizing wisdom or justice. The cherubim was placed in the heavenly hierarchies below the seraphim, a fiery six-winged angel guarding God's throne. Yet even the cherubim who understands everything wonders about God's mercy.
4. The seraphim, whose color is red, represents the ardor of God's burning love.
5. The conclusion is in the form of a prayer and a request to submit to God's will.

### Sonnet III

*To the Holy Virgin*

O Virgin who are peerless, the other[1]
Adornment of man's state, in whom meekness
Did not mar courage nor worth mar meekness,[2]
Mysterious Mother of Your Creator![3]

5   O you, that smashed the head of fell serpent,[4]
When the whole world suffered from its venom,
You are borne above the angels' heaven,[5]

Glorified, you rest in pure contentment.

You are just like the true moon of our souls,[6]
10  In which we sight the timeless mercy's light,
When the terrible sin upon us throws
The grave shadows of the oppressive night.[7]

But you, come to us as the morning light,
Show us the sun's radiance that we invite.[8]

### Notes

1. The first adornment was Christ. The word 'state' implies that she can reach another state, the divine one.
2. A paradox of Mary as a person whose humbleness did not damage her courage nor whose dignity and high position as the Mother of God did not impair the inborn humility of the Lord's servant. "Then Mary said, 'Here am I, the servant of the Lord; let it be with me according to your word'." (Luke 1:37)
3. In Dante's *Paradise* (XXXIII, 1): 'Maiden and Mother, daughter of thine own Son.'
4. This line is directed against the protestants, who did not recognize Mary's role in salvation. A popular medieval metaphor, based on Genesis (3:14-15), showed Mary trampling on the serpent's head.
5. There were nine choirs of angels. Mary was above them; her throne stood next to God's throne.
6. Mary is the moon of the souls, while the planet is the moon of the human bodies. She reflects the rays of God's mercy.
7. For Sęp Szarzyński, the sin had terrible consequences. The shadow and night were associated with mortal sins, they were grave and oppressive.
8. The morning, early light augurs the sunrise. In Christian tradition, Jesus is often described as 'the true light' (John 1:9, 12:46) or the sun (Revelation 12:1): "A great portent appeared in heaven: a woman clothed with the sun, with the moon under her feet, and on her head a crown of twelve stars." Szarzyński is asking Mary to answer people's supplications of attracting God's grace.

## Sonnet IV

### On the War We Wage Against Satan, the World, and the Body

Peace--happiness, but strife our existence
Under the skies.[1] That grim prince of darkness
And the world's enticing vanities press
Forcefully to bring on our decadence.

5　This is not all, O our mighty Ruler!
Our house--this body, for fleeting delight,[2]
Heedlessly envying the spirit its might,
Will not cease striving to fall for ever.

　What shall I do in battle so frightful,
10　Weak, heedless, also divided in two?
O universal King, peace most faithful,
The hope of my salvation is in You!

Put me by Your side, and I will safely
Engage in struggle and win it bravely!

### Notes

1. The first sentence is a paraphrase of the Book of Job (7:1-6), a classic description of the hard life that mortals are subject to, beginning with: "Do not human beings have a hard service on earth, and are not their days like the days of a laborer?"
2. Another reading of this line: "Our house--this body of fleeting desires."

## Sonnet V

### On the Impermanent Love of the Things of This World

It's hard not to love but in love to stay
Poor solace,[1] when our thoughts seduced by lust
Sugarcoat to excess those things which must

Undergo changes and suffer decay.

5 Who will obtain enough satisfaction
From gold, scepter, fame, pleasure, charming face
So that in his heart they would fill much space
And from all fears he would find protection?

Love is the right course of our life on earth,
10 But our body, made of the elements,
Deceives the soul, which ne'er finds sufficience,

When You, eternal and true perfection,
It doesn't see, the aim of its affection.

### Notes

1. The opening line is a paraphrase of Anacreon's *Ode* 46, also paraphrased by Kochanowski in his *Trifles* I, 40: "Ciężko kto nie miłuje, ciężko kto miłuje" ("It is hard if one doesn't love, it is hard if one loves").
2. The body, made of the perishable elements, when it is deceived by the profane love, praises that which it knows is of the same origin, i.e., common or fleeting. By doing this, the body deceives the soul, which aspires to the absolute.

### On the Picture of Stefan Batory, Polish King

Heaven calls him the crown, homeland calls him daring,[1]
    And we, Sarmatians, recognize him as the king.
God, homeland, neighbors, all adorn so much his fame
    He does not need to be lauded with one more name.
5 Yet his spirit, rich in virtues, tells beforehand
    That we will call him father of this new homeland.

### Notes

1. Stefan means in Greek 'a crown', 'bator' in Hungarian means 'courageous'. King Stefan Batory's homeland was Transylvania.

## On Katie and Annie[1]

Katie with Annie, both charming and appealing,
Unsettle my heart with the same fiery feeling:
The manners of both, worthy of commendation,
Are also a big source of my tribulation.
5   And when at certain times they both sit down closely,
I do not know at whom to look more intently.
Annie seems to me more beautiful than Katie,
While Katie seems to be more beautiful than Annie.
One more than the other, the other more charming,
10  In talk I do not know which is more engaging.
This one thing I know: I love both a great deal.
How can it be? I do not know. But love I feel.

### Notes

1. The poem is attributed to Sęp Szarzyński.


*Text*: Sęp Szarzyński, Mikołaj. *Rytmy albo wiersze polskie oraz cykl erotyków*. 2nd ed. Ed. by Julian Krzyżanowski. Wrocław: Ossolineum, Biblioteka Narodowa I 118, 1973, 6-11, 57-58, 80.

## SEBASTIAN GRABOWIECKI (c. 1540-1607)

Grabowiecki was a poet and translator. He was born in Mszczyczyn (Great Poland) in a nobleman's family and was educated abroad. Grabowiecki obtained a position at the court of King Zygmunt August and in 1581 became King Stefan Batory's secretary. After the death of his wife, he became a parish priest and in 1592 the abbot of the Cistercian monastery in Bledzew. In his *Spiritual Rhymes*, a collection of two hundred religious lyrics, published in Cracow in 1590, Grabowiecki introduced new poetic forms, for example, the canzone and the octave.

*Spiritual Rhymes*
(selections)

*VII*

My life measured by a brief span, as with a twine,
Is encircled as if by a firm border line,
So You know how fleeting it is, and water foam
Seems to be properly used for comparison.

5    Tear me from my sins, I beg you, though I'm fallen,
Do not condemn to disdain this light-minded man,
Lighten Your hand for it has attained victory
And it appears was ready to ridicule me.

Full of misery is the life of the sinner,
10   All his affairs are like a web of the spider;
Remorse destroys them as a moth spoils a garment
While bad will thrusts them back from the Omnipotent.

Listen to my supplications and let Your ears
Remain open to attend to my bitter tears,
15   So I could recover, please show some leniency,
'Ere I give You back my soul, the earth my body.

## XI

The Lord--my light, whom I will imitate;
God--my life, whom I will love, venerate;
The Lord--my strength, He makes my powers reign,
That's why my senses will adore His name.

5   Lord, be my guardian and show some lenience,
Hear my voice, as my throat rests in silence,
Do not hide Your eye, so my composure
Does not meet by chance with Your displeasure.

Lord, stay near me, never abandon me,
10  Let me with Your help praise you fearlessly,
Since my father and mother don't know me.
Where to go, if You scorn the refugee?

Judge of all things, see my humility,
You that rule humble hearts with Your mercy;
15  Teach Your will, help me walk bound by its worth,
Or else I wish I hadn't been brought to birth.


## LXXXII

O God, have mercy, Lord, show compassion,
Hear, please, my sorrowful lamentation,
In keeping with Your unbounded pity
And goodness shown in perpetuity.

5   Turn away Your face and Your benign eye,
Choose not to notice any evil try;
All of my sins, whatever they may be,
Wash in the water of Your leniency.

Lord, make my heart in its truth translucent,
10  Let no unclean thoughts dwell in its extent,
My inner spirit, armed with uprightness,
Let it not host lies from any sources.

Do not let me, Father, out of Your sight,
Let me stay always within reach of Your eye.

15   The Holy Spirit, Spirit of Your own,
     Do not take away from my mortal home.

## Book II

### CXII
### *Octonarius*[1]

My Lord, O my Lord, how great has been Your patience,
When I anger You, sinning, You show forbearance.

My Lord, O my Lord, how great Your beneficence,
You give health when through wrath I risk my existence.
5 Lord, Father of mercy, what a man of licence
Can do in his gratitude for Your great lenience?

Let Your goodness bring You glory, let all my days
And my heartfelt powers give You eternal praise.

### Notes

1. An eight-line poem.


*Text*: Sokołowska, Janina. *I w odmianach czasu smak jest. Antologia polskiej poezji epoki baroku.* Warszawa: PIW, 1991, 33, 34, 43, 45.

## SEBASTIAN KLONOWIC (c. 1545-1602)

Klonowic was born in a burgher's family in Sulmierzyce in Great Poland. He was well educated, traveled abroad, and in 1570 settled in Lublin. He began his career as a town notary, then attained the positions of alderman, councillor, and finally, in 1594, mayor of Lublin. Beginning in 1589, Klonowic taught for two years in the Zamość Academy. He supported Arianism, a Protestant movement which preceded the Unitarian Church, and was criticised for it by the Jesuits.

Klonowic's *Roxolania* (1584), a long poem in Latin, is a detailed ethnographic description of Ruthenia and its cities as well as of the work, customs, and habits of its people. In 1584, when Jan Kochanowski died suddenly in Lublin, next door to the house where Klonowic lived, he expressed his sorrow and paid homage to the famous poet in a collection of thirteen *Funeral Laments*, published a year later. His *Sailing, that is Navigating Boats on the Vistula and the Rivers That Flow Into It* (1595), is a descriptive poem about the greatest Polish river and a guidebook for boatmen and merchants sailing with their goods to Gdańsk. *Judas's Bag* (1600), based on Klonowic's knowledge acquired in Lublin courts, is a moralistic treatise depicting with uncompromising realism a gallery of scoundrels who prey on helpless peasants and burghers.

### Lament V

Who is so audacious, tell me, who has the face,
That his hand on your strings would even dare to place?
That would take a chance to touch the reed instrument
With his mouth, or the pipe that's of oats stems blent.

5    Like a sacrilegious man, he would all displease,
Who would dare to put his lips on the grave mouthpiece,
On which you once performed these exceptional songs
That surprised the listening Pan[1] and forest demons.

When you played in tune with the lute held near your breast,
10 Framed in ivory, Phoebus[2] himself was impressed,

All would say Phoebus himself plucks the twisted strings
And on the gut cords the learned god hones his skills.

Pan also looked in from above shaking his horns,
Although for his pipe he is famous among gods,
15 He listened from far, kept his hairy ears covered,
When wonderful songs on a slender reed you played.

Echo, too, stalking you when the evening dew falls,
Gathered in the resonant forest scattered calls;
She tried to pay court with your song to Narcissus
20 In valleys full of beasts, in the clustered reed coppice.

To whom do you pass now the objects that are left,
The lute and heavenly essences, holy poet,
No one has so much inspiration and power
To take on your songs; each of us is a bungler.

25 We wanted to make a gift of your fiddle to the god of shepherds,
By a thorny hawthorn, in Arcadian desert,
He did not accept the gift, didn't feel confident,
Feared to perform poorly, come after you second.

### Notes

1. Pan, the Arcadian god of flocks and shepherds, was represented with the goat horns and hoofs. He invented the musical pipe of seven reeds and once engaged in a musical contest with Apollo. He loved the nymph Echo, who in turn was in love with Narcissus, a beautiful youth. When Echo escaped from Pan, she was changed into a voice that can only repeat the last words spoken to her.

2. Phoebus (Apollo), the god of light, was sometimes identified with the sun. He was also associated with the care of flocks and herds. In Greek mythology he was the god of music, especially the lyre; in Roman religion he appeared as the patron of poetry and music.

*Text*: Klonowic, Sebastian Fabian. *Żale nagrobne*. Ed. by Halina Wiśniewska. Lublin: KAW, 1988, 37.

## Sailing,[1] that is Navigating Boats on the Vistula and the Rivers that Flow Into It
(selection)

Because if one grows once to like sailing,
He will not want to stay home in the spring,
With ice float he'll sail to Gdańsk in a barge,
    He's afraid of shortage.
5 Put the best game on the boatman's table,
He'll still choose the sailor's vegetable,
When he, maybe one time or maybe three,
    Gets a whiff of the pea.
Even if eloquent Mercury[2] poured
10 Golden words for him, the boatman's whole thought
Sails the Vistula behind his bargee,[3]
    As if behind his chief.
The shipowner's head is so long upset
Till he'll thresh a hundred stacks in the shed,
15 Till he brings the grain into granaries,
    In town of Kazimierz.[4]
The eager merchant who has no peasants,
Not to leave children without any funds,
Will trade Polish grain for money in hand,
20     Or for delayed payment.
One will haggle near the forested San,[5]
Another near the Wieprz,[6] complaining some,
Often near the Bug,[7] the Narew[8] maybe,
    And owes lots of money.
25 But although he will lose and wreck his brig,
Though in this trade not everyone grows big,
Do not tell him in this unwise matter,
    Not to be a a trader.
He will still swim like a fish to the hook,
30 He will still say: "Having lost, I'll recoup."
He will not lose, after fixing his vessel,
    His firmness and mettle.
So if he isn't punished by disaster,
By peril or frequent misadventure,
35 I would then leave him in this endeavor,
    The Polish shipowner.
Go where you planned to go, be contented,
My noble countryman and with your bread

XV. Granary in Kazimierz

Feed a foreign tribe; with God's grace yonder
40           You will sell it dearer.
Leave the sea alone, carry merchandise
On the Vistula, keep your trade small size,
Praise the sea, but just be sure to travel
             The familiar river.
45 And before I guide you to the shore there,
I feel obliged to advise you with care.
I'll withhold tears and will feign demeanor,
             Praising your endeavor.
Before any need arises later,
50 I want to tell you, o brave shipowner,
To visit with your wares, though quite paltry,
             The quiet Motława.[9]
Where many windowed granaries await,
Filled with Polish grain, merchants estimate
55 On the bridge, which Germans when they're speaking
             Give the name of the Green.
So first you learn to make headway on rafts,
Do not run against the wholesale merchants,
Get used at first to trade, at the right times,
60           The forest merchandize.
And when in this bargain you make a gain,
Then you can even build a barge for grain.
Float on the river, but not in mast vessels,
             With one thousand bushels.
65 Then when you come to possess your own rye
And your deed with cash, not words, beautify,
Purchase a modest or average sized ship,
             It should not be too big.
When God brings man luck in a small matter,
70 He acts hurriedly, it is no wonder,
But restraint should rule, as things done in haste
             Bring often lots of waste.
So that's why, brother, towards wordly goods
Proceed with measure, since no one disputes:
75 If one wants to rush and be affluent,
             He'll suffer detriment.
He will please with his loss the bad neighbors,
He will nourish envy; all the revels
Of his foes will resound with his chagrin,
80           Although he did not sin.

```
        One should move step by step to happiness,
        To bigger trade, to what you can possess,
        That is why before you build a vessel,
              Do count your money well.
85      I also ask you: load the ships with care,
        Imitate wise Hesiod in this affair,10
        Who teaches thus, pay proper attention,
              In this situation:
        Don't trust the ship with all your property,
90      But leave at home just for security
        More than a half, and load the rest to sail,
              Foresee that you may fail.
        Because if you put all on the schooner,
        You may become in the end a pauper,
95      You may well be deceived both by Neptune,
              As well as by Fortune,
        Whom you trusted with this bold deposit
        Of your possessions and of your profit.
        It will be hard, even if you reach shore,
100           In court to settle score.
        If they do not keep faith in your trading,
        This is your fault; your greed is unending,
        Do not trust winds, you know they hear no sound,
              Keep your trade on dry ground.
105     But if you put the lesser load on deck,
        You will not get poor, even if you wreck,
        You do not have to bow to any drone,
              You can still come back home.
```

## Notes

   1. The title *Flis* has been usually translated into English as 'boatman' or 'raftsman'. In his dedication to the first edition, Klonowic explains the meaning of 'flis' in the following way: "Because that golden *Odyssey* by Homer is nothing else than 'flis,' that is sailing on the sea; Virgil's *Aeneid* not to a small degree occupies itself with Aeneas's sailing or flis. (...) Apollonius, a great poet, described also the same navigation (...)." Klonowic goes on to use a popular medieval metaphor comparing the Church (and the republic) to a boat sailing in the storm (pp. 4-5). In the dedication to the second edition, the author mentions 'sailing or flis' a number of times (p. 12).

In the sixteenth century Polish, 'flis' meant either 'a raftsman' ('boatman') or 'sailing' ('navigation'). It is this second meaning of the word which Klonowic used as the title of his poem.
    2. Mercury, was a god of trade, particularly of corn-trade. He was also the god of dexterity and eloquence.
    3. 'Bargee' was a leader of ships sailing down the river. He sailed in the boat in front of the ship, pointing with his oar where the helmsman should navigate.
    4. Kazimierz on the Vistula (near Lublin) was a center of grain trade. The grain was stored in town granaries along the river and then shipped to Gdańsk.
    5. The San River, joining the Vistula near Sandomierz.
    6. The Wieprz River, joining the Vistula near Dęblin.
    7. The Bug River, in the east of Poland.
    8. The Narew River, joining the Vistula near Modlin.
    9. The Motława River joins the Vistula near Gdańsk, where the old port was situated.
    10. Klonowic refers here to Hesiod, a Greek poet of the eighth century B.C., who wrote:
"And do not put all your substance in ships' holds, but leave the greater part and ship the lesser; for it is a fearful thing to meet with disaster among the waves of the sea (...). Observe due measure; opportuneness is best in everything." (*Works and Days.* Tr. by M.L. West, Oxford: Oxford University Press, 1988, 688-694).

*Text*: Klonowic, Sebastian Fabian. *Flis*. Ed. by Stefan Hrabec. Wrocław: Ossolineum, Biblioteka Narodowa I 137, 1951, 50-54.

*Judas's Bag*
(selection)

Part II
of this Judas's bag[1]
on the hide and nature of the fox

5    And first about those who cheat under the
      cloak of piety

It's now time to talk of the fox's character;
   After that we will talk of the lynx's temper.
In the likeness of fox we count this kind of throng
10   Of which we propose to talk just farther along.
The gang of Judas, that firstly will solicit
   For God, for the destitute, thus gaining profit,
Taking for themselves, what is due to Our Father;
   Though God shows His anger, they don't even bother.
15 He puts on a long face, pleads with a humble voice,
   Wanders from fair to fair with a Judas's purse;
He carries around a tin cup and a brass bell,
   Feigns to raise funds for a new church and hospital;
He entreats for a holy picture, clever soul,
20   Although out of those alms nothing goes for that goal.
Sometimes he feigns in the green or woods a vision
   And promises the simpletons a sure salvation:
"I have seen--he says--the dear Virgin near the brake!
   (And old wives, hearing those fables, begin to quake.)
25 Great radiance became visible in a pine wold,
   On a freshly cut stump, on a mysterious knoll!"
So this loathsome swindler holds it is genuine:
   He saw with his eyes the Immaculate Virgin,
Who gave him orders to multiply God's glory
30   And there, on that spot, to erect a small chantry.
So he'll prattle, drivel, scheme and for this chapel,
   Bread-loaves, money, cheese he manages to swindle.
And all this cheating brings about a good return:
   Bread goes into his basket, mammon to his can.
35 So the skinny clerics and simple clergymen
   Seeing that their flock can grow from this wonderment,
Sometimes will even abandon their ancient shrine:
   Leave their parish for the fair in the wold of pine;
They go after bread and each paltry offering:
40   Hens, eggs, shekels, loaves, candles they are plundering.
They help the simpletons to err as in the past,
   They don't know how to guide these poor souls as is just,
The blind leading the blind and together they'll roll,
   Masters and disciples, down the very same hole.[2]

Notes

1. Legend had it that Judas, considered by many the greatest thief and scoundrel, had a bag sewn from the hides of four animals: wolf, fox, lynx, and lion. In four corresponding parts, Klonowic described a gallery of cheats, thieves, and scoundrels preying on innocent people.
2. Matthew 15:14, Luke 6:39-40.


*Text*: Klonowic, Sebastian Fabian. *Worek Judaszów*. Ed. by Kazimierz Budzyk and Antonina Obrębska-Jabłońska. Wrocław: Ossolineum, Biblioteka Narodowa B 10, 1960, 173-174.

# SZYMON SZYMONOWIC
(1558-1629)

Born in the family of a Lwów burgher, Szymonowic was educated, like his father, at the Cracow Academy. He taught briefly at the Academy and then studied classical literature and medicine in Belgium and France. His poems, written in Latin, gained him an international reputation. In 1586, he found in Jan Zamoyski, the Crown Chancellor of Poland, a powerful patron. In 1590 he was accepted to the ranks of the gentry and awarded the title of royal poet (*poeta regius*). In 1592, he published his first Polish poems.

After settling in Zamość, called "a Padua of the North", Szymonowic was asked by its founder to organize the Zamość Academy. He administered this new institution of higher learning, recruited professors, and established a library and a printing house. Financially independent, he was able to devote more time to his literary work.

Szymonowic's most important work in Polish is his *Idylls* (1614), a collection of twenty poems. Most of these pastoral poems are free translations or paraphrases of Theocritus, the Greek founder of the genre, and Virgil. Three of them, however, namely IX (*The Fair*), XII (*The Wedding Cakes*), and XVII (*The Reapers*) are original. They depart significantly from the idyllic depiction of enamored, singing shepherds. His *Reapers*, for example, shows a grim and realistic scene of peasant women, not shepherdesses, working under the scorching sun, in order to fulfill their villein service.

## The Reapers

Oluchna, Pietrucha, Steward

### Oluchna

The noon is approaching and we are still reaping;
Does the overseer want to see us collapsing?
Indeed, the well-fed man will not please the hungry:
He is walking among us with his club, grunting,

5   And does not know how hard it is to walk the row.
    One thing for the ploughman, another for the crow,
    Though both the ploughman and the crow follow the plough,
    One thing a sickle, another a well-turned club.

### Pietrucha

    Do not speak loudly so that he would not hear it:
10  Cannot you really see the whip in his belt?
    He'll use it quickly; it's a bad exchange--for words
    The whip on your back, I'm not prepared.
    Better not to goad a bad man; so I praise him
    Or flatter him and my back is as yet unbeaten.
15  And now I'll sing for him, though I am not happy;
    The songs do not go well, when the brow is sweating.

    Little sun, lovely eye, eye of the gorgeous day!
    The customs of our steward you do not obey:
    You rise when your time comes, for him it is not right:
20  He would like you to rise as early as midnight.
    You run along towards noon, always on your route,
    And yet he would like to marry[1] evening with noon.
    Our steward, you will not be our sun in the sky,
    A quite different present for you we set aside:
25  We keep a lovely maid or a comely widow,
    Bad to eat at a stranger's, better have one's own.

### Steward

    Pietrucha, I see you do not work willingly,
    Though no swaddled baby whimpers for you sadly.
    Reap along, do not stop, sing this beautiful tune,
30  A meal is not ready yet, it is not yet noon.

### Pietrucha

    Little sun, lovely eye, eye of the gorgeous day!
    The customs of our steward you do not obey.
    You run day after day, till a long year slips away,
    But he wants to have everything done without delay.
35  Sometimes you scorch, sometimes let the breeze blow

swiftly
And in this way you can relieve our drudgery,
But he will always call: "Reap along, do not stop",
Not mindful that with a sickle you sweat a lot.
Our steward, you will not be the sun in the sky!
40 We know well what ails you; but to please your desire
No one here will help you, even if she knew how.
Some of us know a lot, but still won't want to now,
Because you lash freely with a rod. Here's our quip:
We wish you hang limp, just like the strap of the whip.

### Steward

45 Reap along, do not stop. You too would dream away
Of feeling a different whip; you would only play.
Now you taste this! I see you find it quite funny!
Fall behind the others and reap in a hurry!

### Pietrucha

Little sun, lovely eye, eye of the gorgeous day!
50 The customs of our steward you do not obey:
Sometimes you will be covered by a cloudy veil,
But very quickly fair winds will chase it away;
We cannot look boldly into our steward's eyes,
As a cloud and frown dwell on his face at all times.
55 You bring generous dew in the morning, rising,
And once more in the evening, when you are setting.
We are fasting from early morning until dusk,
Don't ask for an afternoon meal, nor for breakfast.
Our steward, you will not be the sun in the sky!
60 Neither maiden nor widow will become your bride.
We'll slander you everywhere, because you beat us,
We'll procure for you an old hag, that's your worth,
The old hag with four teeth! It will be fun to see,
When you sit by her side as if in full majesty,
65 And she will gracefully be giving you a buss,
As if a scraggly frog had licked you on the puss.

### Oluchna

The steward stepped aside, you are quite lucky:

You would have gotten a sound beating most likely[2]
Or your back would be blood-speckled for these requests.
70 Do you hear what kind of breakfast Maruszka gets?
And she is weak, poor soul: three days up and about
And yet her uncaring landlady chased her out
To harvest. That is what can happen in service!
They will seldom today excuse an apprentice.
75 Take a look how he whips her, she covered her head,
Poor soul, he hit her on the head, it's blood-spattered.
She must have told him something, she is quick to scoff
That is what will happen when you talk back a lot.
It's good to keep, they say, your tongue behind your teeth.
80 And though he is joking, better leave him in peace.
Lord's jokes stand for anger, into anger they slip;
You touch him with a word, he'll hit you with a whip.

### Pietrucha

That's good advice. I think he is not against me,
But with him peace is better. What bends frequently,
85 May get broken, when one unfortunate hour draws,
And very often the cause is a minor cause.
He is a very good man, if only not spoiled
By his housekeeper; she indeed has him saddled
And rules him as she wishes, while he has given in
90 And is led by the nose. Sometimes she will scold him.
Whoever she is angry with, may also deem
To suffer something from him which is not pleasing.
She doesn't trust him; at home they are always wrangling;
And no one is allowed to say a word to him.

### Oluchna

95 That's true. We combed flax in the manor some time back,
He stood over us, while two tenant women talked
With him: she eavesdropped from somewhere behind the wall
And like a real hag came running towards us all.
Without any reason she began to beat them

100　And the steward removed himself in that instant,
　　　She scolded all the women, some she chased away;
　　　She gave nothing to eat to those of us who stayed.

### Pietrucha

　　　If she were superior, made of a better mold;
　　　But she's our sister, in the body the same soul.
105　The wrinkles have already deeply marked her face
　　　And the grey streaks in her hair left many a trace.
　　　And yet she will primp, yet with fancy frippery
　　　The bonnet on her head, yet her apron lacy.
　　　She's most funny when she babbles in her chatter;
110　The pig should grunt, the old woman's head should wobble.
　　　Never enough dogs for her,[3] anyone will do,
　　　Not one hired man will wriggle out from her hook.
　　　She nearly went wild about one not long ago,
　　　Until our Czarnucha washed her in herbal flow.
115　The steward sees it, and seeing, he does not see:
　　　Sometimes will talk back, she mocks him openly.
　　　Sorcery is the cause, since with this sorcery
　　　She gets up and lies down: she's in devil's ministry.

### Oluchna

　　　That's what it is indeed, I saw it with my eyes,
120　When she was doing something, naked at sunrise.
　　　Whoever deals with this master, will never come
　　　To a good end; no doubt she too will be undone.
　　　At first it may pay a little, then suddenly
　　　Everything falls down. With God all goes easily,
125　Without God all comes to nought: there is nothing worse
　　　Than the devil, for to what good can he bring birth?

### Pietrucha

　　　Both end and beginning are bad with this master.
　　　Just last year the barns got empty altogether,
　　　This summer pigs and piglets have come to nothing,
130　Neither geese nor chickens will even be hatching.
　　　Everything dies in the sty, dies in the chamber--

You won't even see a poor hen in the manor.

### Oluchna

Not the devil but the hand takes from the chamber,
As for husbandry, I will blame in that matter
135 Negligence which much more than the black magic did,
Because what isn't keenly cared for and attended
Will be damaged; with God, the hand too is needed:
To the hardworking hand, God always gives unasked.
So one year's stock of cattle, our eyes have seen it,
140 Because of their neglectfulness, has just perished.
They didn't want to protect them from pestilent air,
And when they were dropping dead, they would barely care.
With a man on your mind, the household will suffer,
A woman's brain is always weak in this matter.
145 And what kind of a housekeeper is she? I swear
She did not milk a cow with her hand, yet she dare
Talk much of it and squabble in the tenement,
Scold the cooks. She will try all she possibly can,
But nothing wise. Yesterday she wanted to pickle;
150 She did it so that all servants had to chuckle.
But in the inn or the dance no bird can catch her,
When she lets her skirt fly, she will sweep the litter.

### Pietrucha

A good housekeeper is a rare thing in the world,
If she has no husband, she'll be a wicked maid.
155 Even years will not tame her: equally will rave
One who goes out into the world, one who turns grey.
Nothing like a virtuous wife near her husband;
She's faithful to him, to the lord well-intentioned;
She takes proper care of the servants and quarters,
160 She looks at the right time after all the creatures.[4]
Nothing ever gets stolen, because she fears God,
She remembers His judgment and punishing rod.
The honest state brings about scrupulous conscience,
That's why God blesses her, that is why affluence,
165 That is why peaceful life, that is why all is nice,
He who wants to do without God is building on ice.

### Oluchna

I didn't know, Pietrucha, that you were so prudent
And that you were capable of such wise judgment.
You must have been somewhere among students at
    school.
170  Yet a young farm-hand will not be against your rule.

### Pietrucha

I am just a servant and not a housekeeper;
I sin for myself, she doesn't her account render,
But brings to ruin the whole house; and I would like
Never to have caused any serious oversight.

175  But the steward again is towards us coming,
With a surly look, his whip threatening.
So I will sing for him, he likes to hear a song.
He is looking, and stopping, and listening along.

Little sun, lovely eye, eye of a gorgeous day!
180  Please do teach our steward your customs to obey:
You brighten a lovely day with the rays of light
And recommend to the moon a shadowy night;
As you do not live without helpmate in the sky,
Let also our steward accept you as a guide.
185  All matters are arranged properly in the sky:
The moon is your wife, let him also have a wife.

Little sun, lovely eye, eye of a gorgeous day!
Please do teach our steward your customs to obey:
When you climb the sky, the stars give up their places,
190  When the moon arises, they reveal their faces.
The master does much at home, he has great power,
But the servants listen to the housewife better.
Let him have a wife: the servants will stay at home,
They will not too often leave their jobs and go,
195  The doors to the manor will stay open for us.
Pleasant atmosphere attracts all people who pass.[5]

Little sun, lovely eye, eye of a gorgeous day!

Please do teach our steward your customs to obey:
You warm us, you give us everything from the sky,
200 Without you there is night--a bright day, when you rise;
Let him always look at us with a sunny eye,
And let us leave the field early, not at twilight.

### Steward

Well, Pietrucha, you truly got away with it:
Though your back was seriously threatened with this whip.
205 Put down your sickles, then sit to eat in bunches,
Eat together, do not go into the bushes.

### Notes

1. The steward would like to abolish a customary midday meal and an accompanying break.
2. An ambigious expression in the original "to give to a woman for the red boots", meaning to reward her, is used ironically here. It implies that Pietrucha could have been cruelly punished, until her legs were covered with blood.
3. The housekeeper is compared here to a bitch.
4. Another reading: "She looks at the right time after all resources."
5. Cf. Adam Mickiewicz, *Pan Tadeusz*, I, 39-40:
"The gate is wide open, announces to the passers-by
That it's hospitable and invites everyone inside."

*Text*: Szymonowic, Szymon. *Sielanki i pozostałe wiersze polskie*. Ed. by Janusz Pelc. Wrocław: Ossolineum, Biblioteka Narodowa I 182, 1964, 155-165.

## SZYMON ZIMOROWIC (c. 1608-1629)

Zimorowic was born in Lwów, where he received his education and worked in the city office. In 1628 he went to Cracow, where he died next year. His collection of lyrical poems *Roxolans*, or the *Ruthenian Maidens*, written for his brother's wedding, was published in Cracow in 1654.

*Roxolans*
(selection)

### Cycerina

I saw you from my small window pass by,
I thought you wanted to be at my side,
  But you passed my chambers
    And also my quarters
5       With a swift pacing foot,
  And at me, poor maiden,
    Your faithful bondwoman,
  Did not bother to look.

When I saw it I was gripped by sorrow,
10 Thank God, I did not fall dead at the window;
  But I thought the reason
    Was just your distraction
      Or your unwillingness,
  I was looking forward
15     To the evening moment
      With greater eagerness.

Twilight came and found me at the window,
I kept waiting for the full moon to show,
  But you did not come here
20     Nor could I see you near
      With my unhappy eye,
  You did not send a card,
    Nor did you breathe a word,
      O your heart is so vile!

XVI. Engraved view of Cracow from Braun and Hogenberg's *Civitates orbis terrarum*, 1572-1617

25     Where are now your services, where your bows?
Where of the sweet lute those caressing sounds,
    That without much resting
      From dusk until dayspring
      You favored me to hear?
30     Also your good wishes
      And some quiet yearnings
      That you lightly sent here?

No more earlier pastime, no more singing,
Ears full of silence, the heart of longing.
35     Where is usual laughter?
      Where is former pleasure?
      O you unheeding man!
    Don't you know that a chance
      And youthful existence
40       Will so rapidly end?

So since you did not bid me a good night,
My poor eyes did not know in sleep respite;
    And you too, as penance,
      Will never experience
45       A kind night without me,
    Each night you'll be feeling
      Wretched lack of sleeping
      And will sigh frequently.

*Text*: Sokołowska, *I w odmianach czasu smak jest*, 322-323.

# KASPER MIASKOWSKI (c.1550-1620)

Born in a nobleman's family in Smagorzewo in Great Poland, Miaskowski attended probably a Benedictine school in Lubin and the well-known *gymnasium* founded by Bishop Lubrański in Poznań. He spent his whole life managing various country estates.

Miaskowski was the author of political and panegyrical poems, e.g., *Łódź Opaleńska*, but is best known for his *Zbiór rytmów (Collection of Rhythms)*, published in 1612 and 1622. In many carols, psalms, and reflective poems, Miaskowski told of his somber religious experience, using elaborate poetic figures and mythological concepts.

### *The Elegy of Penitence*
### *to the Holiest Virigin and Mother*

O rod without a flaw of the stem of Jesse,[1]
   From which the flower of living God came to be,
You are the second anchor, when the fierce wind whirl
   Carries the ship in the path of the sea breaker.
5 You are, while tempests cover the black firmament,
   Like the gold Cynosure[2] at that very moment,
Which is heralded by the sailors gone astray,
   When fearfulness and death embrace them holding sway.
Now that the heavy waves of my enormous sins
10    Are pouring down on me, my strength quickly lessens!
Into eternal depths I will most likely slip,
   If I will not, saved by You, be able to grip
This cross which Your son on His shoulder had carried,
   And having stained it with blood, death for me suffered;
15 If I do not seize hold of the edge of the rock,
   Where I can see the towering house at the top,
Which is safe and solid, and there (as I desire)
   I'll be able to rest, wash, and dry my attire. (...)

Notes

1. "And there shall come forth a rod out of the stem of Jesse" (Isaiah 11:1).
2. The constellation of Ursa Minor, the polar star.

### On a Painted Glass Goblet

Glass is ash, although painted with colors,
When in glassworks they make from it wonders:
Better than the sun, when it is borne low
By lathered steeds, before it sinks below--
5    When bidding farewell with a serene eye,[1]
It enounters a misty cloud behind--
Grants the world a rainbow of many hues,
Like a craftsman[2] who can a glass produce
With his brush which is green, gold, and sapphire,
10   And shape it grandly to your heart desire.
And yet what of that? The goblet just then,
Before you drink will fall out of your hand;
And that wonderful crystal turns to ash,
What is left behind with blue smoke will flash.
15   Glass is ash, but man is ash just as well,
Even if like Phoenix[3] he could here dwell,
Because this bird created from sun's rays,
Rises from ashes, into ash decays.
But why do I recall Arab wonders?
20   The day will come when this world full of years
Burns down, like straw, into a big fire thrown,
Ere the eternal judge sits on His throne.

Notes

1. In Greek mythology, Helios, the Sun, climbed in his golden chariot the vault of heaven and descended in the evening in the west.
2. The craftsman's artistic work is more colorful than a rainbow.
3. Phoenix was a legendary bird, represented by the ancient Egyptians as living five or six centuries in the Arabian desert. Consumed in fire and reborn from its own

ashes, Phoenix was often regarded as an emblem of immortality or of the resurrection.

Text: Sokołowska, *I w odmianach czasu smak jest*, 86, 90.

## On Harvest

Ceres[1] put under sickle each grain head,
And letting her light blond hair freely spread,
She ties the sheaves in the fertile meadows,
Setting the stacks in the fields in long rows.
5   Like an eager host of black ants in file,
That chose their place and a safe isle,
Carry on their backs for their tribe the goods,
From forest stump or clearing in the woods:
So the legions of industrious reapers,
10   Though it is very hot, wipe their foreheads;
Some put down with a cheer thick manes of hay,
Which a hooked sickle at once clears away;
Others, whose wheat sheaves sear in rays of sun,
Carry them quickly to the rack wagon;
15   Soon with the loud whip it rolls to the barn,
Until the night wraps the fields in black yarn.

### Notes

1. Ceres was the goddess of grain.

Text: Borowy, Wacław. *Od Kochanowskiego do Staffa. Antologia liryki polskiej.* 3rd ed. Warszawa: PIW, 1958, 24.

# For Notes

# For Notes

**For Notes**

## Other Books From Slavica

Oscar E. Swan: *First Year Polish*.

Oscar E. Swan: *Intermediate Polish*.

Wiesław Oleksy and Oscar E. Swan: *W Labiryncie (Labyrinth of Life) opera mydlana w dwudziestu jeden odcinkach oparta na motywach serialu telewizyjnego w reżyserii Pawła Karpińskiego* (a video-based advanced Polish language course).

Ronelle Alexander: *The Structure of Vasko Popa's Poetry*.

*American Contributions to the Eleventh International Congress of Slavists (Bratislava, 1993), Literature, Linguistics, Poetics*, ed. Robert A. Maguire and Alan Timberlake.

*American Contributions to the Tenth International Congress of Slavists, Sofia, September, 1988, Linguistics*, ed. Alexander M. Schenker.

*American Contributions to the Tenth International Congress of Slavists, Sofia, September, 1988, Literature*, ed. Jane Gary Harris.

*American Contributions to the Ninth International Congress of Slavists (Kiev 1983) Vol. 1: Linguistics*, ed. Michael S. Flier.

*American Contributions to the Ninth International Congress of Slavists, (Kiev 1983) Vol. 2: Literature, Poetics, History*, ed. P. Debreczeny.

*American Contributions to the Eighth International Congress of Slavists, Vol 1: Linguistics and Poetics*, ed. Henrik Birnbaum.

*American Contributions to the Eighth International Congress of Slavists Vol. 2: Literature*, ed. Victor Terras.

Patricia M. Arant: *Russian for Reading*.

*James Daniel Armstrong in memoriam*.

Howard I. Aronson: *Georgian: A Reading Grammar*.

Howard I. Aronson, ed.: *Non-Slavic Languages of the USSR Papers from the Fourth Conference*.

Bayara Aroutunova: *Lives in Letters Princess Zinaida Volkonskaya and Her Correspondence*.

James Bailey: *Three Russian Lyric Folk Song Meters*.

## Other Books From Slavica

Natalya Baranskaya: *Неделя как неделя Just Another Week*, ed. *Lora Paperno, Natalie Roklina,* and *Richard Leed.*

Adele Marie Barker: *The Mother Syndrome in the Russian Folk Imagination.*

R. P. Bartlett, A. G. Cross, and Karen Rasmussen, eds.: *Russia and the World of the Eighteenth Century.*

John D. Basil: *The Mensheviks in the Revolution of 1917.*

Christina Y. Bethin: *Polish Syllables The Role of Prosody in Phonology and Morphology.*

Henrik Birnbaum & Thomas Eekman, eds.: *Fiction and Drama in Eastern and Southeastern Europe: Evolution and Experiment in the Postwar Period.*

Henrik Birnbaum and Peter T. Merrill: *Recent Advances in the Reconstruction of Common Slavic (1971-1982).*

Marianna D. Birnbaum: *Humanists in a Shattered World: Croatian and Hungarian Latinity in the Sixteenth Century.*

F. J. Bister and Herbert Kuhner, eds.: *Carinthian Slovenian Poetry.*

K. L. Black, ed.: *A Biobibliographical Handbook of Bulgarian Authors.*

Ralph Bogert: *The Writer as Naysayer Miroslav Krleža and the Aesthetic of Interwar Central Europe.*

Marianna Bogojavlensky: *Russian Review Grammar.*

Rodica C. Botoman, Donald E. Corbin, E. Garrison Walters: *Îmi Place Limba Română/A Romanian Reader.*

Richard D. Brecht and James S. Levine, eds: *Case in Slavic.*

Gary L. Browning: *Workbook to <u>Russian Root List</u>.*

Ranko Bugarski and Celia Hawkesworth, eds.: *Language Planning in Yugoslavia.*

Diana L. Burgin: *Richard Burgin A Life in Verse.*

R. L. Busch: *Humor in the Major Novels of Dostoevsky.*

# Other Books From Slavica

Terence R. Carlton: *Introduction to the Phonological History of the Slavic Languages*.

Catherine V. Chvany and R. D. Brecht, eds.: *Morphosyntax in Slavic*.

Jozef Cíger-Hronský: *Jozef Mak* (a novel), translated from Slovak.

Julian W. Connolly & Sonia I. Ketchian, eds.: *Studies in Honor of Vsevolod Setchkarev*.

Henry R. Cooper, Jr. ed.: *Papers in Slovene Studies 1978*.

Andrew R. Corin: *The New York Missal: A Paleographic and Phonetic Analysis*.

Gary Cox: *Tyrant and Victim in Dostoevsky*.

Anna Lisa Crone and Catherine V. Chvany, eds.: *New Studies in Russian Language and Literature*.

Paul Cubberley: *Handbook of Russian Affixes*.

Carolina De Maegd-Soëp: *Chekhov and Women: Women in the Life and Work of Chekhov*.

William W. Derbyshire: *A Basic Reference Grammar of Slovene*.

Stefana Dimitrova: Исключения в русском языке

Dorothy Disterheft: *The Syntactic Development of the Infinitive in Indo-European*.

Per Durst-Andersen: *Mental Grammar Russian Aspect and Related Issues*.

Thomas Eekman and Dean S. Worth, eds.: *Russian Poetics*.

M. J. Elson: *Macedonian Verbal Morphology A Structural Analysis*.

M. S. Flier and R. D. Brecht, eds.: *Issues in Russian Morphosyntax*.

M. S. Flier and A. Timberlake, eds: *The Scope of Slavic Aspect*.

John M. Foley, ed.: *Oral Traditional Literature A Festschrift for Albert Bates Lord*.

John Miles Foley, ed.: *Comparative Research on Oral Traditions: A Memorial for Milman Parry*.

# Other Books From Slavica

Richard Frucht, ed.: *Labyrinth of Nationalism, Complexities of Diplomacy Essays in Honor of Charles and Barbara Jelavich.*

Isidore Geld: *Dictionary of Omissions for Russian Translators with Examples from Scientific Texts*

Zbigniew Gołąb: *The Origin of the Slavs A Linguist's View.*

Gerald Greenberg: *Beginning Russian Computer Exercises for DOS.*

Diana Greene: *Insidious Intent: An Interpretation of Fedor Sologub's* The Petty Demon.

Charles E. Gribble, ed.: *Medieval Slavic Texts, Vol. 1, Old and Middle Russian Texts.*

Charles E. Gribble: *Reading Bulgarian Through Russian.*

Charles E. Gribble: *Russian Root List with a Sketch of Word Formation.*

Charles E. Gribble: *A Short Dictionary of 18th-Century Russian/ Словарик Русского Языка 18-го Века.*

Charles E. Gribble, ed.: *Studies Presented to Professor Roman Jakobson by His Students.*

George J. Gutsche and Lauren G. Leighton, eds.: *New Perspectives on Nineteenth-Century Russian Prose.*

Morris Halle, ed.: *Roman Jakobson: What He Taught Us.*

Morris Halle, Krystyna Pomorska, Elena Semeka-Pankratov, and Boris Uspenskij, eds.: *Semiotics and the History of Culture In Honor of Jurij Lotman Studies in Russian.*

Charles J. Halperin: *The Tatar Yoke.*

William S. Hamilton: *Introduction to Russian Phonology and Word Structure.*

Pierre R. Hart: *G. R. Derzhavin: A Poet's Progress.*

Michael Heim: *Contemporary Czech.*

Michael Heim, Z. Meyerstein, and Dean Worth: *Readings in Czech.*

Warren H. Held, Jr., William R. Schmalstieg, and Janet E. Gertz: *Beginning Hittite.*

# Other Books From Slavica

Peter Hill: *The Dialect of Gorno Kalenik.*

M. Hubenova & others: *A Course in Modern Bulgarian.*

Martin E. Huld: *Basic Albanian Etymologies.*

Charles Isenberg: *Substantial Proofs of Being: Osip Mandelstam's Literary Prose.*

Roman Jakobson: *Brain and Language*

L. A. Johnson: *The Experience of Time in* Crime and Punishment.

S. J. Kirschbaum, ed.: *East European History (Selected Papers from the Third World Congress for Soviet and East European Studies).*

Emily R. Klenin: *Animacy in Russian: A New Interpretation.*

Andrej Kodjak, Krystyna Pomorska, and Kiril Taranovsky, eds.: *Alexander Puškin Symposium II.*

Andrej Kodjak, Krystyna Pomorska, Stephen Rudy, eds.: *Myth in Literature.*

Andrej Kodjak: *Pushkin's I. P. Belkin.*

Andrej Kodjak, Michael J. Connolly, Krystyna Pomorska, eds.: *Structural Analysis of Narrative Texts.*

Demetrius J. Koubourlis, ed.: *Topics in Slavic Phonology.*

Mark Kulikowski: *A Bibliography of Slavic Mythology.*

Konstantin Kustanovich: *The Artist and the Tyrant: Vassily Aksenov's Works in the Brezhnev Era.*

Ronald D. LeBlanc: *The Russianization of Gil Blas: A Study in Literary Appropriation.*

Richard L. Leed, Alexander D. Nakhimovsky, and Alice S. Nakhimovsky: *Beginning Russian, Second Revised Edition.*

Richard L. Leed and Slava Paperno: *5000 Russian Words With All Their Inflected Forms: A Russian-English Dictionary.*

Edgar H. Lehrman: A *Handbook to Eighty-Six of Chekhov's Stories in Russian.*

Lauren Leighton, ed.: *Studies in Honor of Xenia Gąsiorowska.*

# Other Books From Slavica

Gail Lenhoff: *The Martyred Princes Boris and Gleb: A Social-Cultural Study of the Cult and the Texts.*

Jules F. Levin and Peter D. Haikalis, with Anatole A. Forostenko: *Reading Modern Russian.*

Maurice I. Levin: *Russian Declension and Conjugation: A Structural Description with Exercises.*

Alexander Lipson: *A Russian Course.*

*Alexander Lipson in Memoriam.*

Yvonne R. Lockwood: *Text and Context Folksong in a Bosnian Muslim Village.*

*A Sense of Place Tsarskoe Selo and Its Poets Papers from the 1989 Dartmouth Conference Dedicated to the Centennial of Anna Akhmatova,* ed. Lev Loseff and Barry Scherr.

Sophia Lubensky and Donald K. Jarvis, eds.: *Teaching, Learning, Acquiring Russian.*

Horace G. Lunt: *Fundamentals of Russian.*

Paul Macura: *Russian-English Botanical Dictionary.*

Thomas G. Magner, ed.: *Slavic Linguistics and Language Teaching.*

Robert Mann: *Lances Sing: A Study of the Igor Tale.*

Stephen Marder: *A Supplementary Russian-English Dictionary.*

V. Markov and D. S. Worth, eds.: *From Los Angeles to Kiev Papers on the Occasion of the Ninth International Congress of Slavists.*

Cynthia L. Martin, Joanna Robin, and Donald K. Jarvis: *The Russian Desk: A Listening and Conversation Course.*

Mateja Matejić and Dragan Milivojević: *An Anthology of Medieval Serbian Literature in English.*

Peter J. Mayo: *The Morphology of Aspect in Seventeenth-Century Russian (Based on Texts of the Smutnoe Vremja).*

Arnold McMillin, ed.: *Aspects of Modern Russian and Czech Literature (Selected Papers from the Third World Congress for Soviet and East European Studies).*

## Other Books From Slavica

Gordon M. Messing: *A Glossary of Greek Romany As Spoken in Agia Varvara (Athens).*

Vasa D. Mihailovich and Mateja Matejic: *A Comprehensive Bibliography of Yugoslav Literature in English, 1593-1980.*

Vasa D. Mihailovich: *First Supplement to* A Comprehensive Bibliography of Yugoslav Literature in English *1981-1985.*

Vasa D. Mihailovich: *Second Supplement to* A Comprehensive Bibliography of Yugoslav Literature in English *1981-1985.*

Dragan Milivojević and Vasa D. Mihailovich: *A Bibliography of Yugoslav Linguistics in English 1900-1980.*

Edward Możejko, ed.: *Vasiliy Pavlovich Aksënov: A Writer in Quest of Himself.*

Edward Możejko: *Yordan Yovkov.*

Alexander D. Nakhimovsky and Richard L. Leed: *Advanced Russian, Second Edition, Revised.*

*The Comprehensive Russian Grammar of A. A. Barsov/Обстоятельная грамматика А. А. Барсова, Critical Edition* by Lawrence W. Newman.

Hongor Oulanoff: *The Prose Fiction of Veniamin Kaverin.*

T. Pachmuss: *Russian Literature in the Baltic between the World Wars.*

Lora Paperno: *Getting Around Town in Russian: Situational Dialogs*, English translation and photographs by Richard D. Sylvester.

Slava Paperno, Alexander D. Nakhimovsky, Alice S. Nakhimovsky, and Richard L. Leed: *Intermediate Russian: The Twelve Chairs.*

Ruth L. Pearce: *Russian For Expository Prose.*

Jan L. Perkowski: *The Darkling   A Treatise on Slavic Vampirism.*

Gerald Pirog: *Aleksandr Blok's Итальянские Стихи   Confrontation and Disillusionment.*

Leonard A. Polakiewicz: *Supplemental Materials for First Year Polish.*

# Other Books From Slavica

Stanley J. Rabinowitz: *Sologub's Literary Children: Keys to a Symbolist's Prose.*

Gilbert C. Rappaport: *Grammatical Function and Syntactic Structure: The Adverbial Participle of Russian.*

David F. Robinson: *Lithuanian Reverse Dictionary.*

Klaus Roth and Gabriele Wolf: *South Slavic Folk Culture A Bibliography.*

Don Karl Rowney, ed.: *Imperial Power and Development: Papers on Pre-Revolutionary Russian History (Selected Papers from the Third World Congress for Soviet and East European Studies).*

Don K. Rowney & G. Edward Orchard, eds.: *Russian and Slavic History.*

Klaus Roth and Gabriele Wolf, eds.: *South Slavic Folk Culture A Bibliography.*

Catherine Rudin: *Aspects of Bulgarian Syntax: Complementizers and WH Constructions.*

Norma L. Rudinsky: *Incipient Feminists: Women Writers in the Slovak National Revival.*

Gerald J. Sabo, S.J., ed.: *Valaská Škola, by Hugolin Gavlovič*, with a linguistic sketch by Ľubomír Ďurovič.

Barry P. Scherr and Dean S. Worth, eds.: *Russian Verse Theory.*

William R. Schmalstieg: *Introduction to Old Church Slavic.*

William R. Schmalstieg: *A Lithuanian Historical Syntax.*

R. D. Schupbach: *Lexical Specialization in Russian.*

Elena Semeka-Pankratov, ed.: *Studies in Poetics Commemorative Volume Krystyna Pomorska (1928-1986).*

P. Seyffert: *Soviet Literary Structuralism: Background Debate Issues.*

Kot K. Shangriladze and Erica W. Townsend, eds: *Papers for the V. Congress of Southeast European Studies (Belgrade, September 1984).*

J. Thomas Shaw: *Pushkin A Concordance to the Poetry.*

## Other Books From Slavica

J. Thomas Shaw: *Pushkin's Poetry of the Unexpected: The Nonrhymed Lines in the Rhymed Poetry, and The Rhymed Lines in the Nonrhymed Poetry.*

Efraim Sicher: *Style and Structure in the Prose of Isaak Babel'.*

Rimvydas Šilbajoris: *Tolstoy's Aesthetics and His Art.*

M. S. Simpson: *The Russian Gothic Novel and its British Antecedents.*

David A. Sloane: *Aleksandr Blok and the Dynamics of the Lyric Cycle.*

Greta N. Slobin, ed.: *Aleksej Remizov: Approaches to a Protean Writer.*

Theofanis G. Stavrou and Peter R. Weisensel: *Russian Travelers to the Christian East from the Twelfth to the Twentieth Century.*

G. Stone and D. S. Worth, eds.: *The Formation of the Slavonic Literary Languages, Proceedings of a Conference Held in Memory of Robert Auty and Anne Pennington at Oxford 6-11 July 1981.*

John W. Strong, ed.: *Essays on Revolutionary Culture and Stalinism (Selected Papers from the Third World Congress for Soviet and East European Studies).*

Rudolph M. Susel, ed.: *Papers in Slovene Studies 1977.*

Roland Sussex and J. C. Eade, eds.: *Culture and Nationalism in Nineteenth-Century Eastern Europe.*

Oscar E. Swan and Sylvia Gálová-Lorinc: *Beginning Slovak.*

Jane A. Taubman: *A Life Through Poetry Marina Tsvetaeva's Lyric Diary.*

Charles E. Townsend: *Continuing With Russian.*

Charles E. Townsend: *Czech Through Russian.*

Charles E. Townsend: *A Description of Spoken Prague Czech.*

Charles E. Townsend: *The Memoirs of Princess N. B. Dolgorukaja.*

Charles E. Townsend: *Russian Word Formation.*

Janet G. Tucker: *Innokentij Annenskij and the Acmeist Doctrine.*

# Other Books From Slavica

Boryana Velcheva: *Proto-Slavic and Old Bulgarian Sound Changes.*

Walter N. Vickery, ed.: *Aleksandr Blok Centennial Conference.*

*Essays in Honor of A. A. Zimin*, ed. D. C. Waugh.

Daniel C. Waugh: *The Great Turkes Defiance On the History of the Apocryphal Correspondence of the Ottoman Sultan in its Muscovite and Russian Variants.*

Paul Wexler: *The Ashkenazic Jews: A Slavo-Turkic People in Search of a Jewish Identity.*

Susan Wobst: *Russian Readings and Grammatical Terminology.*

James B. Woodward: *Form and Meaning: Essays on Russian Literature.*

James B. Woodward: *The Symbolic Art of Gogol: Essays on His Short Fiction.*

Dean S. Worth: *Origins of Russian Grammar  Notes on the state of Russian philology before the advent of printed grammars.*

Yordan Yovkov: *The Inn at Antimovo* and *Legends of Stara Planina*, translated from Bulgarian by John Burnip.

*Что я видел  What I Saw* by Boris Zhitkov, annotated and edited by Richard L. Leed and Lora Paperno.

*Twelve Stories* by M. Zoshchenko, selected and annotated for English-speaking students by Lesli LaRocco and Slava Paperno.

## JOURNALS

*The International Journal of Slavic Linguistics and Poetics.*

*Folia Slavica*

*Oral Tradition*

*Balkanistica: Occasional Papers in Southeast European Studies*